THE SPIRIT OF TRUTH
Bible, the Herald of Quran

ESMAIL HEMMATI

Toronto – 2017

Title	The Spirit Of Truth
Subtitle	Bible, the Herald of Quran
Edition	2017-Toronto, Ontario, Canada
Author	Esmail Hemmati
Published by	Author
E-mail	spiritoftruthbook@gmail.com
Copyright	© 2016 Esmail Hemmati, All rights reserved.
ISBN	978-0-9959690-0-1

[Scripture quotations marked (NIV) are taken from the Holy Bible, New International Version®, NIV®. Copyright © 1973, 1978, 1984, 2011 by Biblica, Inc.™ Used by permission of Zondervan. All rights reserved worldwide. www.zondervan.com The "NIV" and "New International Version" are trademarks registered in the United States Patent and Trademark Office by Biblica, Inc.™][a]

---

[a] https://www.harpercollinschristian.com/permissions/#2, accessed 2017 April 11.

Acknowledgment

I am using this opportunity to express my gratitude to everyone who supported me throughout the course of this work. I am thankful for their aspiring guidance, invaluably constructive criticism and advice. I am sincerely grateful to them for sharing their truthful and illuminating views on a number of issues related to the book. I am grateful for those who helped to complete this work by their continuous support in editing it. Those who did not allow me to mention their names will indeed gain the heavenly gratitude.

Thank you

Author

ABBREVIATIONS

ABPE	American Bible in Plain English
Acc	Accusative
Adj	Adjective
Adv	Adverb
BLB	Berean Literal Bible
BSV	Berean Study Bible
DBT	Darby Bible Translation
DRB	Douay-Rheims Bible
ERV	English Revised Version
ESV	English Standard Version
HCSB	Holman Christian Standard Bible
ISV	International Standard Version
JB	Jubilee Bible
KJ200B	King James 2000 Bible
KJB	King James Bible
NASB	New American Standard Bible
NHEB	New Heart English Bible
NIV	New International Version
NLV	New Living Translation
NT	New Testament
OSSP	Old Syriac Sinaitic Palimpsest
OT	Old Testament
pbuh	Peace Be Upon Him / Her
pbut	Peace Be Upon Them
Prep	Preposition
Pro	Pronoun
Prtcl	Particle
Rev.	Revelation (the Book of)
Verb	Verb
WBT	Webster's Bible Translation

WEB	World English Bible
WLC	Westminster Leningrad Codex
WNT	Weymouth New Testament

TABLE OF CONTENTS

Abbreviations v

Preface 1

Chapter 1 – A Brief Review of Biblical Languages 13
   Semitic Languages 16
   Problem of How to Read, Write and Translate 18
   The Triconsonantal Roots of Words 26
   Arabic and Hebrew Letters 29

Chapter 2 – The Prophet and Twelve Princes 35
   The Twelve Princes (Genesis 17:20) 36
      Problems with Genesis 25:13-18 44
      12 Leaders from m-'ōḏ mə-'ōḏ 50
   God Will Not Forsake Seyid (Psalm 37:28) 53
   The 12 Stars of a Lady (Revelation 12) 56
   The 12 Fruits in Mekka (Revelation 22:1, 2) 59
      The Problem with Revelation 22 65
   A Prophet like Moses (Deuteronomy 18:18) 67
   Revelation from Paran (Deuteronomy 33:1, 2) 74
      Where is Paran? 77
   The Three Awaited Figures (John 1:19 - 21) 79
   Prophet Muhammad in the Bible 81
      Hamda and Hem-daṯ 81
      Islam, granted in Kaaba and Qum (Haggai 2:6-9) 84
      Ehmet (Psalm 145:18) 92

Ehmet and Ahmed 95
Mê-ḥam-mā-ṭōw (Psalm 19:6) 100
Mahammadim (Song of Solomon 5:16) 108
Muhammad from Mekka (Ezekiel 24:16) 111
Meka Baka (Psalm 84:6) 116
Ahmed foretold by Jesus 124
    Parakleet 125
    The Spirit of Truth 136
Arise, Descend in Mekka (John 14:31) 146

Chapter 3 – Imam Ali in the Bible 151

A Brief Biography of Imam Ali 152
Ali in the Bible 154
    Eli and the Faithful Priest 155
    Eli of the Bible and Ali of Islam 157
Ali and Well (Numbers 21: 17) 158
hitpa'er Ali (Exodus 8:9) 161
Ali, the King (Deuteronomy 17:14) 165
Yedollah Ali (1 Chronicles 28:19) 167
Majestic Mekka and King Haidar (Psalm 8) 170
    Meka, Shemka, Shameka or Shimka? 176
David Appeals to Ali (Psalm 7:8) 178
Mekka and Haidar Ali Assad (Psalm 21:1-7) 181
Children of Ali, the Judges (Psalm 82:1) 186
The Quran, Haidar and Zulfaqar (Psalm 149) 193
Ghadeer and the Bible 202
    Ghadeer in Arabic and Hebrew 202
    Balaam and Ghadeer (Numbers 22) 204
    Ghadeer and Dhul-Jinaah (Ecclesiastes 10:8, 20) 208

Chapter 4 – Imam Hussain in the Bible 213

   A Short Biography of Imam Hussain 214

   Imam Hussain in the Bible 216
      David Mourns Imam Hussain (Psalm 25:17) 218
      Ghadeer and the Lonely Man (Psalm 62) 221
      The Sacrifice by the River Euphrates (Jeremiah 46) 225
      Ashura in the Bible 232
      Sufyani and Mahdi (Isaiah 21) 234

   Imam Hussain in the New Testament 252
      Hussain Foretold by Jesus (Luke 11:21-22) 252
      John the Baptist and Imam Hussain (Matthew 3:11) 256
      Hussain Foretold by Simon (Acts 2:27) 258
      Triconsonantal Word "Hasin" 260
      Hasin and Great in the Bible 262

Chapter 5 – Quran In The Bible 263

   The Holy Scriptures 264

   The Quran 266
      Qarna ܩܪܢܐ 267
      Qarana קראנא & Ḡrōwn גרון 270

   Furqan 272
      Redemption, Save or Salvation 281

   The Quran Seals It 283

Chapter 6 – Isaiah and Islam 285

   Isaiah, the Prophet of Prophecies 286

   The Everlasting Prince of Islam (Isaiah 9) 289
      Mighty God or Great Counsel 293

   Ali, the Lion (Isaiah 21:8) 297

   The Migration (Isaiah 21:11-17) 303

Quran, the Step by Step Revelation (Isaiah 28) 305
Read! - I cannot read (Isaiah 29) 308
An Everlasting Scroll and Five People (Isaiah 30) 313
My Messenger, My Muslim (Isaiah 42:19) 322
After Ahmed (Isaiah 59) 331

Chapter 7 – Hajj, the Pilgrimage 345
The Symbol of Submission and Unity 346
Moses and Hajj 348
    Moses, the Tradition of Sacrifice and Ashura 350
David and Hajj 351

Chapter 8 – Imam Mahdi in the Bible 353
Who is Imam Mahdi? 354
Mahdi in Different Faiths 355
Mahdi in Avesta 356
    Soshians, Airyaman, Adzan and Islam 356
    Garonemana to the Pure Man of Magkha 359
    Maidyo Mah, Airyaman and Aishyo 364
Mahdi in the Bible 367
    Madai 368
    Ali Elam and Mahdi 369
    Repairer of the Broken Ghadeer 370
    The Occultation and Mahimen 371

A Closing Statement 379

References 381

PREFACE

The prophetic landscape of the Bible is the most significant phenomenon ever explored in the book. According to many scholars, the Bible contains thousands of prophecies, many fulfilled and many reach into the future. Perhaps the most conservative count is given in J. Barton Payne's *Encyclopedia of Biblical Prophecy*[a]. It lists 1,239 prophecies in the Old Testament (OT) and 578 prophecies in the New Testament (NT), for a total of 1,817. These encompass 8,352 verses, representing more than one quarter of the Bible.

It is widely accepted in the Jewish tradition that no prophet is a true prophet if he makes no true prophecy. The prophetic mission of prophets is so important that it has been used as a criterion for distinguishing a true prophet from a false one. As read in Deuteronomy 18:22, New International Version (NIV), "If what a prophet proclaims in the name of the LORD does not take place or come true, that is a message the LORD has not spoken. That prophet has spoken presumptuously, so do not be alarmed." [1]

Some scholars unhesitatingly praise the Bible for its undeniable prophetic qualities: *"Unique among all books ever written, the Bible accurately foretells specific events–in detail–many years, sometimes centuries, before they occur. Approximately 2,500 prophecies appear in the pages of the Bible, about 2,000 of which already have been fulfilled to the letter—no errors"* writes Dr. Hugh Ross in *Fulfilled Prophecy*.[2]

Given that Islam is the fastest growing religion in the world, according to PEW Research Center, and that scholars have called

---

[a] Hodder and Stoughton, 1973

Prophet Muhammad$_{pbuh}$ the most influential man in history, it would be a surprise to find that any intellectual Bible believer had not thought at least once to look for Biblical prophecies about Islam.

Michael H. Hart in his famous book of *"The 100"* writes: *My choice of Muhammad to lead the list of the world's most influential persons may surprise some readers and may be questioned by others, but he was the only man in history who was supremely successful on both the religious and secular levels. Of humble origins, Muhammad founded and promulgated one of the world's great religions, and became an immensely effective political leader. Today, thirteen centuries after his death, his influence is still powerful and pervasive. The majority of the persons in this book had the advantage of being born and raised in centers of civilization, highly cultured or politically pivotal nations. Muhammad, however, was born in the year 570, in the city of Mecca, in southern Arabia, at that time a backward area of the world, far from the centers of trade, art, and learning. Orphaned at age six, he was reared in modest surroundings.*[3]

When I read *"The Bible, The Quran and Science"*, by Dr. Maurice Bucaille[a], I paused at length on Page 129. The author, after a careful examination of the Quran in its original Arabic, declares: *what initially strikes the reader confronted for the first time with a text of this kind is the sheer abundance of subjects discussed: the creation, astronomy, the explanation of certain matters concerning the earth, and the animal and vegetable kingdoms, human*

---

[a] Dr. Maurice Bucaille, 1920 – 1998, a French Medical Doctor and Head of French scientists who were examining the mummy of Pharaoh, found out the accuracy of Quranic verses about Pharaoh's death which led him to deeper studying the Quran in its original Arabic language and eventually he became Muslim.

reproduction. Whereas monumental errors are to be found in the Bible, I could not find a single error in the Quran. I had to stop and ask myself: if a man was the author of the Quran, how could he have written facts in the Seventh century A.D. that today are shown to be in keeping with modern scientific knowledge? [4]

For a book composed 1,400 years ago in the desert of Arabia by an illiterate orphan to have no scientific error at all is not something usual; this is an extraordinary phenomenon.

The great history of Islam for the past 14 centuries should remind us of the most frequently mentioned topic in the Bible, *prophecy*. It is undeniably logical to expect the Bible to prophesy the fastest-growing religion on Earth and the most influential man in the history of mankind, when we know that the book has repeatedly foretold events as insignificant as the drying out of the rivers of the Nile (Ezekiel 30:12) and the Euphrates (Isaiah 19:1-8); Egyptians speaking the language of Canaan (Isaiah 19:18); increase and rumors of war (Joel 3:9-10; Matthew 24:6-7); the rise of false prophets and antichrists (Matthew 24:5, 11; 2 Peter 2:1-2); the king of Jerusalem riding a donkey (Zechariah 9:9), and so on.

In recent years, some political organisations have covertly attempted—with evident success—to make the growth of the Muslim population look like a threat to their society. Some news agencies have been blowing their whistle for decades to falsify the truth of Islam.

Islamophobia, hateful and malicious thoughts, ill-mannered narcissistic propaganda—whatever it is, it has had an unforgettable impact on the relationship between East and West and can be expected to continue its negative effects on civilization if people choose to be absolutely submissive to the false trumpets. Attempts to falsify the real message of Islam are very apparent. Anti-Islam TV and radio channels that broadcast messages of hate and mistrust are proliferating in western countries. To our sorrow, some Christian and Muslim "authorities" have chosen to be silent and, in some occasions, have given their own voices to the propellants of this conflict. The tensions have grown more serious as intrusive agents from both sides have committed crimes against humanity. This pattern has been a reiterative reality throughout history.

I, a humble self-taught researcher, a man born and reared in the East and living in the West, am one of millions who feel that we are in the middle of a tug-of-war game, with beloved family members and friends at both ends of the rope. That, along with my humanistic and religious obligations, motivated me to look up the commonalities between Christianity and Islam, in hopes that I may be a part of the resolution of this dispute.

My own natural desire encouraged me to start my journey from an exploration of the depth of Christianity and Islam. Nothing could satisfy me better than studying the Holy Books of the Bible and Quran. With every verse I read from these two great books, I immersed myself in them with no notion of emerging.

While many have falsely portrayed Islam as the major opponent or competitor to Christianity, the bases of these religions are remarkably similar. Islam is the only non-Christian faith that affirms and makes it an article of faith to believe that $Jesus_{pbuh}$ is the Messiah—the Christ.

The Quran, the Holy Book of Muslims, is the only religious text that explicitly uses this title, Messiah, for $Jesus_{pbuh}$; it also contains a major chapter named $Mary_{pbuh}$, honouring the mother of $Jesus_{pbuh}$. The Quran talks about the birth of $Mary_{pbuh}$ (3:33-36), her childhood (3:37), her devotion (3:42-44), excellence (66:12), and the list goes on. It tells of the visit from the Spirit of God to her and how she and $Jesus_{pbuh}$ are made to be signs of God's might to the world (21:91). The Quran also confirms that Jesus$_{pbuh}$ was born miraculously without any male intervention (19:19-21, 21:91) and was strengthened with the Holy Spirit (2:87).

While the ascension of Jesus$_{pbuh}$ was not even mentioned in the most ancient Gospel of Mark[a], the earliest of all Gospels, the Quran allows no doubt that he ascended to God (4:158).

Muslims are obligated to believe in Jesus$_{pbuh}$ and the miracles he performed without any proof from sources other than the Quran (2:253). Indeed, no Muslim is a Muslim if he or she does not believe that Jesus$_{pbuh}$ is the Messiah (3:45). These are not honeyed words for the purpose of flattery in interactions with Christians; Muslims believe so because the Quran says so.

The verses of the Quran regarding Hebrew prophets including Jesus$_{pbuh}$ have attracted hearts and minds of many. Similarly, numerous Biblical verses prophesying the coming of Islam have led many wise and noble thinkers, scholars and learned men and women of Judaism and Christianity to accept the truthfulness of Islam. Many of those who have converted to Islam found their ways to the faith through the Quran and the Bible. The following names are just a few examples of the countless converts to Islam:

Dr. Maurice Bucaille (an outstanding French medical doctor, and specialist in gastroenterology), author of 'The Bible, the Qur'an and Science'

Nathanel ben Malka[5] (known as Abu'l-Barakāt of Iraq, 12th Century physician and philosopher of Jewish decedent)

---

[a] Mark 16:9-20: The story of Jesus' reappearance and ascension does not exist in the most ancient manuscripts.

Samau'al al-Maghribi [6] (Jewish Philosopher, physician and mathematician of 12th century)

Musha Bin Yuhanna of Iran (known as Muhammad Sadiq Fakhrul Islam – 1844-1912), a Christian scholar who served Vatican and learned that the secret manuscripts, in the private library of Vatican, foretell the coming of Prophet Muhammad$_{pbuh}$. He traveled back to Iran and then to Iraq, studied Islamic theology and became an Islamic scholar as well- written many book in the field of theology.

Leopold Weiss of Austria[7] (20th century – known as Muhammad Assad)

Rashid-al-Din Hamadani [8] of Iran (13th century – Jewish physician)

Muhammad Ali Kelly [9] of America (Olympic and professional boxer and activist of 20th-21st century)

Sachini Y.Stretchen [10] of America (former Pastor of several churches in the USA, renamed herself Sakina Stretchen)

… and more.

The cores of Abrahamic religions – Judaism, Christianity and Islam – are identical to one another. The only serious dividing point between Islam and Christianity is the question of Jesus' identity. In Islam and Judaism there is no one worthy of worship except the One God, the Creator; where in Christianity, despite accepting the oneness of God, it has been dominantly believed that Jesus$_{pbuh}$ himself is also a perfect God. The theory goes on in accepting the Holy Spirit as a perfect God as well. It develops the doctrine of Trinity, where it states that *God the Father, God the*

Son and God the Holy Spirit is not three but one God; each one is a perfect God, yet there is One God not three Gods.

For Muslims, Trinity cannot be the teaching of the Messiah; however, the doctrine of Trinity is indeed the major and the most fundamental element of Christian faith today. How do we know who is right or wrong? It is a long story and not intended to be discussed in this book.

My goal here is mainly to examine parts of the Bible that are prophesying the emergence of Islam, a religion risen from the desert of Arabia, from among people, as a nation, who have been in darkness for most of their history prior to Islam.

On the path of discovering the Bible, which took me more than a decade, I studied hard nights after nights and days after days and it still, God willing, continues to occupy my years to come. It was difficult for me not only because of my limited knowledge about Islamic theology, but also I knew very little about Judaism and Christianity. To make the case even worse, I knew nothing about Hebrew and Aramaic languages, not even a single letter; but my basic knowledge of Greek language sometimes gave me a break.

First, I had to struggle with learning some Hebrew, not modern but the *Ancient Hebrew*, of course without a teacher. Then, I had to figure out the relationship between Arabic and Hebrew, since it is very critical to know what the Quran and Old Testament, in their original languages, have to say about each other. That pushed me to review and practice my basic Quranic knowledge, the meanings and applications of Arabic words, particularly when it was related to the Hebrew texts that I was studying.

It was necessary to study the Bible in its original language because almost all biblical scholars agree on the differences in translations and interpretations of the Bible. Besides, the gradual changes and developments of the Bible reminded me of reviewing the critics and the historic facts in this regards. Therefore, an ocean of questions was in front of me with only a few sources to look for answers. With financial obligations to my family of four, as the only working member of the family and as an immigrant with typical difficulties which most of the newcomers face, financial breakdown and distress, and many unwanted events in the past 16 years of my life, I ended up in dead-end roads several times. I felt that I had to give up. It was a blessing from God that I could continue not just my struggle to overcome the difficulties but also my journey of discovering the truth.

As I furthered my study and research in the Bible, I found many grounds for the claim that Islam is the Greatest Prophecy of the Bible. With so many great Quranic verses talking about the Hebrew prophets, and numerous verses of the bible, in both Old and New Testaments, prophesying the coming of the Prophet of Islam and his family members, I am assured that the three Abrahamic faiths are indeed one in three different eras.

When I looked closely at the Bible, although there were numerous mistranslations of the actual texts and verses concerning the coming of Islam, it was crystal clear that the Bible did speak of Islam and did prophesy the coming of Prophet Muhammad$_{pbuh}$.

There are many verses in the Bible mentioning the names of the prophet of Islam, the Quran, the revelation which was sent down to him, his birth city of Mecca (Mekka), his migration, his death, his successor Imam Ali$_{pbuh}$, the events that took place after him (such as the event of Karbala[a]), and so on.

---

a. The event of Karbala (680 AD – Iraq), where the Prophet's grandson Imam Hossein (Hussain) son of Ali$_{pbuh}$, his 72 men and even his 6 months old son were

Both Old and New Testaments confirm that Prophet Muhammad$_{pbuh}$ was the Promised one. The Twelve Imams and Lady Seddiqa$_{pbuh}$ (daughter of the Prophet) are also foretold in the Bible. Foretelling such events in the Bible has made many to accept Islam as the true message and religion of all prophets.

As I was still writing this book, I had a meeting with three honourable Church fathers in Toronto on Friday, December 16, 2016. After a long discussion, I was questioned if the Bible has mentioned the word "Quran" or not. I personally did not have an answer to it. I find it an unfair prerequisite, because we do not have to see the word "Quran" in the Bible in order to accept it as the book of revelation, knowing that even the word "Bible", as we know it today, is not in the Bible. Having many verses about Islam in the Bible, should make all Bible believers to accept Islam.

After the meeting, my mind was occupied with the question. Many times, I recited prayers and sought God's help. For three days and nights, I re-read the Book of Revelation. Whenever I felt necessary, I compared some of the verses with the Aramaic texts. Then, in the evening of Monday 19th December 2016 around 7 pm, I saw a verse foretelling the Revelation of the Quran. It was the most amazing moment of my Bible study. Then I did the word search, and found even more occasions.

Moreover, even more interestingly, as if I was supernaturally guided, I found myself reading Chapter Mary, the nineteenth

---

massacred and decapitated by tens of thousands of tyrant army, for not giving allegiance to the tyrant ruler, Yazid. Then they were left on the hot sands of dessert, their women and remaining children were taken as prisoners. Today, millions of pilgrims from all over world visit the shrine of Imam Hussain in the city of Karbala, Iraq to pay their respects. Imam Hussain is an honoured and beloved man throughout Christianity as well.

chapter of the Quran. I cannot remember why I started from there and how I decided to read Chapter Mary. What I found there, right at the first verse, shook me for the rest of the night. It is a reference to the Book of Revelation where the word Furqan (another name of Quran) is mentioned. It will be explained in detail later.

Verses from Genesis to Revelation ascertain truthfulness of the Prophet of Islam and his household, quash the false whistles of separation and confrontation, invite people of the Books to coexist and cooperate for a better future.

In hope of peace, love and unity we are obligated to listen to each other, respect different faiths, tolerate opponents and appreciate the diversity. I intend to produce this book not to divide but to unite, not to intensify anyone's mistake but to suggest a correction. I also admit to be in the same line of probability of having mistake(s) on my part, therefore, please do your part of responding and correcting my errors. Your pen may move better than mine.

It is said: *"When the truth is hard to handle; we choose to believe lies instead, because a hopeful heart is better than a broken one."* But I say: When the truth is hard to handle we must choose to share it with others, because a truthful heart is better than a deceitful one. Although I am aware of what Abu Dharr said, *"Telling the truth left me with no friends."* I chose to speak the truth, for Truth is my best friend.

Esmail Hemmati

Toronto 2016

Chapter 1 – A Brief Review of Biblical Languages

It is well known amongst Bible experts that Hebrew/Aramaic[a] is the major language of the Old Testament (OT); and (in my opinion) even the Gospels of the New Testament (NT) must have been written originally in Hebrew/Aramaic. Although majority of Bible scholars believe that the NT was originally written in Greek, the minority has a different opinion. They say that the original language of the NT was Aramaic (or Syriac). The dispute is still on the table. I take the minority's opinion, for two reasons:

First, because the mother tongue of Jesus[pbuh] and the Disciples is Aramaic. Second, in Matthew 10:5, King James Bible (KJB), we read: *These twelve Jesus sent forth, and commanded them, saying, Go not into the way of the Gentiles, and into any city of the Samaritans enter ye not.* If the Disciples were prohibited from going to the gentiles, why they should preach or write in a gentile language.

Eusebius of Caesarea (also known as Eusebius Pamphili), a third and fourth century Greek historian of Christianity declared that *Matthew had begun by preaching to the Hebrews, and when he made up his mind to go to others too, he committed his own Gospel to writing in his native tongue [Aramaic], so that for those with whom he was no longer present the gap left by his departure was filled by what he wrote.*[11] Another historical proof is Papias, a disciple of St. John, who wrote in the 2nd century: *Matthew wrote his Gospel in Hebrew and everyone interpreted it as they were able.*[12]

Most importantly, the Gospels are not the originals, not even copies of the originals but the copies of copies of copies of ... copies. We can't conclude that the originals must have been written

---

[a] Aramaic and Hebrew for most non-Jews were one and the same.

in Greek from the mere fact of having Greek manuscripts; there may be a presumption of that, but not a proof.

After all, if the Disciples of Jesus$_{pbuh}$ were Jews, then why should they preach and write in Greek knowing that all the written books and/or all the spoken words by Hebrew prophets and Jesus$_{pbuh}$ were also in Aramaic/Hebrew. Therefore, most of the NT, possibly with an exception of the letters of Paul in which the Churches in Greece were addressed to, must have been written originally in Hebrew or Aramaic.

We must keep in mind what Jesus himself said: *I have sent to the lost sheep of Israel only.*[a] And the Israelites were not Greek but Hebrew/Aramaic! In summary, if we want to know the authentic words told by the Prophets and written in the original manuscripts, we have to back root them to the original language of Jews. By doing so, we will be bombarded with verses prophesying the emergence of Islam. Understanding the relationship between the three sister languages of Aramaic, Hebrew and Arabic, known as the Semitic Languages, is also essential in bridging the Abrahamic faiths of Judaism, Christianity and Islam.

---

[a] Matthew 15:24

Semitic Languages

Semitic languages (mainly Arabic, Aramaic and Hebrew) are spread throughout Southwest Asia and North Africa and have played a significant role in the linguistic and cultural landscape of Middle East for nearly 5,000 years. They all are originated from one root, Syro-Arabian (some say Afro-Asiatic).

Aron D. Rudin in *A Brief Introduction to the Semitic Languages* shows that these languages are originated from the same root and Changes in these languages are proven facts. For example we read on page 19 of his book: *By the Late Aramaic period several very important Aramaic literary traditions developed, and the dialect differences become even more apparent.*[13]

In today's literature every language is different from one location to another, such as: Arabic of Iraq and Lebanon, Turkish of Iran and Turkey, and so on. Therefore, it is very natural to see differences between various dialects of Aramaic or Hebrew, let alone between Arabic and Aramaic / Hebrew.

Arabic, Aramaic and Hebrew are historically and genetically connected to each other. Daniel Norén, in "An Arabic Hebrew comparative Study of Genesis 1-3" writes:

It's astonishing how similar biblical Hebrew and modern Arabic are. Even if there is a time span of around 3000 years, it is fascinating how much both languages concur in their grammar and the meaning of compatible cognates. Just by learning the Hebrew alphabet and how it corresponds to the Arabic, a modern day Arabic reader would immediately know the meaning of 72 (40.2%) out of the total amount of 179 cognates of verbs, nouns and adjectives of the Hebrew text of Genesis 1-3.[14]

Semitic languages sometimes use same words with similar meaning and sometimes completely different meanings; in many cases, differences have been developed in pronunciations and/or the meanings of words.

The following lines are explaining a few important specifications of these languages. This will help us to understand the close relationship between them.

Problem of How to Read, Write and Translate

Semitic Languages have almost no vowels, all written by consonants, which is feasible for their native speakers because the consonants in Semitic languages are the primary carriers of meaning. As a later development, vowels are notated using diacritic marks added to the consonants, just to make it easy to read. This was a positive improvement at least for future generations; however, it had disadvantages as well. The most common of that is wrong diacritical marking of words that accept multi phonetics and meanings. An example of it in Arabic is من (*m n*); that could mean *who* or *from* if marked as مَن (*man*) or مِن (*men*), respectively. Similarly in Hebrew, the word אדני (*a – d – n y*) can mean *master* or *God*, depending on the way it is marked or said, *adoni* or *adonay* (אֲדֹנִי or אֲדֹנָי)[a] respectively. This simple case of *adoni* or *adonay* is a great dispute between scholars, for it concerns the very base of Christian theology – the nature of Jesus, a man or God? As such, in Psalm 110:1 we read:

Psalm 110:1[1]

נאם יהוה | לַֽאדֹנִי שב לימיני עד־אשית איביך הדם לרגליך׃

The Latin transliteration:

*nə-'um Yah-weh **la-dō-nî**, šêḇ lî-mî-nî; 'aḏ- 'ā-šîṯ 'ō-yə-ḇe-ḵā, hă-ḏōm lə-raḡ-le-ḵā.*

English Standard Version (ESV): (Reads: *adonay*)

---

[a] Note the different diacritic marks under and above the third letter from right: נָ (in "ado*nay*") and נִ (in "ado*ni*")

The LORD says to my Lord: "Sit at my right hand, until I make your enemies your footstool."

On the other hand, if read as *adoni*:

The LORD says to my master: "Sit at my right hand, until I make your enemies your footstool."

Majority of Christian scholars read אדני as *Adonay* (the first translation), but Rabbis read it as *adoni* (the second translation). The difference is extremely staggering. The author of the Gospel of Matthew chose the first reading (*Adonay*), as we read in Matthew 22:44, *The Lord said to my Lord ...*, Christians use this verse to prove Jesus' deity.

Another example is עלי a-l-i, frequently used in the Old Testament, with variety of vocalizations each with a different meaning, such as *almighty, over me, to me, spring up, go up, come up* and so on. Not only in different verses has it been translated differently, but also in a single verse, different translations of the bible have different interpretations to it. An example of that is Exodus 8:9, where Moses$_{pbuh}$ begins his conversation with Pharaoh with a mysterious phrase: *hitpa'er ali* (התפאר עלי). No one, up to this moment, has a clear translation for it. (We will discuss about it later.)

As we could see, it is quite problematic when the grammatical rules cannot protect the original intended form of the word. In short, in Semitic languages, depending on how you mark and read words, you may get the meaning right or end up in total confusion. In this book, we will not be short on bringing examples for that.

The dispute over biblical texts does not end on just how to *read* and how to *vowel*. The problem of how to *write* is even more serious. *Among over 5000 manuscripts of the Bible, not even two are identical. Some say, there are 400,000 variants in the manuscripts, this means the number of differences is greater than the number of words in the entire New Testament*[15]. There are many serious differences between these writings; this makes it extremely challenging to distinguish the right from wrong. *We could go on nearly forever talking about specific places in which the texts of the New Testament came to be changed, either accidentally or intentionally*, says Dr. Bart Ehrman, an outstanding New Testament scholar, in his "Misquoting Jesus" [16].

It will be shown in this book that the Old Testament was not excluded from these changes. Just as an example out of many, *Mekka* has been changed to *shemka* or *shameka* in some manuscripts. It will be explained in Chapter 3 – Imam Ali in the Bible, under "Meka, Shemka, Shameka or Shimka?"

Word combination, in my opinion, in some parts of the manuscripts, has been done suspiciously. One example of that is בעמק הבכא (bemekk hbekka) in Psalm 84:6. It can be "through the valley of Bekka" or "through mekkh bekka". Different versions of the Bible give different interpretations on this, as some say "through the valley of Baka" or "…Baca", "through the valley of Weeping" and "in the vale of tears." Some even say: "through a valley where balsam trees grow". We do not know for sure how it was written in the original text, but what we *can* know is that something is not right. (We will discuss this particular case later.)

Another complication we find in the Bible is *the hidden prophecies*. There are many cases in the Bible where words have different meanings and hidden prophecies within them, but they were never noticed by the translators. Such are *Hashamayim*, *kufato*, *yām*, *hadar*, *hasad*, *ghadeer*, *hassin* and many more.

Scribal intervention has made the situation even worse. Some later Bible copyists have added words, verses and stories to the manuscripts, and have caused fundamental shifts in Christian theology. Example of that is verse 7 chapter 5 in 1 John, the most famous and frequently quoted verse of the Bible to prove the doctrine of Trinity.

1 John 5:7, 8 (KJB)[17]: *7 For there are three that bear record in heaven, the Father, the Word, and the Holy Ghost: and these three are one. 8 And there are three that bear witness in earth, the[b] Spirit, and the water, and the blood: and these three agree in one.*

Today we know that verse 7 was a later insertion because it is not in the earliest manuscripts at all. That is why it has been deleted in the newer versions but, to keep the *number* 7 there, they had to cut the verse after (verse number 8) into two sections and number them as 7 and 8, and, besides, even the verse 8 had to be changed: [a]

1 John 5:7, 8 (NIV)[18]: *7 For there are three that testify: 8 the[b] Spirit, the water and the blood; and the three are in agreement.*

The Bible copyists/translators also did not mind to add articles to words to make it the way they thought that it "should be". An example of that is what you have just read in verse 8, where *the* has been added to *spirit*.[19] The difference is quite fundamental: *a spirit* or *the spirit*? The first one means *any spirit* or *an unknown spirit*, but the second one means *very known spirit* (interpreted as *the Holy Spirit*.)

Furthermore, the story of the adulterous woman brought to Jesus[pbuh] for his judgement (John 8:1-11) and the verse before (John 7:53) were all added by the later copyist(s)[20, 21, 22]. Even the story of Jesus' Ascension – perhaps the mightiest story of all in the

---

[a] Note that there is no mention of "bear witness in earth" (as it was in verse 8 of older versions such as King James Bible).
[b] "*the*" is not found in any Greek manuscript before fourteenth century.

New Testament – was added to the newer copies of the Mark's Gospel[23, 24]. (Mark 16:9-20)

If copyists can add verses to the text, why they should not be able to change or delete the original words and verses, or, better to say, they most likely did change or delete some words and verses. Therefore, it is indispensable to be open to critics and various possible interpretations/corrections of the Bible.

The New Testament has other problems when it comes to the matter of "original" texts. We do not have any original manuscript or even first or second or N^{th} copies of the originals. Even If today we get the original Greek Gospels, it does not perfectly reflect the real message of the original words of Jesus$_{pbuh}$ or his disciples. Because they did not write the Gospels and they did not preach in Greek. Authors wrote these Gospels according to their ability, knowledge and judgement of what they had heard from others decades later. Even if we had a Hebrew or Aramaic Gospel, probably it would be facing the same problems as the Old Testament does; wrong vocalisations and readings, wrong translations, wrong interventions, and omitting / adding words/passages, and so forth.

The last matter of my logos is many mistranslations of the texts of the Bible, particularly in the Old Testament. A very frequently occurred example of this is translating the names of people and places, such as the בעמק הבכא (bemekk hbekka)[a], as mentioned earlier. Sometimes even very obvious words are interpreted wrong, out of context or a metaphorical statement taken literal, and phrases have been translated with no sense of meaning, such as עלי באר ענו־לה ‘ă-lî bə-’êr ‘ĕ-nū- lāh (in Numbers 21:17) translated

---

[a] in Psalms 84:6

differently and with no common sense. (We will examine this verse in detail later.)

Another, perhaps the most serious, occasion of misinterpretation is where Jesus said "I am" to roman soldiers who were looking for him; as we read in the Gospel of John:

John 18:4-8
NIV
4 Jesus, knowing all that was going to happen to him, went out and asked them, "Who is it you want?" 5 "Jesus of Nazareth", they replied. "I am he", Jesus said. (And Judas the traitor was standing there with them.) 6 When Jesus said, "I am he", they drew back and fell to the ground. 7 Again he asked them, "Who is it you want?" "Jesus of Nazareth", they said. 8 Jesus answered, "I told you that I am he. If you are looking for me, then let these men go."

"Because God also said to Moses: *I am*", Christians say, "Therefore Jesus claimed that he is the same God." The whole argument is based on a misunderstanding. They also refer to another occasion where Jesus$_{pbuh}$ said: *"before Abraham was born, I am!"* but again, a close study shows that the statement never literally meant that Jesus claimed deity. One reason to that is the idea of human being created in several stages, metaphysical and physical to be the main ones. In addition, we all are created in God's knowledge prior to our Earthly birth. This might be the case of being Jesus created ahead of others like Abraham. Thirdly, he did not claim to be around before *Adam* was created. In another word, Abraham was not the first man on earth and Jesus did not claim in this verse that he is before Adam.

Another matter worthy of mentioning is that John is the only Gospel that uses the "I am" statements of Jesus as a framework. Scholars have disputes over the matter whether these are the exact words of Jesus$_{pbuh}$ or John's style of interpreting the teachings of Jesus$_{pbuh}$.

Finally, the mysterious priest of Abraham's time named Melchizedek who "had no beginning and no end, no father and no mother" (Hebrews 7:3), yet never called God by anyone including Abraham. How then someone, whose existence supposedly goes to just before Abraham and did have a mother, could be God. Therefore, the meaning of *"before Abraham was born, I am"* must be examined more carefully, particularly according to the Hebrew linguistic and culture of the time not according to a modern western view of the ancient literature.

Dr. Thomas McElwain, comparing Arabic and Hebrew, writes about the issue of misunderstanding Hebrew texts by non-Hebrew readers: *The ancient Hebrew language is extremely poor in expressions indicating the distinction between concrete and abstract. Thus words are used in Hebrew with both an abstract and concrete meaning. By contrast, the Arabic language is very precise in making such distinctions. It is easy to misconstrue the Hebrew meaning of words by giving them concrete connotations where such did not exist at the time of writing.*[25] Although he is comparing the Hebrew with Arabic, it shows how easily Hebrew can be misunderstood, let alone Aramaic, which was mostly a spoken language of Jesus' time.

To make the story short, many words and passages of the Bible are misunderstood by later readers, some translations have also been done with uncertainty and sometimes incorrectly. Furthermore, the manuscripts (the handwritten copies) were altered to such an extent that among 5700 of them no two are identical. With this complex situation, we need to be cut from the mesmerizing tradition of *Hear and Believe* and turn to *Hear and Think*.

Having all these difficulties in the most widely believed holy book makes it extremely challenging to restore the texts to its assumed "original" form. It is even more challenging to correct the views of the believers because the pillars of the faith that are laid on a foundation of numerous mistakes, wrong translations/interpretations, and insertions or omissions of texts / stories to original manuscripts have taken centuries to form. It is a difficult task because changing the foundation can end up in a full-scale demolition. It is simply not an overnight job. The difficulty reformists are facing in dealing with the situation is not how to say the truth but how to penetrate the adamant walls of centuries old belief.

The Triconsonantal Roots of Words

The triconsonantal roots of words in Semitic languages are the main carriers of the meaning and it has stayed relatively intact, such as Hebrew šlām-ā' שְׁלָמָא and Arabic salām- سلام constructed from *s-l-m*, meaning "peace". Another example is חמדה *hemdah* and احمد *ahmad*, both from *h-m-d.* meaning "pleasant" or "most praised". The triconsonantal property of Arabic, Hebrew and Aramaic is very essential when it comes to pairing and correlating these languages. Although almost all words have a three-letter root, some words may carry only two letters, such as אָב *ab* (father). Table 1 demonstrates some of the words used in these languages, much of them identical.

Table 1

		common vocabulary – examples [26,27,29,30]		
English	**Proto-Semitic**	**Arabic**	**Aramaic**[a]	**Hebrew**
father	'ab-	'abb- اَبّ	'aḇ-ā' אבא	'āḇ אָב
heart	lib(a)b-	lubb- لُبّ	lebb-ā' לִבָּהּ	lēḇ(āḇ) לֵב
house	bayt-	bayt بيت	bayt-ā' בַּיְתָא	báyit, bêṯ בַּיִת
peace	šalām-	salām- سلام	šlām-ā' שְׁלָמָא	šālôm שָׁלוֹם
tongue	lišān-/lašān-	lesān- لسان	leššān-ā' לישן	lāšôn לָשׁוֹן
One[b]	'aḥad-, 'išt-	waːḥid- واحد aḥad- أحد	echad אחד achaṯ אַחַת	echad אחד achaṯ אַחַת

[a] Hebrew alphabet is used instead of Aramaic.
[b] Arabic *ahad* changes to *achat* in Hebrew and Aramaic (*h* and *d* becomes *ch* and *ṯ*, respectively).

Table 2 shows a few examples of commonly used words in the Quran and the Bible.

Table 2

Examples of common words in Quran and bible [1, 26, 27]		
English	**Quran**	**Bible**
spirit	ruh- روح	(ruach) רוּחַ
God	Allah الله	(eloah) אלוה or in Aramaic Ĕlāhā
From me	men-ni مَنّی	(mimeni) ממני
prophet	nabi نبی	(navi) נביא
Jesus	Eisa عیسی	(yshv) ישו
Isaac	Is-haq اسحاق	(yitz'chak) יצחק

Considering the fact that these languages have a common root and have gone through changes during the past millenniums, hence it is natural to see both similar and different words in them. There was a time where Arabic and Hebrew / Aramaic might have been understood as merely different dialects of a single language. However, throughout time many identical words have been changed significantly in pronunciation and meaning, such as the following examples. (See Table 3)

Table 3

Arabic	Pronunciation / Meaning	Hebrew	Pronunciation / Meaning
ثُغرَة	soghrah(t) / crack	שַׁעַר	šā-ar / gate
غَضَب	ghadzab / anger	עֶצֶב	ezev / sadness
نَعيم	naeim / gentle	נָעִים	naeim / pleasant
اَحمد	aḥmed / praised	אֱמֶת	'ĕ-met̠ / truth
صداقة	sidaqah(t) / friendship	צְדָקָה	ṣə-d̠ā-qāh / justice
شغر	shaghar / void	שֶׁקֶר	sheqer / falsehood
امين	Ameen / trustworthy	אָמַן	aman / trusted

Meaning / Pronunciation Changes [1,27,30]

Arabic and Hebrew Letters

Letters in Hebrew and Arabic are mostly related to each other - 16 letters from a total of 22 in Hebrew and 28 in Arabic, to be specific. However, there are other Hebrew letters that correspond to two or more different letters of the Arabic alphabet and it is this type of relation that is the cause of most of the seeming dissimilarities.

Six Arabic letters have disappeared from Hebrew. For these letters similar phonetics are used in Hebrew. The missing Arabic letters are ث th, خ kh (ch), ذ dh, غ gh, ض ḍ (or ze), and ظ ẓ, which have completely disappeared in Hebrew pronunciation, and instead merged with similar sounds represented by surviving Hebrew letters שׁ š (sh), ח ḥ, ז z, ע ', and צ ṣ, respectively. Three Arabic letters ظ ẓ, ض ḍ, and ص ṣ would all come to merge in the single Hebrew letter צ ṣ.

Some letters exchange their sounds in these languages, such as S and Sh. Arabic ش š (sh) turns to Hebrew שׂ ś (s) and sometimes Hebrew שׁ š (sh) to Arabic س s. Arabic carries many more sounds than Hebrew but there is one Hebrew letter which is not identified with any specific Arabic letter, that is ס s; it is somewhat between س s and ص ṣ or even both.

Table 4 lists the synopsis of Arabic and Hebrew consonants.

Arabic غ gh is one of the six letters that has disappeared in Hebrew, and replaced with two letters: ג or ע. In addition, خ kh and ח ḥ, remaining separate in Arabic, would both come to be pronounced in Hebrew as ח ḥ. (Table 4 and Table 5).

Table 4

| \multicolumn{4}{c}{Synopsis of the consonantal system[a, 28, 29]} |
Hebrew	Hebrew Transliterated	Arabic	Arabic Transliterated
א	ʼ (A)	ا	ʼ (A)
ע	ʻ (A)	ع	ʻ (A)
ב	b	ب	b
ד	d	د	d
ז	z	ذ	ḏ
ג	g / gh	ج	ǧ
ע	ġ = gh	غ	ġ = gh
ה	h	ه	h
ח	ḥ	ح	ḥ
ח	ḫ / ḥ	خ	ḫ = kh
כ	k	ك	k
ל	l	ل	l
מ	m	م	m
נ	n	ن	n
פ	p	ف	f
ק	q	ق	q
ר	r	ر	r
ס	s	س	s
צ	ṣ	ص	ṣ
שׂ	ś	ش	š = sh
צ	ṣ	ض	ḍ
שׁ	š = sh	س	s
ת	t	ت	t
ט	ṭ	ط	ṭ
שׁ	š	ث	ṯ
צ	ṣ	ظ	ẓ
ו	w	و	w
י	y	ي	y
ז	z	ز	z

---

[a] The transliterations may differ depending on sources.

Table 5 lists a few examples of خ kh and ح ḥ merged into ח ḥ; note the slight differences in meanings.

Table 5

Examples of خ kh and ح ḥ merged into ח ḥ [27, 30]			
Arabic	Pronunciation / Meaning	Hebrew	Pronunciation / Meaning
حَفَرَ	ḥafar / to dig	חָפַר	ḥafar / to dig
خَفَرَ	khafera / to be bashful	חָפַר	ḥafar / to be ashamed
حَبل	ḥabl / rope	חֶבֶל	ḥevel / rope
خَبَلَ	khabala / to confuse	חָבַל	ḥaval / to damage

Table 6 gives a few examples of other changes.

Table 6

Arabic ظ ẓ, ض ḍ, and ص ṣ merg into Hebrew צ ṣ [27,30]		
Arabic	Hebrew	Meaning
ظِرّ zirr	צר ṣor	Flint
صُرّة ṣurrah	צרו ṣror	Bundle
ضرّة dharrah	צרה ṣarah	Rival/Second wife

31

The changes did not stop there. Another development in Hebrew pronunciation was the transformation of the sounds represented by the letters ב *b*, ג *g*, ד *d*, כ *k*, פ *p*, and ת *t*. Depending upon where they occur within a word, they would come to be pronounced as "softer" versions of themselves: ב *v*, ג *gh*, ד *dh*, כ *kh*, פ *f*, and ת *th*. This would have the effect of distancing the sound of Hebrew now slightly even further from her sister language, Arabic. (An exception exists in the case of the Hebrew letter פ *p*. Hebrew פ *p* corresponds to Arabic ف *f*, so in a word where פ *p* turns into פ *f*, this actually makes it *closer* to its Arabic counterpart).

In contemporary spoken Hebrew, three of the six softer variants have dropped away, but distinctions do continue to exist for ב/ב *b/v*, כ/כ *k/kh*, and פ/פ *p/f*, as shown in Table 7, which provides one example for each sound change.

Table 7

Hebrew ב /b, כ /k, and פ /f change to ב /v, כ /kh and פ /p [27,30]		
Arabic	Hebrew	Meaning
ابّ 'abb	אָב 'āb̲	father
حكمة ḥikmah	חוכמה ḥokhmah	wisdom
فتح fataḥa	פתח pataḥ	to open

Lastly, see the pairs below (Table 8), in which the Arabic letter ن *n* is present in the Arabic words, but the Hebrew letter נ *n* is mysteriously absent in the Hebrew words.

Table 8

Arabic letter ن n missing in Hebrew [27,30]		
Arabic	Hebrew	Meaning
أنتَ anta	אתה attah	you
خنفس khunfus	היפושית ḥippušit	beetle
إنسان insan	איש iš	man

Having all these developments in the Semitic languages, we still see many similarities between Hebrew, Aramaic and Arabic texts but no rational thinker would expect to see *all words* identical in these languages.

It is a fact that every language has a variety of accents and spelling differences, therefore, it is very natural to see variations in sister languages such as Arabic, Hebrew and Aramaic.

Chapter 2 – The Prophet and Twelve Princes

The Twelve Princes (Genesis 17:20)

The history of biblical prophecies about Islam starts with Abraham$_{pbuh}$. He was 86 when his first son Ishmael$_{pbuh}$ was born from his second wife, Hagar$_{pbuh}$. Abraham's first-born son was named "Ishmael" by God; it means "God hears (him)". As we read in the Bible:

Genesis 16:10, 11
NIV
10 The angel added (talking to Hagar), "I will increase your descendants so much that they will be too numerous to count."
11 The angel of the Lord also said to her:
"You are now pregnant and you will give birth to a son. You shall name him Ishmael, for the Lord has heard of your misery.

Genesis 16:15
NIV
"So Hagar bore Abram a son, and Abram gave the name Ishmael to the son she had borne. Abram was eighty-six years old when Hagar bore him Ishmael."

The bible says that Abraham$_{pbuh}$ prayed to God to shelter Ishmael$_{pbuh}$ with His blessings: *And Abraham said to God, "If only Ishmael might live under your blessing!"* (Genesis 17:18), and God promised him that the descendants of Ishmael$_{pbuh}$ will start and become a great nation. It's quoted in the Bible, Genesis 17:20, *"As for Ishmael, I have heard you; behold, I will bless him and make him fruitful and multiply him "exceedingly"; he shall be the father of twelve princes, and I will make him a great nation."*

In the above verse, there are two facts worthy of mentioning: "the 12 princes", and "exceedingly". God accepts Abraham's prayer for blessing Ishmael$_{pbuh}$ and promises him that he will be fruitful. His fruitfulness is expected to come to reality through "the 12 princes".

The original Hebrew text reveals two secrets in the verse (Note the bolded words below and Table 8[1]):

Genesis 17:20
WLC (Consonants Only) [1]

וּלְיִשְׁמָעֵאל֮ שְׁמַעְתִּ֒יךָ֒ הִנֵּ֣ה ׀ בֵּרַ֣כְתִּי אֹת֗וֹ וְהִפְרֵיתִ֥י אֹת֛וֹ וְהִרְבֵּיתִ֥י אֹת֖וֹ **בִּמְאֹ֣ד מְאֹ֑ד** שְׁנֵים־עָשָׂ֤ר **נְשִׂיאִם֙** יוֹלִ֔יד וּנְתַתִּ֖יו לְג֥וֹי גָּדֽוֹל׃

Table 8[1]

966 [e]	bim-'ōḏ	בִּמְאֹד	exceedingly	Adj
3966 [e]	mə-'ōḏ;	מְאֹד	greatly	Adj
5387 [e]	nə-śî-'im	נְשִׂיאִם	princes	Noun

The above bolded words are essential into understanding the real meaning of the verse. Even though the translations do not regard the seriousness of these words but by examining the roots and meanings of them we can uncover the hidden secret.

The first word, בִּמְאֹד מְאֹד (bim-'ōḏ mə-'ōḏ), is translated to *"exceedingly."* A careful examination unveils the inaccuracy of the translation. Let us start with the second phrase first: the 12 princes or נְשִׂיאִם (nə-śî-'im). However, before that, it is necessary to know that *twelve* is a characteristic number that is repeatedly used in the Bible. These series are specifically "the twelve reigning patriarchs of the Book of Genesis", "the twelve sons of Ishmael and those of Jacob", "the twelve judges in The Book of Judges", "the twelve disciples of Jesus", and so forth. The following is just a few examples of these biblical verses: (all these verses are from New International Version)

Revelation 21:12
*It had a great, high wall with **twelve gates**, and with **twelve angels** at the gates. On the gates were written the names of the **twelve tribes** of Israel.*

Revelation 21:14
*The wall of the city had **twelve foundations**, and on them were the names of the **twelve apostles** of the Lamb.*

John 6:13
*So they gathered them and filled **twelve baskets** with the pieces of the five barley loaves left over by those who had eaten.*

Jeremiah 52:20
Verse Concepts
*The two pillars, the one sea, and **the twelve bronze** bulls that were under the sea, and the stands, which King Solomon had made for the house of the LORD--the bronze of all these vessels was beyond weight.*

Numbers 7:86
*The **twelve gold dishes** filled with incense weighed ten shekels each, according to the sanctuary shekel. Altogether, the gold dishes weighed a hundred and twenty shekels.*

John 11:9
*Jesus answered, "Are there not **twelve hours** of daylight? Anyone who walks in the daytime will not stumble, for they see by this world's light.*

Joshua 3:12
*Now then, choose **twelve men** from the tribes of Israel, one from each tribe.*

Exodus 24:4
Moses then wrote down everything the LORD had said. He got up early the next morning and built an altar at the foot of the

mountain and set up **twelve stone pillars** representing the **twelve tribes** of Israel.

Genesis 17:20
*And as for Ishmael, I have heard you: I will surely bless him; I will make him fruitful and will greatly increase his numbers. He will be the father of **twelve rulers**, and I will make him into a great nation.*

Numbers 17:2
*"Speak to the Israelites and get **twelve staffs** from them, one from the leader of each of their ancestral tribes. Write the name of each man on his staff.*

Numbers 7:84
*These were the offerings of the Israelite leaders for the dedication of the altar when it was anointed: **twelve** silver plates, **twelve** silver sprinkling bowls and **twelve** gold dishes.*

Numbers 33:9
*They left Marah and went to Elim, where there were **twelve springs** and seventy palm trees, and they camped there.*

Luke 22:30
*so that you may eat and drink at my table in my kingdom and sit on thrones, judging the **twelve tribes** of Israel.*

Exodus 15:27
*Then they came to Elim, where there were **twelve springs** and seventy palm trees, and they camped there near the water.*

Luke 2:42
*When he was **twelve years** old, they went up to the festival, according to the custom.*

1 Kings 4:7
*Solomon had **twelve district governors** over all Israel, who supplied provisions for the king and the royal household. Each one had to provide supplies for one month in the year.*

1 Kings 10:20
Twelve lions *stood on the six steps, one at either end of each step. Nothing like it had ever been made for any other kingdom.*

1 Kings 11:30
*and Ahijah took hold of the new cloak he was wearing and tore it into **twelve pieces**.*

Matthew 26:53
*Do you think I cannot call on my Father, and he will at once put at my disposal more than **twelve legions** of angels?*

Revelation 12:1
*A great sign appeared in heaven: a woman clothed with the sun, with the moon under her feet and a crown of **twelve stars** on her head.*

Revelation 22:2
*down the middle of the great street of the city. On each side of the river stood the tree of life, bearing **twelve crops** of fruit, yielding its fruit every month. And the leaves of the tree are for the healing of the nations.*

(Revelation 22:2, in Aramaic, is mentioning the name of Mekka, or Mecca, twice. We will discuss it shortly.)

The *Twelve rhythmic* prophecy of the Bible starts from Ishmael$_{pbuh}$, the first son of Abraham$_{pbuh}$.

Genesis 17:20
And as for Ishmael, I have heard you: I will surely bless him; I will make him fruitful and will greatly increase his numbers. He will be the father of twelve rulers, and I will make him into a great nation.

Applying *prince* to the sons of Ishmael$_{pbuh}$ can only mean a metaphor, because they never became princes. If we take it to "the sons of Ishmael" as a metaphor, it means that the twelve sons were metaphorically *princes*, therefore, the promised *blessing* would be only metaphoric not literal. This claim does not satisfy any neutral thinker.

If we take it literally, meaning that all twelve sons were indeed princes, lack of historical evidence dismisses the claim because, although Ishmael$_{pbuh}$ had twelve sons, based on the evidence from the Bible, the title *princes* did not refer to his sons. According to Bible Hub, the word used for son is בֵּן (ben). It occurs 4932 times in entire Bible; and in no cases meant "prince" or "leader".

On the other hand, the word used for "princes" in Genesis 17:2 is נְשִׂיאִם (nə-śî-'im), plural form of נָשִׂיא (nasiy'). The singular form, נָשִׂיא (nasiy'), occurs 134 times in entire Bible, and translated to leader, ruler, chief, Sheikh and captain. None of these words referred to "son" except, according to the common bible interpretations, in Genesis 17:20. It is a serious question that why out of 134 cases only once the word נָשִׂיא (nasiy') is attributed to *son*?

As shown in Figure 1, Strong's Exhaustive Concordance makes it clear that נָשָׂא *nasa'* (the root of nasiy') means *an exalted one, a king* or *sheik*. None of the 12 sons of Ishmael became sheik or exalted one. On the contrary, according to Genesis 25:18, they lived in hostility toward each other:

Genesis 25:18
NIV
His descendants settled in the area from Havilah to Shur, near the eastern border of Egypt, as you go toward Ashur. And they lived in hostility toward all the tribes related to them.

Figure 1
5387. nasiy' [1]

Strong's Exhaustive Concordance

captain, chief, cloud, governor, prince, ruler, vapor

Or nasi' {naw-see'}; from nasa'; properly, an exalted one, i.e. A king or sheik; also a rising mist -- captain, chief, cloud, governor, prince, ruler, vapour.

Strong's Concordance
nasiy': captain
Original Word: נָשִׂיא
Part of Speech: Noun Masculine
Transliteration: nasiy'
Phonetic Spelling: (naw-see')
Short Definition: captain

Ishmael's sons cannot be *the promised 12 nə-śî-'im*, for two reasons:

Firstly, Ishmael's sons were all under his wardship until his death. None of them had so called nations at their lifetime. As the book of Jasher Chapter 25 explains, all 12 sons of Ishmael[pbuh] lived together with him and had 2 to 4 children each. Ishmael[pbuh] died at the age of 137. There is no mention of having tribes and towns at the time of Ishmael[pbuh], not even at the time of his 12 children. All civilizations and tribes emerged many generations later. Being a leader for four children at most, twelve leaders at the same time and almost same geographical location can only be a childish game.

Therefore, if we apply the meaning of נְשִׂיאִם (nə-śî-'im) to the 12 sons of Ishmael_pbuh, there will be no historical evidence to prove it.

Secondly, the plural form of the word, נְשִׂיאִם (nə-śî-'im), occurs 8 times in the Bible, 4 times as "princes" (Genesis 17:20, 25:16, Joshua 22:14, 1 Chronicles 4:38) and 4 times as "clouds" (Psalm 135:7, Proverbs 25:14, Jeremiah 10:13, Jeremiah 51:16). The root meaning of it is "vapour", *the highest of all on the earth*. It does make sense to use it for *leaders, captains, sheikhs, priests, Imams* and so on.

It seems that Genesis 25:16 is the only place this title of נְשִׂיאִם (nə-śî-'im) is given to the sons of Ishmael. At first, it might be taken as an evidence to claim that Genesis 17:20 also meant the same, "the sons of Ishmael_pbuh are the princes". However, when we carefully study Genesis 25 verses 13-18, we realise a few problems.

Problems with Genesis 25:13-18

In Genesis 25 we read: (NIV)

13 These are the names of the sons of Ishmael, listed in the order of their birth: Nebaioth the firstborn of Ishmael, Kedar, Adbeel, Mibsam, 14 Mishma, Dumah, Massa, 15 Hadad, Tema, Jetur, Naphish and Kedemah. 16 These are the sons of Ishmael, and these are the names of the twelve tribal rulers according to their settlements and camps. 17 Ishmael lived a hundred and thirty-seven years. He breathed his last and died, and he was gathered to his people 18 His descendants settled in the area from Havilah to Shur, near the eastern border of Egypt, as you go toward Ashur. And they lived in hostility toward all the tribes related to them.

Problem 1: Repetition and Insertion

Any critical reader can easily notice that verse 16 is a later insertion to the text because its first portion repeats the same words in verse 13. Then it continues with what I think could be an insertion: *"and these are the names of the twelve tribal **rulers** (נְשִׂיאִם nə-śî-'im) according to their settlements and camps"*.

The purpose behind this insertion can only be found in the real application of the title נְשִׂיאִם (nə-śî-'im), the *Leaders, Rulers, Sheikhs* and *Imams*. The copyist(s) did not like the idea of the twelve leaders from Ishmael's offspring, therefore it seemed very satisfying to apply the title of Leader to dead sons of Ishmael_pbuh and close the case.

We know that the book of Genesis is written many centuries after Abraham_pbuh; this makes a lot of sense why the author or copyist would prefer to do so. No waiting for the Leaders from Ishmaelite, because they had already come and died!

Problem 2: 12 leaders for 55 people?!

Please read the second statement of verse 16:

...and these are the names of the twelve tribal rulers according to their settlements and camps.

This statement is written centuries, if not millenniums, after the death of Ishmael$_{pbuh}$, when many tribes and huge populations came from him. Nevertheless, it was not the case when he or his sons were around. If we take it to the time of Ishmael$_{pbuh}$ or his twelve sons, and assume that all his twelve sons were old enough to marry and have children (2 to 4 children for each son)[a] before any of them pass away, adding up their wives, Ishmael$_{pbuh}$ and his wife, the highest number we can get is 55. Having twelve rulers in a tribe of 55 people is simply not realistic, neither if we make it 12 tribes of 5 people.

I think either the author/copyist did not realize that hundreds of years before his time, Ishmael$_{pbuh}$ lived in a tent in wilderness with his family; and he would be very happy if he could afford a few tents for his extended family; or maybe the author/copyist forgot that *tribe* is a totally different word than *family*. A leader of a tribe with no tribe is not a leader at all, let alone 12 leaders for a family or for "a tribe" at most.

I can only guess one possibility, positively, and that is only attributing names of the twelve sons to the 12 tribes, which came from Ishamel$_{pbuh}$. It does not mean if his sons were called princes at their lifetime. Their names might have taken as the names of 12 tribes of Arabs but they were not rulers of any tribe.

---

[a] Book Of Jasher Chapter 25

Problem 3: blessing turned into hostility!

The scribe(s) also made sure that hundreds and thousands of years after Ishmael$_{pbuh}$, his descendants should never have a blessed-hood image in the Bible; they did it by adding/changing the verse 18, as we read:

Genesis 25:18
His descendants settled in the area from Havilah to Shur, near the eastern border of Egypt, as you go toward Ashur. <u>And they lived in hostility toward all the tribes related to them</u>.

It is not the first times Ishmael$_{pbuh}$ becomes victimized for being the son of Hagar. His character was already assassinated earlier in Genesis 16:12, giving him title of "wild ..."

The reputation of Ishmaelite in fact made Isaac's first son (Esau) to marry with Mahalath, the daughter of Ishmael$_{pbuh}$, in hope of receiving blessings of his father; (Genesis 28:9) although some commentators have twisted the message by interpreting it as "he only made bad worse"! (See below)

Jamieson-Fausset-Brown Bible Commentary on Genesis 28:6-9

6-9. when Esau saw that Isaac had blessed Jacob, &c.—Desirous to humor his parents and, if possible, get the last will revoked, he became wise when too late (see Mt 25:10), and hoped by gratifying his parents in one thing to atone for all his former delinquencies. But <u>he only made bad worse</u>, and though he did not marry a "wife of the daughters of Canaan", <u>he married into a family which God had rejected.</u> [1]

I think instead of saying: "we have rejected", they said: "God had rejected". This reminds me Matthew 21:42-44, NIV:

42 Jesus said to them, Have you never read in the Scriptures: The stone the builders rejected has become the cornerstone; the Lord has done this, and it is marvelous in our eyes? 43 "Therefore I tell you that the kingdom of God will be taken away from you and given to a people who will produce its fruit. 44 Anyone who falls on this stone will be broken to pieces; anyone on whom it falls will be crushed [a]."

In Genesis 21:15-20 we read something contrary to what Bible commentators write. It is the story of Ishmael[pbuh] and his mother in the wilderness, alone and thirsty, in the hands of Lord. God speaks with Hagar[pbuh] and ensures her what He had promised before, "to make her son into a great nation"; God was with Ishmael[pbuh] as he grew up:

Genesis 21:15-21
NIV
15 When the water in the skin was gone, she put the boy under one of the bushes.
16 Then she went off and sat down about a bowshot away, for she thought, "I cannot watch the boy die." And as she sat there, shec began to sob.
17 God heard the boy crying, and the angel of God called to Hagar from heaven and said to her, "What is the matter, Hagar? Do not be afraid; God has heard the boy crying as he lies there.
18 Lift the boy up and take him by the hand, for <u>I will make him into a great nation</u>."
19 Then God opened her eyes and she saw a well of water. So she went and filled the skin with water and gave the boy a drink. 20 <u>God was with the boy as he grew up</u>. He lived in the desert and became an archer. 21 While he was living in the Desert of Paran, his mother got a wife for him from Egypt.

---

[a] Some manuscripts do not have Matthew 21 verse 44

Is this called "rejected by God"? I wonder how some people can afford such a comment that creates tensions, and misleads nations. Is not it time people to consider their own journey of searching for truth rather than following the false prophets?

Coming back to the 12 princes from Ishmael$_{pbuh}$: if the twelve sons and twelve tribes of Ishmael$_{pbuh}$ were the blessing that God promised to Abraham$_{pbuh}$, as the translations claim, then how this "only" blessing of God to Abraham$_{pbuh}$ regarding his first son turned out to be "hostility" and "rejection"? No answer is given in anywhere in the Bible!

Problem 4: First-born son with no heritage!

We read in the Bible that the first-born son has a very special status, even if he is from a disliked wife. He inherits twice as others; he is the first sign of his father's strength:

Deuteronomy 21:15-17
NIV
15 If a man has two wives, and he loves one but not the other, and both bear him sons but the firstborn is the son of the wife he does not love, 16 when he wills his property to his sons, he must not give the rights of the firstborn to the son of the wife he loves in preference to his actual firstborn, the son of the wife he does not love. 17 He must acknowledge the son of his unloved wife as the firstborn by giving him a double share of all he has. ***That son is the first sign of his father's strength. The right of the firstborn belongs to him***.

The entire Bible regards Isaac$_{pbuh}$ as the true heir of Abraham$_{pbuh}$, as if Ishmael$_{pbuh}$ was not son of Abraham$_{pbuh}$, let alone his first son. This is contrary to God's promise and the law of first-born son.

The greatness of the bilateral respect between Isaac$_{pbuh}$ and Ishmael$_{pbuh}$, and their children, cannot be ignored by any learned man unless the politics becomes a priority. A later storey of Abraham's burial ceremony also confirms the special status of Ishmael$_{pbuh}$, where Isaac$_{pbuh}$ waited for him to bury their father. (Genesis 25:9)

[The Quran gives the highest respect and honor to the Hebrew Prophets. For instance, Moses$_{pbuh}$ is mentioned in the Quran 136 times, Jesus$_{pbuh}$ 25 times while Prophet Muhammad$_{pbuh}$ only 5 times. No disrespect is given to any of the prophets in the Quran, contrary to the Bible in which we can find plenty of it.]

12 Leaders from m-'ōḏ mə-'ōḏ

Genesis 17:20 mentions that Ishmael_pbuh through "m-'ōḏ mə-'ōḏ" will be the father of 12 princes but, in translations, it is interpreted "exceedingly." Following lines are examining the case.

The words בִּמְאֹד (bim-'ōḏ) and מְאֹד (mə-'ōḏ) have been used 300 times throughout the Old Testament in five forms. (Table 9[1])

Table 9[1]

Form	Occurrence	Place	Meaning
מְאֹד (mə-'ōḏ)	291 times	Throughout the Bible	very, greatly, exceedingly
לִמְאֹד (lim·'ōḏ)	1 time	2 Chronicles 16:14	a very
מְאֹדֶךָ (mə·'ō·ḏe·ḵā)	1 time	Deuteronomy 6:5	your might
מְאֹדוֹ (mə·'ō·ḏōw)	1 time	2 Kings 23:25	his might
בִּמְאֹד מְאֹד (bim-'ōḏ mə-'ōḏ)	6 times	Throughout the Bible	"very very" "exceedingly" "exceedingly exceedingly"
בִּמְאֹד (bim-'ōḏ)	nil	nil	

The word בִּמְאֹד (bim-'ōḏ) has never been used apart form מְאֹד (mə-'ōḏ) while מְאֹד (mə-'ōḏ) used 291 times by itself, as well as once with the prefix "li" (lim·'ōḏ) and twice with the suffixes "ḵā" and "ōw" (mə·'ō·ḏe·ḵā and mə·'ō·ḏōw). I must emphasize that בִּמְאֹד (bim-'ōḏ) has always followed by מְאֹד (mə-'ōḏ) as "bim-'ōḏ mə-'ōḏ".

The fact that בִּמְאֹד (bim-'ōḏ) is always with מְאֹד (mə-'ōḏ) reminds that it is a completely different word rather than repetition of a word ("exceedingly exceedingly"). Why did not bim-'ōḏ occur alone, if it means "exceedingly", knowing that in almost all Bible versions, both בִּמְאֹד (bim-'ōḏ) and מְאֹד (mə-'ōḏ) translated to "exceedingly"?

Since מְאֹד (mə-'ōḏ) alone has been used 291 times in the Bible, naturally we expect בִּמְאֹד (bim-'ōḏ) to be also used alone, *at least once*. However, it is not the case. What it portrays is that בִּמְאֹד (bim-'ōḏ) never did have an independent use and meaning. Was it a very different word but has been altered to what we see now? We do not know for sure. What we know is that בִּמְאֹד מְאֹד (bim-'ōḏ mə-'ōḏ) is conveniently translated to "exceedingly". Particularly when we look at the prefix בְּ (bi) – meaning *by, through* – it becomes obvious that בְּ (bi) acts as an adverb and it is not a part of the מְאֹד (mə-'ōḏ), neither does it mean bi + exceedingly. That is why we never see בִּמְאֹד (bim-'ōḏ) alone in entire Bible, and no translator has interpreted it to *by exceedingly*. Having that said, מְאֹד בִּמְאֹד (bim-'ōḏ mə-'ōḏ) should be translated to *by* or *through m-'ōḏ mə-'ōḏ*. Therefore, the verse should be translated as following:

Rendered translation
Genesis 17:20
"As for Ishmael, I have heard you; behold, I will bless him and make him fruitful and multiply him through m-'ōḏ mə-'ōḏ; he shall be the father of twelve leaders (exalted ones/Sheikhs), and I will make him a great nation."

When we look at the Hebrew Bible, it becomes more apparent that the translations have been done with uncertainty. Here is what we see in the common translations:

*"As for Ishmael, I have heard you; behold, I will bless him and make him fruitful and multiply him **exceedingly**; he shall be the father of twelve princes, and I will make him a great nation."*

The word מְאֹד (mə-'ōḏ) by itself means: *exceedingly* or *greatly*. The word בִּמְאֹד (bim-'ōḏ), in the other hand, supposed to mean: *in / by exceedingly*. Again, it is translated to "exceedingly". (Table 10[1])

Both words together, בִּמְאֹד מְאֹד (bim-'ōḏ mə-'ōḏ), supposed to mean "by exceedingly exceedingly"; However, it does not make sense, as even the Bible translators agree with it. That is why they did not translate it "by exceedingly exceedingly", instead they wrote: "exceedingly."

Table 10[1]

| 3966 [e] | bim-'ōḏ | בִּמְאֹד | exceedingly | Adj |
| 3966 [e] | mə-'ōḏ; | מְאֹד | greatly | Adj |

In my opinion, the only occasion Ishmael[pbuh] could be receiving the promised blessing of the twelve princes is through his offspring, Prophet Muhammad[pbuh], from whom the twelve Imams are descended. But how m-'ōḏ mə-'ōḏ possibly refer to Prophet Muhammad[pbuh], it is as simple as *Yeshua* becoming *Eisa* عيسى (Jesus) and *yitz'chak* becoming *Is-haq* اسحاق (Isaac). Interestingly, even today Muhammad is pronounced differently in different parts of world, such as: Mammad and Mahammad (in Azerbaijan), Mohammad-d'o (in Japan), Mehmet (in Turkey) and so on.

As a closing statement, bim-'ōḏ mə-'ōḏ is referring to a person and does not mean "exceedingly". The nearest candidate for it is Prophet Muhammad[pbuh], contextually, linguistically and historically.

God Will Not Forsake Seyid (Psalm 37:28)

There is another verse in the Bible somehow related to Genesis 17:20; it is Psalm 37:28.

Psalm 37:28
NIV
For the LORD loves the just and will not forsake his faithful ones. Wrongdoers will be completely destroyed; the offspring of the wicked will perish.

In the Hebrew text, the word used for *faithful* is "ḥă-sî", from ḥă-sî-ḏāw (means "The Seyid of Him" or "the Holy one of Him"). The word ḥă-sî-ḏ is identical to Arabic السّيد (As-Seyid). (See Table 11 and Figure 2)

Below is the rendered translation of Psalm 37:28.

For the LORD loves the just and will not forsake His Seyid. Wrongdoers will be completely destroyed; the offspring of the wicked will perish.

Seyid (or Sayed) is the title of Prophet Muhammad$_{pbuh}$ and his direct descendants; Psalm 37:28 is synonymous with Chapter 108 of the Quran.

Quran 108[26]
(1) To thee have We granted the Fount (of Abundance). (2) Therefore to thy Lord turn in Prayer and Sacrifice. (3) For he who hateth thee, he will be cut off.

Table 11
Text Analysis[1]   Psalm 37:28

Str	Translit	Hebrew	English	Morph
3588 [e]	kî	כִּ֥י	For	Conj
3068 [e]	Yah-weh	יְהוָ֨ה ׀	the LORD	Noun
157 [e]	'ō-hêb	אֹ֘הֵ֤ב	loves	Verb
4941 [e]	miš-pāṭ,	מִשְׁפָּ֗ט	judgment	Noun
3808 [e]	wə-lō-	וְלֹא־	and not	Adv
5800 [e]	ya-'ă-zōb	יַעֲזֹ֣ב	do forsakes	Verb
853 [e]	'et-	אֶת־	-	Acc
2623 [e]	hă-sî-dāw	חֲ֭סִידָיו	his saints	Adj
5769 [e]	lə-'ō-w-lām	לְעוֹלָ֣ם	forever	Noun
8104 [e]	niš-mā-rū;	נִשְׁמָ֑רוּ	they are preserved	Verb
2233 [e]	wə-ze-ra'	וְזֶ֖רַע	but the offspring	Noun
7563 [e]	rə-šā-'îm	רְשָׁעִ֣ים	of the wicked	Adj
3772 [e]	nik-rāt.	נִכְרָֽת׃	shall be cut off	Verb

Figure 2

2623. chasid[1]

Strong's Concordance

chasid: kind, pious

Original Word: חָסִיד
Part of Speech: Adjective
Transliteration: chasid
Phonetic Spelling: (khaw-seed')
Short Definition: ones

NAS Exhaustive Concordance

WordOrigin
from chasad
Definition
kind, pious

The 12 Stars of a Lady (Revelation 12)

Revelation 12
NIV
1 A great sign appeared in heaven: a woman clothed with the sun, with the moon under her feet and a crown of twelve stars on her head. 2 She was pregnant and cried out in pain as she was about to give birth. 3 Then another sign appeared in heaven: an enormous red dragon with seven heads and ten horns and seven crowns on its heads. 4 Its tail swept a third of the stars out of the sky and flung them to the earth. The dragon stood in front of the woman who was about to give birth, so that it might devour her child the moment he was born. 5 She gave birth to a son, a male child, who "will rule all the nations with an iron scepter." And her child was snatched up to God and to his throne. 6 The woman fled into the wilderness to a place prepared for her by God, where she might be taken care of for 1,260 days.
7 Then war broke out in heaven. Michael and his angels fought against the dragon, and the dragon and his angels fought back. 8 But he was not strong enough, and they lost their place in heaven. 9 The great dragon was hurled down—that ancient serpent called the devil, or Satan, who leads the whole world astray. He was hurled to the earth, and his angels with him.
10 Then I heard a loud voice in heaven say:
"Now have come the salvation and the power and the kingdom of our God, and the authority of his Messiah. For the accuser of our brothers and sisters, who accuses them before our God day and night, has been hurled down. 11 They triumphed over him by the blood of the Lamb and by the word of their testimony; they did not love their lives so much as to shrink from death.
12 Therefore rejoice, you heavens and you who dwell in them! But woe to the earth and the sea, because the devil has gone down to you! He is filled with fury, because he knows that his time is short." 13 When the dragon saw that he had been hurled to the earth, he pursued the woman who had given birth to the male child. 14 The woman was given the two wings of a great eagle, so that she might fly to the place prepared for her in the wilderness, where

she would be taken care of for a time, times and half a time, out of the serpent's reach. 15 Then from his mouth the serpent spewed water like a river, to overtake the woman and sweep her away with the torrent. 16 But the earth helped the woman by opening its mouth and swallowing the river that the dragon had spewed out of his mouth. 17 Then the dragon was enraged at the woman and went off to wage war against the rest of her offspring—those who keep God's commands and hold fast their testimony about Jesus.

The last book of the Protestant Bible, the Book of Revelation, in chapter 12, portrays a war between Dragon, a symbol of tyrant rulers, and a Holy woman with 12 stars on her crown. She is clothed with sun (meaning *under the guidance of her father*) and the moon under her feet (*her mother passed away*).

The offspring of the Lady triumphed over Dragon by the blood of the Lamb and by the word of their testimony and giving their lives. This can picture the event of Karbala where Imam Hussain$_{pbuh}$ gave everything he had, including his life. All 11 Imams were martyred and some believe that the last and 12th Imam, Al-Mahdi$_{pbuh}$, will also be martyred.

She brings forth a son, who will rule all the nations with an iron sword, who has the authority of Messiah. She is given two wings (symbol of two Divine powers, one through her offspring and one through a revelation; it could also mean two holy sons.) It may also indicate the beloved mother of Al-Mahdi, Lady Narjes$_{pbuh}$, who is from the offspring of Simon$_{pbuh}$ (the first Disciple of Jesus$_{pbuh}$), having the honour of marriage with the eleventh Imam, Al-Hassan al Askari$_{pbuh}$. The two wings, in her case, can be Islam and Christianity; both combined and brought forth a son who will bring justice and peace to the Earth.

Her son goes to hiding for periods. The Devil is angry with the woman. He rages wars against the rest of her offspring, those who keep God's commands and hold fast their testimony about Jesus.

Unfortunately, almost all Christians believe that this is a second coming prophecy. They have not thought about the "iron sword", "12 stars", "the war between Devil and the woman"; no logical explanation has given to "the offspring of her and having the authority of Jesus".

These prophecies perfectly fit in the story of Lady Fatimah$_{pbuh}$, the beloved daughter of the Prophet, and the 12 Imams as her stars. Her mother died when she was a child and her father, Prophet Muhammad$_{pbuh}$, was with her most of her life. Soon after prophet's death, she was also martyred. The last Imam, Al-Mahdi$_{pbuh}$, is the one who is on the Occultation and will come to stablish Justice on the Earth.

This chapter alongside with other passages, such as Revelation 19, Isaiah 21, 42, and 58 – to be discussed shortly, with no doubt, is about the coming of Imam Al-Mahdi$_{pbuh}$. The "coming of Jesus" is far from this prophecy for many reasons such as: the book of revelation is not about the past but future, Jesus$_{pbuh}$ has no offspring, he (according to Christian theology) will not fight, his mother was not chased by the ruler, she had no 12 stars, and so on. If we try to relate it to his second coming, the question of 12 stars on the lady's crown will still remain unanswered.

The 12 Fruits in Mekka (Revelation 22:1, 2)

Not only do the Biblical prophecies about Islam start with twelve princes, it also ends with a similar statement, *the twelve fruits from the tree of life standing on the water of life **in Mekka**.*

Chapter 22 of Revelation has all we need to know about the truthfulness of Islam. It is an excellent document for all Christians to examine and find the truth. Islam is the outstanding prophecy of this chapter.

I must remind that the author of Revelation, St. John, was a Jew, whose mother tongue was Aramaic. Some scholars even argue that Revelation was a Hebrew apocalypse that has been changed to fit Christian faith. Therefore, we have to look at the Aramaic or Hebrew version of the book, otherwise the translations have very little to offer, as we see below.

Revelation 22:1, 2
NIV
1 Then the angel showed me the river of the water of life, as clear as crystal, flowing from the throne of God and of the Lamb. 2 down the middle of the great street of the city. On each side of the river stood the tree of life, bearing twelve crops of fruit, yielding its fruit every month. And the leaves of the tree are for the healing of the nations.

What we do not see in these verses are indeed what the entire chapter is crying about, *Allah and the twelve fruits from the tree of life in Mekka.*

Figure 3 is taken from one of the most credible Christian sources, Dukhrana Biblical Research Society, Department of Linguistics and Philosophy at Uppsala University. It lists verses 1 and 2 in Aramaic text (called Peshitta[a]) with Arabic, Hebrew and Latin transliterations. The boxed words are the missing points of the verses in the translations: "mekkā wəmekkā", translated to "On each side"; and "alaha" translated to "God".

Every learned person, with no doubt, would know that the word *mekkā wəmekkā* is the city of Mekka in Arabian peninsulas, the city of the prophet of Islam. The repetition of "Mekka" emphasizes its importance in the context: Mekka and *only* Mekka.

"The 12 fruits in 12 months" means "the 12 Imams for all eras". Let us read it again:

Revelation 22:1, 2
*1 Then the angel showed me the river of the water of life, as clear as crystal, flowing from the throne of **Allah** and of the Lamb. 2 in the middle of the great street of **Mekka and Mekka**, on the river stood the tree of life, bearing **twelve crops of fruit**, yielding its fruit every month. And the leaves of the tree are for the healing of the nations.*

Healing of the nations indicates its global application; no race, skin color, language or background can be barriers for its healing remedy. *The twelve crops of fruits from Mekka* can be fulfilled by the Twelve Imams only. In addition, the lamb is a symbol of sacrifice referring to Imam Hussain$_{pbuh}$, the beloved grandson of the Prophet.

---

[a] Peshitta, (Syriac: "simple", or "common"), Syriac version of the Bible, the accepted Bible of Syrian Christian churches from the end of the 3rd century AD.

Figure 3
Peshitta[31]

- Revelation 22:1

ܘܚܘܝܢܝ ܢܗܪܐ ܕܡܝܐ ܚܝܐ ܕܟܝܐ ܐܦ ܢܗܝܪܐ ܐܝܟ ܓܠܝܕܐ ܘܢܦܩ
ܡܢ ܟܘܪܣܝܗ ܕܐܠܗܐ ܘܕܐܡܪܐ ܀

Revelation 22:1 - وخَوِينِي نَهرَا دمَيَا خيَا دَكيَا أپ نَهِيرَا أَيك جلِيدَا ونَاپِق مِن كُورسيه دَ الآهَا ودامرَا .

Revelation 22:1 - וחויני נהרא דמיא חיא דכיא אף נהירא איך גלידא ונפק מן כורסיה דאלהא ודאמרא .

Revelation 22:1
- wəḥawyan nahrā dəmayyā ḥayye daḵyā ʾāp̄ nahīrā ʾayḵ gəlīdā wənāp̄eq men kūrsəyēh d'ālāhā wədemrā .

Revelation 22:2-

ܘܒܡܨܥܬ ܫܘܩܝܗ ܡܟܐ ܘܡܟܐ ܥܠ ܢܗܪܐ ܩܝܣܐ ܕܚܝܐ ܕܥܒܕ ܦܐܪܐ ܬܪܥܣܪ ܘܒܟܠ ܝܪܚ ܝܗܒ ܦܐܪܘܗܝ ܘܛܪܦܘܗܝ ܠܐܣܝܘܬܐ ܕܥܡܡܐ

Revelation 22:2 - ومِصعَت شُوقيه مكا ومكا عَل نَهرَا قَيسَا دخَيا دعَابِد پارا ترعسَر وَبكُل يرَخ يَاهِب پَاروهي وطَرپَوهي لَاسيُوتَا دعَممِا .

Revelation 22:2 - ומצעת שוקיה מכא ומכא על נהרא קיסא דחיא דעבד פארא תרעסר ובכל ירח יהב פארוהי וטרפוהי לאסיותא דעממא .

Revelation 22:2
- wəmeṣʿat šūqēh mekkā wəmekkā ʿal nahrā qaysā dəḥayye dəʿāḇeḏ pīre tərəʿsar waḇkul yīraḥ yāheḇ pīraw wəṭarpaw lāsyūṯā dəʿamme .

61

The remaining verses of Revelation 22 are complementary to verses 1 and 2.

Revelation 22:8-9
NIV
I, John, am the one who heard and saw these things. And when I had heard and seen them, I fell down to worship at the feet of the angel who had been showing them to me. 9 But he said to me, "Don't do that! I am a fellow servant with you and with your fellow prophets and with all who keep the words of this scroll. Worship God!"

The original word for God in Aramaic is ܐܠܗܐ ālāhā ("Allah" in Arabic). Figure 4 is verse 9 in Peshitta.

Figure 4

Peshitta[31]

- Revelation 22:9

ܘܐܡܪ ܠܝ ܚܙܝ ܠܐ ܟܢܬܟ ܐܝܬܝ ܘܕܐܚܝܟ ܢܒܝܐ ܘܕܐܝܠܝܢ ܕܢܛܪܝܢ ܗܠܝܢ ܡܠܐ ܕܟܬܒܐ ܗܢܐ ܠܐܠܗܐ ܣܓܘܕ ܀

Revelation 22:9 - وَامَر لِي خزِي لَا كَنَاتَاك اِيتَي ودَاخِيك نِبِيا ودَاِيلِين دنَاطرِين هَالِين مِلا دكتَابَا هَانَا لَاَلَاهَا سجُود .

Revelation 22:9 - wemmar lī ḥəzī lā kənātāk ʾītay wədaḥayk nəḇīe wədaylēn dənāṭrīn hālēn melle daktāḇā hānā lālāhā səgūd .

Revelation 22:9 - Then saith he unto me, See thou do it not: for I am thy fellowservant, and of thy brethren the prophets, and of them which keep the sayings of this book: worship God.

The Bible commentators could not deny the strong concept of monotheism in this verse. We clearly understand that no one is worthy of worship except God, not even the Angel who brings the revelation to the Prophets or Disciples. Remember this Angel is called the Holy Spirit in most of the NT, as even today Christian leaders claim that all truth revealed to the Disciples are from the Holy Spirit, but how they can worship the Holy Spirit when he himself forbids it. Similar statement is given in Revelation 19:10.

Revelation 19:10
At this I fell at his feet to worship him. But he said to me, "Don't do that! I am a fellow servant with you and with your brothers and sisters who hold to the testimony of Jesus. Worship God! For it is the Spirit of prophecy who bears testimony to Jesus".

The verse also is emphasizing the prophethood of Jesus$_{pbuh}$, although the translations are confusing.

Revelation 19 is a great prophetic passage about Islam; it is discussed in Chapter 5 – Quran In The Bible, under "Furqan".

Revelation 22:10 prohibits closing the prophecy of the scroll: "*Do not seal up the words of the prophecy of this scroll, because the time is near.*" This indicates the coming of another Revelation in near future. Christianity, Contrary to this verse, believes that the New Testament is the Last Testament and no more revelation is to come. Verse 14 talks about the blessing of entering to *the city*, those who worship God alone will enter to it. (Figure 5)

All translators, with no exception, use the definite article "the" for "city", indicating that the chapter has talked about it already; but when we go back to read the previous verses in the translations, we find no mention of any city name. Unless we examine the Peshitta, in which the word Mekka is mentioned in verse 2.

Figure 5

Peshitta[31]

- Revelation 22:14

ܛܘܒܝܗܘܢ ܠܕܥܒܕܝܢ ܦܘܩܕܢܘ̈ܗܝ ܢܗܘܐ ܫܘܠܛܢܗܘܢ ܥܠ ܩܝܣܐ ܕܚ̈ܝܐ ܘܒܬܪܥܐ ܢܥܠܘܢ ܠܡܕܝܢܬܐ܀

Revelation 22:14 - طُوبَيهُون لَدعَابِدِين فُوقدَانَوهي نِهوا شُولطَانهُون عَل قَيسَا دخَيا وَبتَرعَا نِعلُون لَمدِينتَا .

Revelation 22:14 - ṭūḇayhon laḏ‘āḇdīn pūqdānaw nehwe šūlṭānhon ‘al qaysā dǝḥayye waḇtar‘ā ne‘lon lamḏīttā .

Revelation 22:14 - Blessed are they that do his commandments, that they may have right to the tree of life, and may enter in through the gates into the city.

"Blessed are those do his commandments" makes the criterion for salvation and having permission to enter the city. Obviously the commandment is: "Do not worship anyone but God, not even the Angel who brings the revelation". It reminds us what Jesus$_{pbuh}$ also said in numerous places to worship and love God only. (Luke 4:8, Mark 12:29, Matthew 22:37) Jesus$_{pbuh}$ also made it clear that his God is the same One God of all. (See John 20:17)

John 20:17
NIV
Jesus said, "Do not hold on to me, for I have not yet ascended to the Father. Go instead to my brothers and tell them, **'I am ascending to my Father and your Father, to my God and your God.'"**

The Problem with Revelation 22

Chapter 22 of Revelation is a conversation between John and the Angel; this is ONLY up to verse 11. However, from verse 12 all in sudden God himself is the speaker and in verse 16 it changes to Jesus$_{pbuh}$, then in verses 17 to 21 it is not clear who is the speaker. It illustrates a later change in the text to serve a purpose.

Revelation 22:12-21
NIV
12 "Look, I am coming soon! My reward is with me, and I will give to each person according to what they have done. 13 I am the Alpha and the Omega, the First and the Last, the Beginning and the End. 14 "Blessed are those who wash their robes[a], that they may have the right to the tree of life and may go through the gates into the city. 15 Outside are the dogs, those who practice magic arts, the sexually immoral, the murderers, the idolaters and everyone who loves and practices falsehood. 16 "I, Jesus, have sent my angel to give you this testimony for the churches. I am the Root and the Offspring of David, and the bright Morning Star." 17 The Spirit and the bride say, "Come!" And let the one who hears say, "Come!" Let the one who is thirsty come; and let the one who wishes take the free gift of the water of life. 18 I warn everyone who hears the words of the prophecy of this scroll: If anyone adds anything to them, God will add to that person the plagues described in this scroll. 19And if anyone takes words away from this scroll of prophecy, God will take away from that person any share in the tree of life and in the Holy City, which are described in this scroll. 20 He who testifies to these things says, "Yes, I am coming soon." Amen. Come, Lord Jesus. 21 The grace of the Lord Jesus be with God's people. Amen.

---

[a] In Peshitta it says: "Blessed are those do his commandments"

Chapter 22 verse 18 says that God will add plagues to who adds anything to the scroll; the history shows there were many plague epidemics in the world particularly in Europe. Is it related to the verse 18 or not? I have no answer.

Revelation 22:18
NIV
I warn everyone who hears the words of the prophecy of this scroll: If anyone adds anything to them, God will add to that person the plagues described in this scroll.

No wonder why we do not see "Mekka" in verse 1 in Greek manuscripts, the only surviving key word in the entire chapter. Subsequently, other translations, which follow the Greek, make no mention of "Mekka".

A Prophet like Moses (Deuteronomy 18:18)

Deuteronomy, the fifth book of Torah, teaches us that God have informed Moses$_{pbuh}$ the advent of Prophet Muhammad$_{pbuh}$. We read in Deuteronomy 18 that Moses asked God not to show his fire and the great sound again for he would die from it. God accepted Moses' request and informed him coming of a Prophet from the Israelites Brethren:

Deuteronomy 18:16-19
NIV
16 For this is what you asked of the LORD your God at Horeb on the day of the assembly when you said, "Let us not hear the voice of the LORD our God nor see this great fire anymore, or we will die." 17 The LORD said to me: "What they say is good. 18 I will raise up for them a prophet like you from among their brothers; I will put my words in his mouth, and he will tell them everything I command him. 19 If anyone does not listen to my words that the prophet speaks in my name, I myself will call him to account."

I must emphasize that God responded to the request of Moses to "not hear the voice of the Lord nor see the great fire"; that is the great fiery revelation.

The prophecy has the following five characteristics:

1) He will be like Moses$_{pbuh}$.
2) He will come from the brothers of the Israelites.
3) God will put His words in the mouth of the prophet and he will declare what God commands him.
4) He will speak in God's name.
5) If someone does not listen to these words, God will call him to account.

Let us examine these characteristics in depth.

1) A prophet like Moses$_{pbuh}$.

Moses and Muhammad $_{pbut}$ are very much alike, because:

1) Both were born naturally, from human parents.
2) Both lived most of their lives without parents.
3) Both were married and had children.
4) Both were given a comprehensive law and code of life.
5) Both encountered their enemies and were victorious in miraculous ways.
6) Both were accepted as prophets and statesmen by their people.
7) Both migrated following conspiracies to assassinate them.
8) Both were king and prophet same time.
9) Both had direct occasion of inspiration from God, Moses$_{pbuh}$ in Mt. Sinai and Muhammad$_{pbuh}$ in Me'raaj.
10) None of them were mistaken as Divine beings by their people.
11) Both died and buried.

Christians claim that this prophecy is about Jesus$_{pbuh}$, because he was an Israelite. Nevertheless, they are puzzled when we ask about any other commonality between Moses and Jesus $_{pbut}$. If we look at the differences between them, it will be impossible to consider Jesus$_{pbuh}$ the promised prophet of Deuteronomy 18:18.

Below is a list of differences between Moses and Jesus $_{pbut}$:

1) Their birth was different; Moses$_{pbuh}$ with human father and mother while Jesus$_{pbuh}$ had only Mother.
2) Moses$_{pbuh}$ migrated but Jesus$_{pbuh}$ never did.
3) Moses$_{pbuh}$ revived a set of laws, but Jesus$_{pbuh}$ was only to stablish the laws. Although modern Christianity even does not believe that Jesus$_{pbuh}$ had anything to do with the laws of

Moses_pbuh_, except to void it; "He came to save mankind from the Torah" they say.

4) Moses_pbuh_ fought with his enemies, Jesus_pbuh_ never did.
5) Moses_pbuh_ was accepted by his people, Jesus_pbuh_ was rejected.
6) Moses_pbuh_ was the king and commander of his people, Jesus_pbuh_ was not.
7) Moses married (had at least two wives) and had children, there is no evidence if Jesus_pbuh_ married.
8) Moses_pbuh_ is a prophet but Christians call Jesus_pbuh_ "God"[a].
9) Moses_pbuh_ died but Jesus_pbuh_ ascended to Heaven.

2) From the brothers of the Israelites.

Abraham_pbuh_ had two sons from Hagar and Sarah, Ishmael and Isaac _pbut_ (Genesis 21). Ishmael_pbuh_ became the grandfather of the Arab nation, and Isaac_pbuh_ became the grandfather of the Jewish nation. The prophet spoken of was not to come from among the Jews themselves, but from among their brothers, i.e. the Ishmaelite. Muhammad_pbuh_, a descendant of Ishmael, is indeed this prophet.

Also, Isaiah 42:1-13, to be discussed in Chapter 6 – Isaiah and Islam, speaks of the servant of God, His "chosen one" and "messenger" who will bring down a law. "He will not falter or be discouraged till he establishes justice on earth. In his law the islands will put their hope." (Isaiah 42:4). Verse 11, connects the awaited one with the descendants of Kedar (second son of Ishmael_pbuh_), the ancestor of the Prophet Muhammad_pbuh_.

---

[a] Jehovah Witnesses calls him "a god", with so-called "small g".

3) God will put His words in the mouth of His Prophet.

The words of God (the Holy Quran) were truly put into Prophet Muhammad's mouth $_{pbuh}$. God sent Angel Gabriel to teach Prophet Muhammad$_{pbuh}$ the exact words of God (the Holy Quran) and asked him to dictate them to people as he heard them. He replied: "I cannot read". They did not come from his own thoughts, but were put into his mouth by the Angel. For second time, the Angel asked him to read; "I am not learned" he replied; then the Angel revealed him the first passage of the Quran, five verses from Chapter 96 (Al-Alaq):

The Quran 96:1-5[26]
In the name of Allah, Most Gracious, Most Merciful
1 Proclaim! (or read!) in the name of thy Lord and Cherisher, Who created- 2 Created man, out of a (mere) clot of congealed blood: 3 Proclaim! And thy Lord is Most Bountiful, 4 He Who taught (the use of) the pen, 5 Taught man that which he knew not.

During the lifetime of Prophet Muhammad$_{pbuh}$, and under his supervision, these words were then memorized and written down by his companions.

A similar prophecy has been made by Jesus$_{pbuh}$:

John 16:13
NIV
But when he, the Spirit of truth, comes, he will guide you into all the truth. He will not speak on his own; he will speak only what he hears, and he will tell you what is yet to come.

We will discuss about this verse in this chapter under "The Spirit of Truth".

4) He will speak in God's name.

The Quran is the only Holy Book starts with the statement: *In the name of God*. Indeed 113 chapters out of 114 begin with the phrase, "In the Name of God, the Most Gracious, the Most Merciful." Even the chapter, which does not start with the exact statement, chapter 9, do have the word "Allah" (God) at the very first line.

One must keep in mind that there are many passages related to the advent of the Prophet. For example, Isaiah relates the messenger to Kedar who will sing a new song (a scripture in a new language) (Isaiah 42:10-11)[a]. This is mentioned more clearly in the prophecy of Isaiah: "and another tongue, will he speak to this people" (Isaiah 28:11)[b]. Isaiah even explains that the revelation will be sent down in parts and complex rules: *For it is: Do this, do that, a rule for this, a rule for that; a little here, a little there."* (Isaiah 28:10, NIV). The Quran was revealed in sections over a span of twenty-three years in different locations and occasions.

5) If someone does not listen to these words, God will call him to account.

This, the very last statement, shows that God will send rules and laws that require people to obey them. No book can compete with the Quran in perfection of Divine laws and rules.

Can the Gospels be another candidate? By examining the Gospels we know that they do not pass the criteria of Deuteronomy 18:18. The Gospels do not bring new laws because Jesus[pbuh] did not come

---

[a] See Chapter 6 – Isaiah and Islam- My Messenger, My Muslim
[b] See Chapter 6 – Isaiah and Islam- Quran,

to do so but to revive the laws of Moses_pbuh. He was to stablish the laws of Moses (Matthew 5:17), although it did not work out because people rejected him.

It is believed in Christianity that Jesus_pbuh came to be crucified; "his mission was not to bring laws or a scripture but to pay for the inherited sin of mankind", Christians say; it is what the Churches teach. How then they can consider Deuteronomy 18:18 a prophecy concerning Jesus_pbuh, knowing that his mission was not to tell people what to do and what no to do, because people already knew those from the OT. He was simply reminding them the laws of Moses_pbuh.

As a closing word for Deuteronomy 18:15-18, I must emphasize a few things again:

1. In Deut. 18:15 the original word: me·'a·chei·cha מֵאַחֶיךָ (similar to Arabic: من اخيك), meaning "from your brother", refers to someone who is not within the Israelite (the audience), otherwise should say: "from you" or "from Israelites". Some versions, such as NIV, interpreted it "from your fellow Israelites"!

2. In Deut. 18:16 we read: (NIV)

For this is what you asked of the LORD your God at Horeb on the day of the assembly when you said, "Let us not hear the voice of the LORD our God nor see this great fire anymore, or we will die."

It explains the fact that Moses_pbuh asked neither to hear nor to see the great fire of God anymore. In another word, no more Laws to be seen by Israelites.

3. In Deuteronomy 18:17 we read:

The LORD said to me: "What they say is good.

God accepts Moses request and therefore no more Laws to come from Israelites.

4. In 18:18 we read:

I will raise up for them a prophet like you from among their brothers. And I will put my words in his mouth, and he shall speak to them all that I commend him.

God tells that the revelation will continue from "a·chei·hem אֲחֵיהֶם"; it means: "their brothers", similar to Arabic: اخيهم (akhihem or achihem). The question is: Whose brothers? Well, of course, the Israelites' brother.

God will raise up (not will "give birth" and not "will beget"). God will raise up *a prophet*, not "a god". "*I will raise up for them a prophet*" He says, not "a begotten son"! Not "a god in flesh"!

… "*like you*" (Moses)

Was Jesus$_{pbuh}$ like Moses$_{pbuh}$? Moses$_{pbuh}$ was a man, Period. Christians claim that Jesus$_{pbuh}$ was "a man and God"! Moses$_{pbuh}$ was born naturally and he died a natural death. Did Jesus$_{pbuh}$ also was born and died like him? Moses$_{pbuh}$ migrated, fought, made his kingdom, judged, killed, and so many things that Jesus$_{pbuh}$ did none of them. Moses$_{pbuh}$ did not rise after death, but Christians claim that Jesus$_{pbuh}$ did!

Was Jesus$_{pbuh}$ Like Moses$_{pbuh}$?!

Revelation from Paran (Deuteronomy 33:1, 2)

Moses_{pbuh} announces the blessing of God: revelations from three different locations, Sinai, Seir and Paran. Deuteronomy 33 verse 2 is such a significant prophecy to all Bible believers. Unfortunately, interpretations widely differ for two very obvious reasons: presence of codded words and "Paran". Below are just a few examples of the different translations.

NIV
He said: "The LORD came from Sinai and dawned over them from Seir; he shone forth from Mount Paran. He came with myriads of holy ones from the south, from his mountain slopes.

NLT
The LORD came from Mount Sinai and dawned upon us from Mount Seir; he shone forth from Mount Paran and came from Meribah-kadesh with flaming fire at his right hand.

ESV
He said, "The LORD came from Sinai and dawned from Seir upon us; he shone forth from Mount Paran; he came from the ten thousands of holy ones, with flaming fire at his right hand.

KJB
And he said, The LORD came from Sinai, and rose up from Seir unto them; he shined forth from mount Paran, and he came with ten thousands of saints: from his right hand went a fiery law for them.

Followings are the Hebrew and text analysis of Deuteronomy 33:2.

33:2 דברים Hebrew OT: WLC (Consonants Only)[1]
ויאמר יהוה מסיני בא וזרח משעיר למו הופיע מהר פארן ואתה מרבבת
קדש מימינו [אשדת כ] (אש ק) (דת ק) למו:

Table 12

Text Analysis[1]   Deuteronomy 33:2

Str	Translit	Hebrew	English	Morph
559 [e]	way-yō-mar,	וַיֹּאמַר	And he said	Verb
3068 [e]	Yah-weh	יְהוָה	The LORD	Noun
5514 [e]	mis-sî-nay	מִסִּינַי	from Sinai	Noun
935 [e]	bā	בָּא	came	Verb
2224 [e]	wə-zā-raḥ	וְזָרַח	and rose up	Verb
8165 [e]	miś-śê-'îr	מִשֵּׂעִיר	on them from Seir	Noun
	lā-mōw,	לָמוֹ	to them	Prep
3313 [e]	hō-w-p̄î-a'	הוֹפִיעַ	he shined forth	Verb
2022 [e]	mê-har	מֵהַר	from Mount	Noun
6290 [e]	pā-rān,	פָּארָן	Paran	Noun
857 [e]	wə-'ā-tāh	וְאָתָה	and he came	Verb
7233 [e]	mê-rib-bōt	מֵרִבְבֹת	from the midst of ten	Noun

6944 [e]	qō-ḏeš;	קֹדֶשׁ	of saints	Noun
3225 [e]	mî-mî-nōw	מִימִינוֹ	At His right	Noun
	[ʾê-šə-ḏāt	[אֵשְׁדָּת	-	
	k]	כ]	-	
	(ʾêš	(אֵשׁ	-	
	q)	ק)	-	
799 [e]	(ḏāt	(דָּת	there was flashing	Noun
	q)	ק)	-	
	lā-mōw.	לָמוֹ:	to	Prep

Where is Paran?

In Genesis 21:21, we read that Ishmael and his Mother Hagar ₚbut settled in the wilderness of Paran:

Genesis 21:17:21 (NIV)
*17 God heard the boy crying, and the angel of God called to Hagar from heaven and said to her, "What is the matter, Hagar? Do not be afraid; God has heard the boy crying as he lies there. 18 Lift the boy up and take him by the hand, for I will make him into a great nation." 19 Then God opened her eyes and she saw a well of water. So she went and filled the skin with water and gave the boy a drink. 20 God was with the boy as he grew up. He lived in the desert and became an archer. 21 While **he was living in the Desert of Paran**, his mother got a wife for him from Egypt.*

King James Version Lexicon confirms that Paran is the dessert of Arabia. (See Figure 6)

Figure 6

KJV Lexicon[1]

And he dwelt
yashab (yaw-shab')
to sit down (specifically as judge. in ambush, in quiet); by implication, to dwell, to remain; causatively, to settle, to marry

in the wilderness
midbar (mid-bawr')
a pasture (i.e. open field, whither cattle are driven); by implication, a desert; also speech (including its organs) -- desert, south, speech, wilderness.

of Paran
Pa'ran (paw-rawn')
ornamental; Paran, a desert of Arabia -- Paran.

Some other references, such as *The Historical Geography of Arabia*, by Charles Forester, also confirm that Paran is the desert of Arabia. Seir is where Jesus$_{pbuh}$ received his revelation, in Palestine. Mount Sinai is widely believed to be in Egypt, however there are also lines of evidence that relate the Biblical Mount Sinai to the Arabian Peninsula; among them is the Paul's letter to Galatians- Chapter 4 verse 25. Some Bible believers interpret Deuteronomy 33:2 as the revelation to Moses and Jesus $_{pbut}$ only, "because Paran is located in Israel", they say. The problems with this claim cannot be ignored if we accept the credibility of historical facts. Even Bible itself affirms that Paran is in Arabia, let alone nonbiblical sources. Besides that, there is no evidence of any revelation, fiery law, from so-called "Israeli dessert of Paran".

One of the main reasons many Jews migrated to Arabia is indeed the prophecy of advent of the final messenger from the region. Moving from green Palestine to yellow dessert of Arabia can be explained only by having a strong faith in such prophecy.

Paran is also mentioned in Habakkuk as a place of revelation:

Habakkuk 3:3 (NIV)
God came from Teman, the Holy One from Mount Paran. His glory covered the heavens and his praise filled the earth.

Interestingly, Tema is the ninth son of Ishmael. (Genesis 25:13-15) It is also a prophecy of Isaiah in chapter 21 verse 14.

Isaiah 21:14 (NIV)
bring water for the thirsty; you who live in Tema, bring food for the fugitives.

Isaiah 21:14 is talking about the migration of Prophet Muhammad$_{pbuh}$. (See Chapter 6 – Isaiah and Islam - The Migration)

The Three Awaited Figures (John 1:19 - 21)

We learn from the Gospel of John that the Jews were waiting for the fulfillment of three *distinct* prophecies; the first was the coming of the Christ$_{pbuh}$, the second was Elijah$_{pbuh}$, and the third was *the* Prophet$_{pbuh}$. This is apparent from the three questions posed to John the Baptist$_{pbuh}$:

John 1:19 – 21 (NIV)
"Now this was John's testimony, when the Jews of Jerusalem sent priests and Levites to ask him who he was. He did not fail to confess, but confessed freely, "I am not the Christ." They asked him, "Then who are you? Are you Elijah?" He said, "I am not." "Are you the Prophet?" He answered, "No".

In Greek texts, both "Christ" and "Prophet" preceded by "Ho", a definite article, translated to "the". It explains the whole argument that the Jews were familiar with these prophecies. They were waiting for the Meshiach (Christ), Elijah and the Prophet.

Were Jews confused?

Some Christians say that the Jewish Rabbis of the time did not know these three are one; "that is why they asked John if he is any of the three!"

If this is true, it means even John the Baptist$_{pbuh}$ did not know that, because he showed no reaction to the Jews who repeated the question over and over.

I am very surprised to hear such a claim! The Bible has explicit stories about Elijah and the Christ as two completely different persons. It prophesies the coming of the Christ and Elijah and the

Prophet in very different passages with different specifications. Not a single passage of the Bible uses these three synonymously.

During the reign of Ahab, nine centuries before the Christ, Elijah was a prophet, but not *the prophet*. The Book of Malachi prophesies return of Elijah "before the coming of the great and terrible day of Yahweh" (Malachi 4:5). Many references have given to him in various religious texts such as Mishnah and Talmud, the New Testament, and the Quran; none of them confuses him with the Christ or John the Baptist, with an exception, *the only exception*, of a suspicious statement assumed to be made by Jesus$_{pbuh}$, in which John the Baptist is called Elijah:

Matthew 11:13 – 14 (NIV)
13 For all the Prophets and the Law prophesied until John, 14 And if you are willing to accept it, he is the Elijah who was to come.

Although it does not make sense, because John himself rejected such claim (John 1:19-21) but if ever Jesus$_{pbuh}$ said so, then it strongly proves that Elijah and the Christ are two different persons.

Jesus says, in Matthew 11:11 (NLV):

"I tell you the truth, of all who have ever lived, none is greater than John the Baptist ..."

If "the greatest man", John the Baptist$_{pbuh}$, Jesus$_{pbuh}$ and Jewish Rabbis of 2000 years ago did not know the difference between Elijah, the Christ and the Prophet, I think that no Christian can claim to know it either.

Prophet Muhammad in the Bible

There are several words in the Old Testament referring to Prophet Muhammad$_{pbuh}$: *m-'ōd mə-'ōd* (explained earlier), *Hamda* or *Hemda* (Aramaic), equivalent to *Ha-ehmet / -ehmet* (Hebrew)[a], *mê-ḥam-mā-tōw*, *Mahamadim* and *maḥ-mad* or *maḥ-mada*. These words are found in several places in the Bible. The following lines are examining only some of the cases.

Hamda and Hem-dat

Hamda, in the OT, translated to "promised" and "desirable", is symbol of the fulfilment of a Divine plan and promise, a belief to the promised one to come, and the ultimate blessing. It occurs in several places in the Bible. Followings are just a few examples:

Psalms 106:24 (KJB)
Yea, they despised the pleasant land, they believed not his word.

By keeping "Hamda" untranslated, the verse becomes a symbolic statement, referring to a man, Hamda (translated to "pleasant"). Particularly the second part, "they believed not *his* word", reflects the human nature of the Hamda and focuses on him rather than "the land". In another word, the verse is emphasizing a person not land. Below is the rendered translation.

Rendered translation

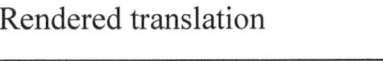

---

[a] The definite article is a suffixed -ā (א) in Aramaic (an emphatic or determined state), and a prefixed h- (ה) in Hebrew.

Psalms 106:24
Yea, they despised the land of Hamda, they believed not his word.

Figure 7 is the text analysis of the verse. Note the morphology of Hamda, which is Noun.

Figure 7

Text Analysis[1]   Psalm 106:24

Str	Translit	Hebrew	English	Morph
3988 [e]	way-yim-'ă-sū	וַיִּמְאֲסוּ	they despised	Verb
776 [e]	bə-'e-reṣ	בְּאֶרֶץ	land	Noun
2532 [e]	ḥem-dāh;	חֶמְדָּה	the pleasant	Noun
3808 [e]	lō-	לֹא־	not	Adv
539 [e]	he-'ĕ-mî-nū,	הֶאֱמִינוּ	do they believed	Verb
1697 [e]	liḏ-ḇā-rōw.	לִדְבָרוֹ׃	in His word	Noun

Another example of Hamda is 2 Chronicles 21:20, which is talking about the death of Jehoram. The verse says that Jehoram died without being Hamda (translated to "desired"). This can mean that he could not reach the expectation of being the promised one or, in my opinion, it means that he died without believing in Hamda. In Hebrew, the phrase used for it is בלא חמדה (blaa hemda), expressing the detachment from "the idea of Hamda" (Figure 8).

2 Chronicles 21:20
He was thirty and two years old when he began to reign, and he reigned in Jerusalem eight years, and departed blaahamda. They buried him in the city of David, but not in the sepulchres of the kings.

There is another coherent link between the verse and Prophet Muhammad_{pbuh} and that is the age of Jehoram when he died, 40. He could not become Hamda when he died. Interestingly, Prophet Muhammad_{pbuh} did receive revelation at the age of 40, *fulfilling the expectation.*

No matter what meaning we take from the numerous verses where the word Hamda occurs, one thing is undeniable; that is *people were expecting a promised person to come*, as the meaning of the word Hamda also suggests so.

Figure 8

Text Analysis[1] 2 Chronicles 21:20

Str	Translit	Hebrew	English	Morph
4427 [e]	mā-lak	מָלַךְ	he reigned	Verb
3389 [e]	bî-rū-šā-lim;	בִּירוּשָׁלֵם	in Jerusalem	Noun
1980 [e]	way-yê-lek	וַיֵּלֶךְ	and departed	Verb
3808 [e]	bə-lō	בְּלֹא	with no	Adv
2532 [e]	ḥem-dāh,	חֶמְדָּה	being desired	Noun
6912 [e]	way-yiq-bə-ru-hū	וַיִּקְבְּרֻהוּ	and however they buried him	Verb

83

Islam, granted in Kaaba and Qum (Haggai 2:6-9)

Book of Haggai[a] has a very interesting passage on the matter; not only does it mention Hem-daṯ but also the coming of Islam in the house of God, Kaaba, and granting it through Qum[b].

> Haggai 2:6-9
> NIV
> 6 *"This is what the LORD Almighty says: 'In a little while I will once more shake the heavens and the earth, the sea and **the dry land**.*
> *7 I will shake all nations, and what is **desired** by all nations will come, and I will fill this house with **glory**,' says the LORD Almighty.*
> *8 The silver is mine and the gold is mine,' declares the LORD Almighty.*
> *9 The glory of **this present house** will be greater than the glory of the former house,' says the LORD Almighty. 'And **in this place** I will grant **peace**,' declares the LORD Almighty."*

These four verses are suspiciously interpreted. There are at least four occasions of omissions (one in each verse) and five cases of ambiguous spellings and translations. (See Figure 11 to Figure 14)

Verse 6 ends with הֶחָרָבָה he-ḥā-rā-ḇāh translated to "the dry land". Does this mean "the desert"? May be it does, particularly if we look at the meaning of it. It could also be a metaphoric word for an abandoned place; similar to Persian خرابه (kharabeh). Another possible interpretation is that the Hebrew he-ḥā-rā-ḇāh could relate

---

[a] The Book of Haggai is a short 2-chapter book, written in 520 BC by preassumingly prophet Haggai. It is the third book to last of the OT.
[b] Qum, or Qom, is a holy city in Iran, a center of Islamic school of theology and propagation center, located south of Tehran.

to Arabah or the Arabia. In any case, it is pretty close to the desert of Arabia, which is also a dry land.

All four occurrences of word ṣə-bā-'ō-wṯ (meaning "hosts") are omitted, or replaced with "Almighty" in all four verses. It can only be a cover up maneuver rather than a mistake.

Verse 7 is where word Hem-daṯ translated to *what is desired*; another word that caught my attention is כבוד kā-ḇō-wḏ (translated to *"with glory"*). I guess its original form might have been changed to what we see today. Perhaps it was כבה kabah (Kaaba or Ka'ba, the holy house of God in Mekka) but the scribes "corrected it".

In verse 9, the very same word כבוד kā-ḇō-wḏ is repeated. Verse 9 has another important word, ובמקום ū-ḇam-mā-qō-wm (translated to *"and place"*). Its word origin, according to NAS Exhaustive Concordance, is "qum", meaning "place". ū-ḇam-mā-qō-wm should be translated to *and through Qum*. (See below)

Figure 9

4725. maqom[1]

NAS Exhaustive Concordance

Word Origin
from qum
Definition
a standing place, place

Finally, Shalom שלום, in Arabic "Islam", translated to "peace". If we keep the original words as they are, the passage will be turned out like this:

Haggai 2:6-9
6 *"This is what the LORD of hosts (armies) says: 'In a little while I will once more shake the heavens and the earth, the sea and the* **ḥā-rā-ḇāh** *(abandoned place and/or arabah).*
7 *I will shake all nations, and shall come* **Hem-daṯ** *(hemda) of all nations and the residents of this house of* **Kaaba** *(kābat), says the LORD of hosts.*
8 *The silver is mine and the gold is mine,' declares the LORD of hosts.*
9 *This latter house of* **Kaaba** *will be greater than the former house,' says the LORD of the hosts. 'And through* **Qum** *I will grant* **Islam**,*' declares the LORD of hosts."*

The word "Haggai" is from "chag" (Figure 10). Hebrew "chag" is cognate of Arabic "Hajj" (حج), both mean "festival" and "pilgrimage". This word is repeated in a few places throughout the Bible. It will be discussed in Chapter 7 – Hajj, the Pilgrimage.

In summary, Haggai chapter 2 gives five signs of Islam: Hajj, Hamda, Kaaba, Qum and Islam.

Figure 10

Strong's Exhaustive Concordance[1]

Haggai

From chag; festive; Chaggai, a Heb. Prophet -- Haggai.

see HEBREW chag

Brown-Driver-Briggs

חַג *noun masculine*[Isaiah 29:1] *festival-gathering, feast, pilgrim-feast* (Late Hebrew id.; Aramaic ܚܓܐ, חַגָּא;

Arabic حَجّ *pilgrimage;*

Figure 11

Haggai 2:6[1]

Haggai 2 Interlinear

▲ Haggai 2:6 ▼

3588 [e]	3541 [e]	559 [e]	3068 [e]	6635 [e]	5750 [e]	259 [e]	4592 [e]	
kî	kōh	'ā·mar	Yah·weh	ṣə·ḇā·'ō·wṯ,	'ō·wḏ	'a·ḥaṯ	mə·'aṭ	
כִּי	כֹה	אָמַר	יְהוָה	צְבָאֹות	עֹוד	אַחַת	מְעַט	
For	Thus	says	the LORD	of hosts	Yet	Once	in a little	
Conj	Adv	Verb	Noun	Noun	Subst	Adj	Subst	

1931 [e]	589 [e]	7493 [e]	853 [e]		
hî;	wa·'ă·nî,	mar·'îš	'eṯ-		
הִיא	וַאֲנִי	מַרְעִישׁ	אֶת־		
it	and I	will shake [is]	-		
Pro	Pro	Verb	Acc		

8064 [e]	853 [e]	776 [e]	853 [e]	3220 [e]	853 [e]	2724 [e]
haš·šā·ma·yim	wə·'eṯ-	hā·'ā·reṣ,	wə·'eṯ-	hay·yām	wə·'eṯ-	he·ḥā·rā·ḇāh.
הַשָּׁמַיִם	וְאֶת־	הָאָרֶץ	וְאֶת־	הַיָּם	וְאֶת־	הֶחָרָבָה
the heavens	and	the earth	and	the sea	and	the dry
Noun	Acc	Noun	Acc	Noun	Acc	Noun

Figure 12

Haggai 2:7[1]

◄ **Haggai 2:7** ►

Haggai 2 Interlinear

853 [e]	4390 [e]	1471 [e]	3605 [e]	2532 [e]	935 [e]	1471 [e]	3605 [e]	853 [e]	7493 [e]
'eṯ-	ū·mil·lê·ṯî	hag·gō·w·yim,	kāl-	ḥem·daṯ	ū·ḇā·'ū	hag·gō·w·yim,	kāl-	'eṯ-	wə·hir·'aš·tî 7
אֶת־	וּמִלֵּאתִי	הַגּוֹיִם֔	כָּל־	חֶמְדַּ֣ת	וּבָ֙אוּ֙	הַגּוֹיִ֔ם	כָּל־	אֶת־	וְהִרְעַשְׁתִּ֖י
-	and I will fill	nations	all	the desire	and shall come	nations	all	-	And I will shake
Acc	Verb	Noun	Noun	Noun	Verb	Noun	Acc	-	Verb

6635 [e]	3068 [e]	559 [e]	3519 [e]	2088 [e]	1004 [e]
ṣə·ḇā·'ō·wṯ.	Yah·weh	'ā·mar	kā·ḇō·wḏ,	haz·zeh	hab·ba·yiṯ
צְבָאֽוֹת׃	יְהוָ֖ה	אָמַ֥ר	כָּב֔וֹד	הַזֶּ֣ה	הַבַּ֧יִת
of hosts	the LORD	said	with glory	this	house
Noun	Noun	Verb	Noun	Pro	Noun

Figure 13

Haggai 2:8[1]

THE SPIRIT OF TRUTH   Chapter 2 – The Prophet and Twelve Princes

Figure 14

Haggai 2:9[1]

Ehmet (Psalm 145:18)

Ehmet with all its derivatives has 127 occurrences in the OT. It means truth, righteous, faith/faithful, trustworthy-ness, and so on. Only the verses with close relation to Ahmed (another name for Prophet Muhammad$_{pbuh}$) will be examined here, which namely are Psalm 145:18 and Isaiah 59:14-15. The book of Isaiah will be discussed in Chapter 6 – Isaiah and Islam.

The word "Ehmet" has some relations to prophetic texts in some parts of the Bible, if not all. For example, in Psalm 145:18 we read: (See Table 13)

Psalm 145:18
The LORD is near to all who call upon Him, to all who call upon Him through Ehmet.

It is fascinating how the verse reflects the Shi'ite view of Shafaat (plead) through Prophet Muhammad$_{pbuh}$.

We also have verses in the NT providing evidence that the word Ehmet is indeed Ahmed, such as John 14:16 and 16:13. These verses will be discussed under "Ahmed foretold by Jesus" in this chapter.

Table 13
Text Analysis[1]   Psalm 145:18

Str	Translit	Hebrew	English	Morph
7138 [e]	qā-rō-wb	קָרוֹב	[is] near	Adj
3068 [e]	Yah-weh	יְהוָה	The LORD	Noun
3605 [e]	lə-kāl	לְכָל־	to all	Noun
7121 [e]	qō-rə-'āw;	קֹרְאָיו	those who call	Verb
3605 [e]	lə-kōl	לְכֹל	To all	Noun
834 [e]	'ă-šer	אֲשֶׁר	that	Prt
7121 [e]	yiq-rā-'u-hū	יִקְרָאֻהוּ	call	Verb
571 [e]	be-'ĕ-met.	בֶאֱמֶת׃	upon Him in truth	Noun

There are a few significant specifications of "Ehmet" and 'Ahmad":

1. Both pronounced almost identical.
2. Ehmet means "truth" and "trustworthy". The second meaning is identical to Arabic "Ameen", that is the nickname of Prophet Muhammad_pbuh.
3. The root word of Ehmet, *aman*, is also the nickname of Prophet Muhammad_pbuh (*Ameen* in Arabic). Both "aman" and "ameen" have similar meanings, such as "truthfulness" and "trustworthy'.
4. There are some passages in the Bible where the word Ehmet occurs within a context that can be prophecies related to the history of Islam (such as Isaiah 59:14-15[a] and Psalm 145:18).
5. The Hebrew version (Ehmet) has also developed a different meaning than the Arabic (Ahmed). Ehmet means *truth*; Ahmad means *praise*. This is a common phenomenon in the Semitic languages. An example of that is Arabic صداقه (sidaqah) and Hebrew צְדָקָה (ṣə-dā-qāh); both have similar root but different meanings (*friendship* in Arabic, *justice* in Hebrew).
6. The belief in Shafaat (plead) through Prophet Muhammad_pbuh is strongly backed by Psalm 145:18 when Ehmet is written without translating. (*The LORD is near to all who call upon Him, To all who call upon Him through Ehmet.*)
7. In the NT, we have verses foretelling the coming of "The Spirit of Truth". This, if translated back to Hebrew, is indeed the spirit of Ehmet or Ahmed; backed by historical evidence, it strongly explains the real application of the Psalm 145:18.

The following lines are explaining the aforementioned matters.

---

[a] Isaiah 59 will be discussed in Chapter 6 – Isaiah and Islam.

Ehmet̲ and Ahmed

According to King James Version Lexicon, אמת ('ĕ-met̲) literally means "truth" and "trustworthiness" (Figure 15). It is the exact meaning of Arabic "Ameen". The pronunciation of 'ĕ-met̲ is eh'-meth, a stretched *eh* in the beginning and soft *th* at the end.(Figure 16) The ending letter of ת "tav" is a "soft t"; in Syriac it is also pronounced something in between t and d. No English letter can represent it accurately; that is why it is underlined as a substitution.

The Midrash[a] explains that 'ĕ-met̲ is made of the first, middle, and last letters of the Hebrew alphabet (aleph, mem, and tav: אמת); a very interesting composition. Can it be the same Arabic احمد *Ahmed*? For the following four reasons the answer is positive.

First reason: the pronunciation of *Ehmet̲* אמת and *Ahmed* احمد is almost identical. We must not forget the differences in the pronunciations of names in Hebrew and Arabic, such as *î-šū-'āh* ישועה and *Eisa* عيسى (Jesus) or *yitz'chak* יצחק and *Is-haq* اسحاق (Isaac). Although it appears to have a different starting and ending letters in the English transliteration but, as mentioned earlier, אמת ('ĕ-met̲) starts with the first Hebrew alphabet א "a" (aleph), similar to *Ahmed*, then comes the מ "mem" and ends with ת "tav".

What we may think is missing in אמת ('ĕ-met̲) is the actual "h" sound existed in *Ahmed*. A close look at the phonetic spelling of אמת ('ĕ-met̲) (Figure 16) shows that "h" of Arabic *Ahmed* is covered in the pronunciation of Hebrew אמת ('ĕ-met̲) (as eh'-meth). The difference between the "h" sounds in *Ehmet̲* and *Ahmed* is very insignificant.

---

[a] Midrash is the genre of rabbinic literature containing interpretations of Torah and other religious laws and literature.

Another objection might be given about the pronunciation of these two words is that the ending letters of *Ehmet* and *Ahmed* are not identical (ת *t* and ד *d*, respectively). As shown in Table 1 and bellow, Hebrew ת *t* in some words becomes *d* in its Arabic cognate, such as אַחַת *achat* and أحد *ahad* or *wahed* (meaning "one"). Note that the end letter of אַחַת *achat* is transformed into *d* in أحد *ahad*.

English	Proto-Semitic	Arabic	Aramaic[a]	Hebrew
One[b]	'aḥad-, 'išt-	واحد wa:ḥid- أحد aḥad-	echad אחד achat אחת	echad אחד achat אַחַת

Genesis 11:1 is an example of the two paralleling letters of *t* (ת) and *d* (ד). The Hebrew אַחַת *achat* translated to Arabic واحدا *waheda* or أحد *ahad*. (*d* in *waheda* represents *t* in *achat*)

Genesis 11:1[1]
WLC (Consonants Only)

ויהי כל־הארץ שפה אחת ודברים אחדים:

New International Version
Now the whole world had one *language and a common speech.*

تكوين ١:١١ Arabic: Smith & Van Dyke

وكانت الارض كلها لسانا واحدا ولغة واحدة.

Table 14 shows the text analysis of Genesis 11:1.

---

[a] Hebrew alphabet is used instead of Aramaic.
[b] Arabic *ahad* changes to *achat* in Hebrew and Aramaic (*h* and *d* becomes *ch* and *t*, respectively).

Table 14
Text Analysis[1]   Genesis 11:1

Str	Translit	Hebrew	English	Morph
1961 [e]	way-hî	וַיְהִי	And had	Verb
3605 [e]	kāl	כָּל-	all	Noun
776 [e]	hā-'ā-reṣ	הָאָרֶץ	earth	Noun
8193 [e]	śā-p̄āh	שָׂפָה	language	Noun
259 [e]	'e-ḥāṯ;	אֶחָת	one	Adj
1697 [e]	ū-ḏə-ḇā-rîm	וּדְבָרִים	and speech	Noun
259 [e]	'ă-ḥā-dîm.	אֲחָדִים:	one	Adj

Second reason: meaning of *Ehmeṯ* אמת, which is "truth", "trustworthy" or "trustworthiness", is exactly same as the meaning of *Ameen,* the nickname of Prophet Muhammad$_{pbuh}$ (Figure 15 and Figure 16).

Figure 15

KJV Lexicon[1]

Yea truth
'emeth (eh'-meth)
stability; (figuratively) certainty, truth, trustworthiness -- assured(-ly), establishment, faithful, right, sure, true (-ly, -th), verity.

Figure 16

571. emeth[1]

Strong's Concordance

emeth: firmness, faithfulness, truth

Original Word: אֱמֶת
Part of Speech: noun feminine; adverb
Transliteration: emeth
Phonetic Spelling: (eh'-meth)
Short Definition: truth

NAS Exhaustive Concordance

Word Origin
from aman
Definition
firmness, faithfulness, truth

Third reason is hidden in the word origin of *Ehmet*. According to NAS Exhaustive Concordance (Figure 16), the word origin of *Ehmet* is "aman". It is the cognate of Arabic امین "ameen"; both "aman" and "ameen" are form triconsonantal word of *"a m n"*, means "faith", "sure", "trust", etc.

Fourth reason for equating *Ehmet* and *Ahmed* is the context of Psalm 145 and Isaiah 59. Not only are the verses, where the word occurs, portraying the exact history of early Islam, but also the entire chapter is fitting to the Islamic history. Isaiah 59 mentions outstanding characters of Islam such as Imam Naqi$_{pbuh}$, Ahmed (Prophet Muhammad$_{pbuh}$), and Lady Sediqa$_{pbuh}$ (the Prophet's daughter). We will review Isaiah 59 in Chapter 6 – Isaiah and Islam, under "After Ahmed (Isaiah 59)".

Mê-ḥam-mā-ṯōw (Psalm 19:6)

The word מחמתו (mê-ḥam-mā-ṯōw) occurs only once in the Bible, in Psalm 19:6. It is translated to "of its warmth". (See below)

Psalm 19:1-6
NIV
1 For the director of music. A psalm of David. The heavens declare the glory of God; the skies proclaim the work of his hands. 2 Day after day they pour forth speech; night after night they reveal knowledge. 3 They have no speech, they use no words; no sound is heard from them. 4 Yet their voice goes out into all the earth, their words to the ends of the world. In the heavens God has pitched a tent for the sun. 5 It is like a bridegroom coming out of his chamber, like a champion rejoicing to run his course. 6 It rises at one end of the heavens and makes its circuit to the other; nothing is deprived of its warmth.

There are two problems with the common translations of Psalm 19:1-6: wrong translation of mê-ḥam-mā-ṯōw and distortion in the statements' order of verse 1.

First Problem: Wrong translation of mê-ḥam-mā-ṯōw (see Table 15)

מחמתו mê-ḥam-mā-ṯōw is assumed to be a compound word containing three parts: מ (me), חמ (ḥam or kham) and תו (tow) meaning *from, heat, its (from its heat*, collectively). The word appears nowhere else in the Bible. The similar and assumed derivative words exist in the Bible in two forms: Noun and Adjective.

1. As Noun there are five occurrences as following:

ḥam·māh חַמָּה — 1 Occurrence, Job 30:28, translated to "the sun"
ha·ḥam·māh הַחַמָּה — 3 Occurrences, Isaiah 24:23, Isaiah 30:26 (twice), translated to "the sun"
ka·ḥam·māh כַּחַמָּה — 1 Occurrence, Song 6:10, translated to "as the sun"

In the above cases, all three words end with ה "h". However, mê-ḥam-mā-ṯōw lacks the ending letter of ה "h".

2. As Adjective, there are two occurrences:

In Joshua 9:12, חָם ḥawm (singular), and In Job 37:17, חַמִּים ḥam-mîm (plural). Both words lack the ending letter of ה "h" and are translated to "warmth" or "hot".

In short words, since mê-ḥam-mā-ṯōw, in Psalm 19:6, is a noun but not similar to the three forms of ḥam·māh, ha·ḥam·māh and ka·ḥam·māh, hence we cannot reject other possible application of it.

Second Problem: Distortion

A close look at verse 1 exposes an issue. It has three statements, as the Hebrew text below shows. (See also Figure 17)

Psalm 19:1
WLC (Consonants Only) [1]
למנצח מזמור לדוד: השמים מספרים כבוד־אל ומעשה ידיו מגיד הרקיע:

Statement 1: למנצח מזמור לדוד:
lam-naṣ-ṣê-aḥ, miz-mō-wr lə-ḏā-wiḏ.
For the director of music. A psalm of David.

Statement 2: השמים מספרים כבוד־אל
haš-šā-ma-yim, mə-sap-pə-rîm kə-ḇō-wḏ- 'êl
The heavens declare the glory of God

Statement 3: ומעשה ידיו מגיד הרקיע׃
ū-ma-'ă-śêh yā-daw, mag-gîd hā-rā-qî-a'.
and the work of his hand shows the skies.

The last statement, *and the work of his hand shows the skies*, does not make sense. It is the equivalent to saying: *The work of the artist's hand shows the painting*. It should be other way around: *The painting shows the work of the artist's hand*.

Cause of the Problems with Verse 1

"Hashemayim" (translated to *the heavens*) is the subject for the second and third statements. In the translations, the third statement, *and the work of his hand shows the skies*, is changed to: *the skies proclaim the work of his hands*. They have done this to make sense of the verse and to comply with the translation of the preceding statement: *the heavens declare the glory of God*.

In another word, the structure of the last statement has been changed to hide a problem. Look how it is going to be if we keep the structure of the verse as it appears in the original language:

The heavens declare the glory of God, and the work of his hand shows the skies.

In the above translation, the subject in the first part is *heavens*, but in the second part, it is *his hand* (referring to *God*). This sentence, *and the work of his hand shows the skies*, theologically does not make sense. *The sky* supposed to show *the work of God's hand*, not the other way around. This could expose the mistranslation. Therefore, the flip-over-magic had to be done to cover it up.

Solution for the problem of the last part is hidden in the word *HASHAMAYIM (Hashemite)* הַשָּׁמַיִם. If we keep it as is, just like the word הַנְּפִלִים han-nə-p̄i-lîm in Genesis 6:4, the real meaning of the verse will be apparent.

HASHAMAYIM (Hashemite) הַשָּׁמַיִם *declare the glory of God; the work of his hand reveals the skies.*

That means the *Hashemite* glorify God and reveal knowledge of the heavens. The statement is perfectly consonant with verse 6, where it says: ... *nothing is deprived of mê-ḥam-mā-ṯōw (his Muhammad).* (This verse will be discussed shortly.)

[In a narration of Prophet Muhammad$_{pbuh}$ we read: *I am the city of knowledge and Ali is the gate to it.*]

The word הַשָּׁמַיִם haš-šā-ma-yim occurred 236 times in the Old Testament. It is translated to *the heavens.* Suffix *im* makes the word plural but it is also an affix for respect. If we write it as a name, *The Hashamies* or *Hashamite,* and apply it to Psalm 19:1 – 6, alongside with other parts of these verses, it foretells a great story of the early Islam, uprising of Imam Hussain$_{pbuh}$, the grandson of The Prophet, against the tyrant ruler, Yazid son of Moawia.

Table 15

Text Analysis[1]   Psalm 19:6

Str	Translit	Hebrew	English	Morph
7097 [e]	miq-ṣêh	מִקְצֵה	[is] from the end	Noun
8064 [e]	haš-šā-ma-yim	הַשָּׁמַיִם ׀	of the heaven	Noun
4161 [e]	mō-w-ṣā-'ōw,	מוֹצָאוֹ	His going forth	Noun
8622 [e]	ū-tə-qū-p̄ā-tōw	וּתְקוּפָתוֹ	and his circuit	Noun
5921 [e]	'al-	עַל-	to	Prep
7098 [e]	qə-ṣō-w-tām;	קְצוֹתָם	the ends	Noun
369 [e]	wə-'ên	וְאֵין	and there is nothing	Prt
5641 [e]	nis-tār,	נִסְתָּר	hid	Verb
2535 [e]	mê-ḥam-mā-tōw	מֵחַמָּתוֹ׃	from its heat	Noun

Figure 17

Psalm 19:1[1]

Psalm 19:1

Psalm 19 Interlinear

Strong's	Hebrew	Transliteration	English	Part of Speech
5329 [e]	לַמְנַצֵּחַ	lam·naṣ·ṣê·aḥ,	To the chief Musician	Verb
4210 [e]	מִזְמוֹר	miz·mō·wr	A Psalm	Noun
1732 [e]	לְדָוִד׃	lə·ḏā·wiḏ.	of David	Noun
8064 [e]	הַשָּׁמַיִם	haš·šā·ma·yim,	The heavens	Noun
5608 [e]	מְסַפְּרִים	mə·sap·pə·rîm	declare	Verb
3519 [e]	כְּבוֹד־	kə·ḇō·wḏ-	of the glory	Noun
410 [e]	אֵל	'êl;	of God	Noun
4639 [e]	וּמַעֲשֵׂה	ū·ma·'ă·śêh	and the work	Noun
3027 [e]	יָדָיו	yā·ḏāw,	of His hands	Noun
5046 [e]	מַגִּיד	mag·gîḏ	shows	Verb
7549 [e]	הָרָקִיעַ׃	hā·rā·qî·a'.	the firmament	Noun

105

By reading the verses 1 to 6 of Psalm chapter 19, without changing or translating the key words, every learned man who knows a bit about the history of Islam will immediately remember the Prophet_pbuh and his Grandson Imam Hussain_pbuh.

Rendered translation
PSALM 19:1-6
HASHAMAYIM (Hashemite) הַשָּׁמַיִם *declare the glory of God; the work of his hand reveals the skies. 2 Day after day they pour forth speech; night after night they reveal knowledge. 3 They have no speech, they use no words; no sound is heard from them. 4 Yet their standard (*קַוָּם *qaw-wām) goes out into all the earth, their words to the ends of the world. In SHAM* שָׂם *God has a tent for the sun. 5 It is like a bridegroom coming out of his chamber, like a champion rejoicing IN ARUSUR. 6 It rises at one end of HASHAMAYIM (Hashemite)* הַשָּׁמַיִם *and he is going forth to KUFATO* אָרח לָרוּץ*; nothing is deprived of mê-ḥam-mā-tōw (his Muhammad)* (מֵחַמָּתוֹ)*.*

Psalm 19:1-6 in summary:

1. The morphology of מחמתו mê-ḥam-mā-tōw in psalm 19:6 is Noun (Table 15). To consider it as a derivative of ḥam·māh חַמָּה, it had to have the ending letter ה h after מחם mê-ḥam, just like other 3 derivatives do; or it has to be an adjective without ה h at the end, similar to חָם ḥawm (singular) and חַמִּים ḥam-mîm (plural). In another words, if it was מחמהתו mê-ḥam-māh-tōw or an adjective, it could mean *"from its heat"*. However, it is not.

2. The context of Psalm 19 strongly recommends that the topic is not the heavens but Hashamayim (Hashemite) if the key phrases are written without translating.

If any Muslim were to read these verses, they would immediately remember the story of Karbala. Verse 3 exhibits an era of corruption in Islamic history where tyrant rulers took over the power and distorted the Law.

The fourth verse explains how Imams were reviving the Divine message even under the oppressive rulers. Verse 5 is portraying a young man coming out of his chamber like a champion in *Arusura*, quite similar to *Ashura*, the day that the event of Karbala took place. It is assimilated to Sun appearing in the sky. (Imam Hussain_pbuh was the fifth member of the Prophet's household.)

In verse 6, we read that he is moving toward Kufato, a city in Iraq where the event of Karbala took place near it. The word translated to *"moving"* is מוֹצָאוֹ mō-w-ṣā-'ōw, meaning *"his move toward"*. It clearly shows an action of moving toward a place. The ending statement of verse 6, *"nothing is deprived of mê-ḥam-mā-tōw* מֵחַמָּתוֹ *(his Muhammad)"*, is also what narrations say about foretelling the event of Karbala by Prophet Muhammad_pbuh.

No doubt, these verses are not as simple as mainstream Christianity think. The prophetic message in these verses is apparent.

han-nə-p̄i-lîm הַנְּפִלִים and haš-šā-ma-yim הַשָּׁמַיִם

In Genesis 6:4, word הַנְּפִלִים han-nə-p̄i-lîm is kept intact as "The Nephilim" though it means "the Giants", despite its word root, which is נָפַל (naphal – meaning "to fall, lie"). But the word הַשָּׁמַיִם haš-šā-ma-yim, in Psalm 19, translated to "the heavens". I wonder why a word with a certain meaning is kept as is but another word with similar situation ("with meaning") has been translated instead of applying the same rule – keeping as the original form.

Mahammadim (Song of Solomon 5:16)

A well-known name to all, a favourite to Muslims; he is the beloved of Solomon. You might already know where it is in the Bible; Song of Solomon 5:16. (See Table 16)

Apparently, the word is in plural form as "mahammadim". The suffix *im* not only is used to pluralize a word but also for respect. There are many examples in the Bible to prove the case. Genesis 1:1 is the best one, where we read: *In the beginning **Elohim** created the heavens and the earth.* No translators interpreted *Elohim* as plural (Gods), including the Arabic.

Genesis 1:1
NIV
In the beginning God created the heavens and the earth.

The Arabic translation also uses singular form: Allah (The God).

تكوين ١:١ Arabic: Smith & Van Dyke [1]

في البدء خلق الله السموات والارض.

Chapter 5 of Song of Solomon is talking about a beloved (5:4, 5, 10): (NIV)

*My beloved is radiant and ruddy, outstanding among ten thousand (5:10); His mouth is sweetness itself; he is **altogether lovely**. This is my beloved, this is my friend, daughters of Jerusalem (5:16).*

No Bible believer has a logical answer to the question of whom this chapter is talking about. Who is the beloved man? What is the purpose of this chapter? What do we learn from it? How is it going to help the reader? Can we get any benefit from it? And so forth. There is no answer given to these questions. Some whispering that it is a drama! You do not say it loud because some believers might call you a heretic.

The chapter, in translations, ends with no clue on whom is Solomon talking about. Is it just a show time? Is it a poem for an anonymous beloved? Do any one expect from a wise man like Solomon to parade? Not the Jews of that time. The chapter ends with *this is my friend, daughters of Jerusalem*. Nevertheless, we do not find in the translations whom does *"this"* refer to.

The verse 16 is unequivocally introducing the beloved as ma-ḥă-mad-dîm. It says: wə-ḵul-lōw ma-ḥă-mad-dîm; that means *"and all (of these are) Muhammad;* all *the beauty and sweetness and brightness ... are him, Oh daughters of Jerusalem"*. Why daughters of Jerusalem, not men and women? Because it concerns future generations; *it is a prophecy*. By keeping "Mahammadim" as is in the ending verse, whole chapter becomes full of meaning. Below is the rendered translation of the verse. (See Table 16 for text analysis.)

Song of Solomon 5:16
His mouth is sweetness itself; and all (these are) Mahammadim.
This is my beloved, this is my friend, oh daughters of Jerusalem.

Christians claim that the chapter is a love poem of a woman (assumed to be the Solomon's wife) addressed to her Husband. What does make a love poem get into the Book of God? How they can justify the claim; it depends on how they are going to define the Bible as a whole, "the word of God" or "contains some words of God". This is extremely crucial to Christianity because it will question the "absolute credibility of the Bible"; perhaps wherever suits the believers it is the word of God, wherever does not then it is not the word of God!

Table 16

Text Analysis[1] **Song of Solomon 5:16**

Str	Translit	Hebrew	English	Morph
2441 [e]	hik-kōw	חִכּוֹ	His mouth	Noun
4477 [e]	mam-taq-qîm,	מַמְתַקִּים	[is] most sweet	Noun
3605 [e]	wə-kul-lōw	וְכֻלּוֹ	he altogether	Noun
4261 [e]	ma-hă-mad-dîm;	מַחֲמַדִּים	[is] lovely	Noun
2088 [e]	zeh	זֶה	This	Pro
1730 [e]	dō-w-dî	דוֹדִי	[is] my beloved	Noun
2088 [e]	wə-zeh	וְזֶה	and this	Pro
7453 [e]	rê-'î,	רֵעִי	[is] my friend	Noun
1323 [e]	bə-nō-wt	בְּנוֹת	O daughers	Noun
3389 [e]	yə-rū-šā-lim.	יְרוּשָׁלָ͏ִם׃	of Jerusalem	Noun

Muhammad from Mekka (Ezekiel 24:16)

The word maḥ-mad מחמד occurs in five verses: 1 King 20:6, Ezekiel 24:16, 21, 25 and Hosea 9:6. It is translated to *"favour"*, *"pleasure"* and *"desire"*. Ezekiel 24:21, 25 is a nostalgic prophecy of the Israelite where God proclaims that he will take away their eyes' maḥ-mad (translated to "delight").

A careful study of these five verses ascertains that maḥ-mad was a symbol of favour and pleasure to Israelite. Ezekiel 24:16 is the most relevant to our topic:

Ezekiel 24:16
NIV
"Son of man, with one blow I am about to take away from you the delight of your eyes. Yet do not lament or weep or shed any tears."

Text analysis of the verse (Table 17) shows a very interesting dual word combination: "mim-mə-kā 'et- maḥ-mad"; although it is translated to "from you the delight" but if we keep mə-kā and maḥ-mad the way it is, the hidden message will be revealed: "from mə-kā maḥ-mad".

Another important word in the verse is לקח (lō-qê-aḥ or laqach). This word is translated to "take away". It is used for a variety of meanings including: *accept, bring, supply, take*, and so on. (Figure 18) The Arabic cognate of it is لقح (leqah), meaning "to conceive" and "to bring forth". If we pick "to bring" for it, the verse will be perfectly predicting the coming of Prophet Muhammad$_{pbuh}$ from Mekka:

Ezekiel 24:16
"Son of man, with a stroke in your eye I am about to bring Muhammad from Mekka. So do not lament or weep or shed any tears."

Table 17

Text Analysis[1]   Ezekiel 24:16

Str	Translit	Hebrew	English	Morph
1121 [e]	ben-	בֶּן־	Son	Noun
120 [e]	'ā-dām	אָדָ֕ם	of man	Noun
2005 [e]	hin-nî	הִנְנִ֨י	I am about	Adv
3947 [e]	lō-qê-aḥ	לֹקֵ֧חַ	I take away	Verb
4480 [e]	mim-mə-kā	מִמְּךָ֛	from	Prep
853 [e]	'et-	אֶת־	-	Acc
4261 [e]	maḥ-maḏ	מַחְמַ֥ד	from you the desire	Noun
5869 [e]	'ê-ne-kā	עֵינֶ֖יךָ	of your eyes	Noun
4046 [e]	bə-mag-gê-p̄āh;	בְּמַגֵּפָ֑ה	with a blow	Noun
3808 [e]	wə-lō	וְלֹ֤א	and not	Adv
5594 [e]	tis-pōḏ	תִסְפֹּד֙	shall you mourn	Verb
3808 [e]	wə-lō	וְלֹ֣א	nor	Adv
1058 [e]	tiḇ-keh,	תִבְכֶּ֔ה	weep	Verb
3808 [e]	wə-lō-w	וְל֥וֹא	neither	Adv
935 [e]	tā-ḇō-w	תָב֖וֹא	shall run down	Verb
1832 [e]	ḏim-'ā-te-kā.	דִּמְעָתֶֽךָ׃	your tears	Noun

Figure 18

3947. laqach[1]

Strong's Concordance

laqach: to take

Original Word: לָקַח
Part of Speech: Verb
Transliteration: laqach
Phonetic Spelling: (law-kakh')
Short Definition: take

NAS Exhaustive Concordance

Word Origin
a prim. root
Definition
to take
NASB Translation
accept (8), accepted (3), accepts (2), bring (18), brought (13), buy (1), buys (1), capture (2), captured (2), carry (3), caught (2), exact (1), find (1), flashing (1), flashing forth (1), get (25), gets (1), got (2), has (1), keep (1), married (9), married* (6), marries (1), marry (5), obtain (1), placed (2), procured (2), put (1), raise (3), receive (20), received (12), receives (3), receiving (1), seize (3), seized (2), select (1), selected (1), sent (1), supply (1), take (355), taken (74), takes (15), taking (2), took (352), took away (1), use (1), used (1), wins (1).

Although in Modern Hebrew the word "Mekka" may be written slightly different from what we see in this verse, but we must not forget that many developments and changes have occurred in the Semitic languages in the past.

Some Arabic bibles have translated maḥ-maḏ, in this verse, to *"lust"* (شهوة *shahwat*), a common word used for lower animal (sexual) desire; what a deceitful choice! I cannot figure out how they chose such a word over the true meaning of maḥ-maḏ. Its root goes to *h m d* means *praise*, same in Arabic: حمد *hamd*.

Below is the Arabic translation of Smith & Van Dyke.

- Ezekiel 24:16

حزقيال ٢٤:١٦ Arabic: Smith & Van Dyke[1]
يا ابن آدم هانذا آخذ عنك شهوة عينيك بضربة فلا تنح ولا تبك ولا تنزل دموعك.

There are other places maḥ-maḏ is used but translated slightly different:

- In 1 King 20:6, maḥ-maḏ is translated to "delicate" (شهي *shahi*), a bit less irrelevant than *lust* (شهوة *shahwat*).

1 King 20:6
الملوك الأول ٢٠:٦ Arabic: Smith & Van Dyke[1]
فاني في نحو هذا الوقت غدا ارسل عبيدي اليك فيفتشون بيتك وبيوت عبيدك وكل ما هو شهي في عينيك يضعونه في ايديهم وياخذونه

- The third attempt of the Arabic translators is "treasures" (نفائس *nefa'es*), as we see in Hosea 9:6.

Hosea 9:6
هوشع ٩:٦ Arabic: Smith & Van Dyke[1]
انهم قد ذهبوا من الخراب. تجمعهم مصر. تدفنهم موف. يرث القريص نفائس فضتهم يكون العوسج في منازلهم.

I understand why Arabic Smith & Van Dyke has picked *lust* (شهوة *shahwat*) for maḥ-maḏ in Ezekiel 24:16 but *delicate* (شهي *shahi*) and *treasures* (نفائس *nefa'es*) in other places, because it is too obvious that Ezekiel 24:16 is prophesying Prophet Muhammad[pbuh] and most certainly מִמְּךָ mim-mə-ḵā (*from Mekka*) buzzes the alarm. "It seemed *safer* to be clear from any of these words in Arabic translations!"

Meka Baka (Psalm 84:6)

David_pbuh wishes to be a porter in the house of God; he praises the one who passes by Mekka.

Psalm 84 (NIV)
1 How lovely is your dwelling place, Lord Almighty!
2 My soul yearns, even faints, for the courts of the Lord; my heart and my flesh cry out for the living God.
3 Even the sparrow has found a home, and the swallow a nest for herself, where she may have her young— a place near your altar, Lord Almighty, my King and my God.
4 blessed are those who dwell in your house; they are ever praising you with Sellah

At the end of verse 4, there is a word, familiar to Muslims: סלה "Sellah". In Arabic, it means *prayer*. The Bible translations do not mention it at all.

5 Blessed is he whose strength is in you, in his heart are the highways.

Some translations put a few extra words to verse 5, such as New Living Translation and English Standard Version, as it reads:

Psalm 84:5 (NLT)
What joy for those whose strength comes from the LORD, who has set their minds on a pilgrimage to Jerusalem.

ESV
Blessed are those whose strength is in you, in whose heart are the highways to Zion.

In Hebrew Bible, there is nothing even close to "Zion" or "Jerusalem" in this verse. (See below and Table 18)

THE SPIRIT OF TRUTH — Chapter 2 – The Prophet and Twelve Princes

84:5 תהילים Hebrew OT: WLC (Consonants Only)[1]

אשרי אדם עוז־לו בך מסלות בלבבם:

It reads: 'aš-rê 'ā-dām 'ō-wz- lōw bāk mə-sil-lō-wt bil-bā-bām.

Table 18

Text Analysis[1]   Psalm 84:5

Str	Translit	Hebrew	English	Morph
835 [e]	'aš-rê	אַשְׁרֵי	Blessed	Noun
120 [e]	'ā-dām	אָדָם	[is] the man	Noun
5797 [e]	'ō-wz-	עוֹז־	whose strength	Noun
	lōw	לוֹ	to	Prep
	bāk	בָּךְ	in [are]	Prep
4546 [e]	mə-sil-lō-wt,	מְסִלּוֹת	the ways	Noun
3824 [e]	bil-bā-bām.	בִּלְבָבָם:	in whose heart	Noun

Verse 6 clarifies where the blessed person will be passing through: (NIV)

6 As he passes through the Valley of Baka, he makes it a place of springs; the autumn rains also cover it with pools (bǝ-rā-ḵō-wṯ or "blessings").

"The Valley of Baka" is a greatly disputed word among Bible scholars. Some believe that it means "weeping" (NLV and ASV), relating to Arabic بكاء (bokaa), some have a different opinion: "a place where balsam trees grow" (GOD'S WORD® Translation); others believe that it is name of a location ("Baka" in NIV) or ("Baca" in ESV, KJB).

Bible scholars have reached no conclusion on the real application of this verse. I believe it is because they are not presenting the original Hebrew words. A close look at the Hebrew text explains it very well: (Also see Table 19)

84:6 תהילים Hebrew OT: WLC (Consonants Only) [1]

עברי | בעמק הבכא מעין ישיתוהו גם־ברכות יעטה מורה:

It reads:

'ō-ḇǝ-rê ḇǝ-'ê-meq hab-bā-ḵā ma'-yān yǝ-šî-ṯū-hū; gam- bǝ-rā-ḵō-wṯ, ya'-ṭeh mō-w-reh.

"bǝ-'ê-meq hab-bā-ḵā" is very close to "bǝ meka baka" meaning "through Mekka Bakka"; it is the city of Mekka in Arabian Peninsula. The entire chapter is contextually talking about Mekka. Some might oppose the idea of Mekka being the subject in the verse by referring to the ending statement, *the autumn rains also cover it with pools*; "since Mekka is a very dry land and therefore it cannot be subject of the verse", they may say. Nevertheless, a close look at the comments on the verse proves contrary. For example in Ellicott's Commentary for English Readers we read:

Figure 19

Ellicott's Commentary for English Readers[1]

The rain also filleth the pools.—That rain *is the right rendering of the Hebrew word here appears from* Joel 2:23. *The rendering* pools *follows the reading,* berechóth; *but the text has* berachóth, *"blessings", as read by the LXX. and generally adopted now. Render* yea, as the autumn rain covers *(it)* with blessings, i.e., just as the benign showers turn a wilderness into a garden, so resolution and faith turn disadvantage to profit. *(Comp.* Isaiah 35:6-8; Isaiah 43:18 seq.*)*

It is obvious that the place is not well habitable, but the faith of man will turn the land to a blessed place as the rainwater turns a wilderness into a garden.

Note the different readings of a very simple word, berachóth, meaning "blessings" or in Arabic: بركة barakat, but translated to "pools"; that is the case of many other disputes when it comes to the Hebrew texts.

Moreover, same commentary insists the significance of *Baca* in the verse as well as the importance of *a place of spring*:

Figure 20
Ellicott's Commentary for English Readers[1]

(6) Who passing through the valley of Baca.—All the ancient versions have "valley of weeping", which, through the Vulg. vallis lacrymosa, *has passed into the religious language of Europe as a synonym for life. And* Baca (bākha) *seems to have this signification, whatever origin we give the word. The valley has been variously identified—with the valley of* Achor (Hosea 2:15; Joshua 7:24); *the valley of* Rephaim (2Samuel 5:22)—*a valley found by Burckhardt in the neighbourhood of Sinai; and one, more recently, by Renan, the last station of the present caravan route from the north to Jerusalem. Of these, the valley of Rephaim is most probably in the poet's mind, since it is described (*Isaiah 17:5*) as sterile, and as the text stands, we think of some place devoid of water, but which the courage and faith of the pilgrims treats as if it were well supplied with that indispensable requisite, thus turning adversity itself into a blessing. He either plays on the sound of the word (*Baca, *and* becaîm*) or the exudations of the* balsam *shrub gave the valley its name.*

Both Makka and Bakka are the names of the city of Mekka but they are completely ignored by the commentators. In the Holy Quran we read:

The Quran 3:96[26]
The first House (of worship) appointed for men was that at Bakka: Full of blessing and of guidance for all kinds of beings.

Note how both Psalm and the Quran mention it with blessing.

The King James Version has another interesting word in the verse:

Psalm 84:6
KJB
Who passing through the valley of Baca make it a well*; the rain also filleth the pools.*

"A Well" is indeed what the Hebrew text says, מעין (ma'-yān). (See Table 19) It is from עין (ayin), meaning "spring" or "eye", similar to Arabic عين (ayin). It refers to the Well of Zamzam, located within the Masjid al-Haram in Mecca (Mekka), 20 m (66 ft) east of Kaaba.

Zamzam is a miraculous source of water, which sprang from thousands of years ago, since Abraham's son Ishmael and his mother, Haggar $_{pbut}$, arrived there thirsty. She, with no water left, was desperately seeking water for her son, but she could not find any. Hagar ran seven times back and forth between the two hills of Safa and Marwah, looking for water. Getting thirstier by the second, the infant Ishmael scraped the ground with his feet, where suddenly water sprang out.

Verse 7 exhibits a suspicious text: (NIV)

7 They go from strength to strength, till each appears before God in Zion.

Some scholars believe that the verse is very suspicious. Ellicott's Commentary for English Readers is one of them. (See Figure 21)

Figure 21

Ellicott's Commentary for English Readers[1]

(7) **They go from strength to strength**—*i.e.*, each difficulty surmounted adds fresh courage and vigour. ...

The marginal "from company to company" follows the alternative meaning of the Hebrew word, and suggests a picture of the actual progress of the various bands composing a caravan. But the expression in either sense is hardly Hebrew, and the text is suspicious. ...

Continuing to Psalm 84: (NIV)

8 Hear my prayer, Lord God Almighty; listen to me, God of Jacob.
9 Look on our shield, O God; look with favor on your anointed one.
10 Better is one day in your courts than a thousand elsewhere; I would rather be a doorkeeper in the house of my God than dwell in the tents of the wicked. 11 For the Lord God is a sun and shield; the Lord bestows favor and honor; no good thing does he withhold from those whose walk is blameless.
12 Lord Almighty, blessed is the one who trusts in you.

In verse 9, as well as Psalm 18:50 and 2 Samuel 22:51, David$_{pbuh}$ is called משיח *meshikh*, or Messiah. He is not the only person called Messiah in the bible. The Persian King Cyrus (Isaiah 45:1) and Saul[a] (1 Samuel 24:6) was also given the title of משיח *meshikh* (Messiah). What Christians do not know is that the Quran is the only holy book that uses this title, Messiah, *exclusively* for Jesus$_{pbuh}$.

---

[a] Saul, King David's father in law, was the first king of the Kingdom of Israel and Judah. (11th century BC) David called him *Messiah*.

Table 19
Text Analysis[1]   Psalm 84:6

Str	Translit	Hebrew	English	Morph
5674 [e]	'ō-bə-rê	עֹבְרֵי ׀	[Who] Passing	Verb
6010 [e]	bə-'ê-meq	בְּעֵמֶק	through the valley	Noun
1056 [e]	hab-bā-kā	הַבָּכָא	of Baca	Noun
4599 [e]	ma'-yān	מַעְיָן	it a well	Noun
7896 [e]	yə-šî-tū-hū;	יְשִׁיתוּהוּ	make	Verb
1571 [e]	gam-	גַּם-	also	Adv
1293 [e]	bə-rā-kō-wt,	בְּרָכוֹת	the pools	Noun
5844 [e]	ya'-teh	יַעְטֶה	fills	Verb
4175 [e]	mō-w-reh.	מוֹרֶה:	the rain	Noun

Ahmed foretold by Jesus

The Gospel of John is apparently the only Gospel in the canon foretells openly coming of a person after the departure of Jesus[pbuh]. It calls him Parakleet [a], translated to *advocate, helper* and *councillor* (John 14:16, 14:26 and 16:7). Another name given to him is "the Spirit of Truth", a translation of the Greek τὸ πνεῦμα τῆς ἀληθείας (to pneuma tēs alētheias), (John 14:17, 16:13 and 1 John 4:6).

John 15:26 makes it clear that these two (Parakleet and the Spirit of Truth) are the same. Today, all Christian denominations believe that this person is the Holy Spirit. They reason it using some verses from the same Gospel, such as 14:17, 14:26 and sometimes by quoting verses of 1 John 5:6-10 as well as Revelation 22:1, 2.

Jesus[pbuh], in my opinion, did not mean that the Holy Spirit is the one who is supposed to come after him. He meant that the Parakleet or the Spirit of Truth is a man who will be sent by God after him. I also believe that the Spirit of Truth must be from Hebrew רוח אמת (rū-aḥ 'ĕ-meṯ); it is identical to *the spirit of Ahmed*. I will reason my claim using the verses of the Bible only. For ease of understanding, the argument is divided into two major parts: Parakleet and the Spirit of Truth.

---

[a] Other spellings: Paraklete, Paraclete, Paracleet, Faraglete and Faragleet

Parakleet

The Greek παράκλητ- (paraklét), translated to *advocate* and *helper*, appears five times in the New Testament, all of them as Noun; twice as παράκλητον paraklēton (John 14:16, and 1 John 2:1) which is the accusative masculine singular form of the word, and thrice as παράκλητος paraklētos (John 14:26, 15:26, 16:7), the nominative masculine singular. These two words never been used in any of the other three Gospels, known as the Synoptic Gospels.

It is not clear why the Synoptic Gospels, which were written even before the Gospel of John, have nothing to say about Parakleet or the Spirit of Truth. Is it a later amendment to the Gospel of John or it is omitted from the other Gospels; I have no answer. What we know today is that the identity of Parakleet has been the subject of debates among numerous theologians. I could not clarify the truth about the matter from any of the proposed reasonings. Therefore, I decided to do my own way of examining the texts by word search and contextual study; then by considering some known facts, I could come up with clear evidence. The whole image is yet to be composed by finding some missing parts of the puzzle, but the existing pieces are sufficient to identify the message.

Christians believe that Parakleet is a *Johannine term* used only for the Holy Spirit and Jesus$_{pbuh}$. For example, we read in 1 John 2:1 that Jesus Christ is a parakleet (translated to "advocate").

1 John 2:1
NIV
My dear children, I write this to you so that you will not sin. But if anybody does sin, we have an advocate with the Father--Jesus Christ, the Righteous One.

Finally, it has been used even in the OT referring to the friends of Job_pbuh (Job 16:2). The Hebrew word for parakleet is מנחמי mə-na-hă-mê. (Figure 22)

Figure 22

5162 [e] [1]	mə-na-hă-mê	מְנַחֲמָי	comforters	Verb

The matter of dispute is the application of the verses foretelling the coming of "the future Parakleet" not who is a prakleet, because there are more than one parakleet, according to the Bible. In the verses of the Bible where the Parakleet is a promised figure, Christians say that it is the Holy Spirit but Muslims say that it is Prophet Muhammad_pbuh. The solution is not very complicated; however, it requires a deep study of these verses.

I begin with John 14; the passage related to the topic starts from verse 15 and continues to the end of the chapter. These verses are ambiguous and sometimes controversial. In verse 16 Jesus_pbuh explains that God *will send* another advocate (Parakleet).

John 14:15-16
NIV
15 If you love me, keep my commands. 16 And I will ask the Father, and <u>he will give you another advocate</u> to help you and be with you forever.

Next verse turns out to be contrary to verse 16.

17 the Spirit of truth. The world cannot accept him, because it neither sees him nor knows him. But you know him, for <u>he lives with you and will be in you</u>.

Verse 16 is talking about a promise, a prophecy, to be fulfilled in the future (God *will* give another Parakleet to be with the Disciples), but verse 17 explains that the Disciples already have the Parakleet.

In verse 19, Jesus says that only you (the disciples) will see him not the world; then Judas asks the reason:

19 Before long, the world will not see me anymore, but you will see me. Because I live, you also will live. 22 Then Judas (not Judas Iscariot) said, "But, Lord, why do you intend to show yourself to us and not to the world?"

Jesus$_{pbuh}$ answers:

23 Jesus replied, "Anyone who loves me will obey my teaching. My Father will love them, and we will come to them and make our home with them. 24 Anyone who does not love me will not obey my teaching. These words you hear are not my own; they belong to the Father who sent me.

Apparently verse 23 makes a big shift in Jesus' previous statement (verse 19: *…the world will not see me anymore…*). In my opinion, this is either another scribal "correction" or perhaps Jesus did mean that world will not believe him; therefore he will not show himself to world.

Verse 26 makes a significant shift in defining the Parakleet by calling him *the Holy Spirit*.

26 But the Advocate (Parakleet), the Holy Spirit, whom the Father will send in my name, will teach you all things and will remind you of everything I have said to you;

It is contrary to John 20:22, where Jesus himself sends the Holy Spirit to the Disciples not the Father.

John 20:22
NIV
And with that he breathed on them and said, "Receive the Holy Spirit".

We know that the Jews and the Disciples in particular knew the Holy Spirit but the Parakleet in John 14 is unknown because, in Greek text, there is no definite article with Parakleet. (We will discuss on this topic shortly.) Furthermore, verse 26 emphasizes that God will send him in Jesus' name, that raises Jesus' position higher than God.

Verse 27 reads:

27 Peace I leave with you; my peace I give you. I do not give to you as the world gives. Do not let your hearts be troubled and do not be afraid.

"Peace" in Hebrew and Aramaic is "shalowm" from *sh l m,* same as "Islam".

The chapter ends with verse 28, a troublesome one to Trinitarians:

28 "You heard me say, 'I am going away and I am coming back to you.' If you loved me, you would be glad that I am going to the Father, for the Father is greater than I.

Jesus$_{pbuh}$ calls himself smaller than God, contrary to verse 26.

A Troublesome Question

When we question Christians about the identity of Jesus$_{pbuh}$, they often say that he had two parts or identities: Jesus the son of Mary or "the man Jesus"; and Jesus the Son of God or "the Divine Jesus", "the Christ"; combined together became a "fully human and fully God". "Whenever Jesus says: *I and the Father are one,* he means the second Jesus (the Son of God) is one with God, and whenever he says *Father is Greater than I*, or *the son does not know when the end time comes*, he means the first Jesus, the son of Mary, the Man not the Divine Jesus."

If we believe in duality of Jesus, verse 28 of John 14 raises a big troublesome question:

Which Jesus is in the John 14:28? Is "Jesus the Divine" going to Father or Jesus the Man?

Well, no one is prepared for consequences of either answer. If Jesus the Man is going to Father, then where has his Divinity gone? Why he mentions ascension of his body instead of his Divine being? No Scholar, not even a laity, will give such an answer. Because Christianity believes, "no man can be God but Jesus because he was and is God, and after the resurrection he went back to his place as God." That means the Divine Jesus; the son of God is the Jesus of John 14:28, not the Jesus son of Mary. Some might say both part of Jesus (Man and God), the Whole Jesus, ascended to Father.

No matter what we pick for John 14:28, the Divine Jesus alone or the Whole Jesus, the result is same: Jesus (the Son of God or Jesus as a Whole) is not equal to God; there is no escape form this statement *"for the Father is greater than I"*. If Jesus$_{pbuh}$ said that statement, it means that God is greater than him, no matter what we think of the *"I"*.

Coming back to John 14, we read that Jesus$_{pbuh}$ is talking about a prophecy that did not happen at his time:

Verse 29: I have told you now before it happens, so that when it does happen you will believe.

The phrase "before it happens" emphasizes that it is a prophecy and has not "happened yet" (the coming of Parakleet). If we think the Parakleet in these verses is the Holy Spirit, we are claiming that Jesus$_{pbuh}$ did not know that the Holy Spirit was already there. Besides that, the Disciples already knew him; they did believe in him. It does not make sense to think that Jesus$_{pbuh}$ saying these things so when the Holy Spirit comes, the Disciples should remember what Jesus$_{pbuh}$ said, and should believe him - the Holy Spirit or Jesus$_{pbuh}$. They already knew the Holy Spirit and believed it and Jesus$_{pbuh}$. We read in the Bible that the Disciples believed him from very beginning:

John 2:11
Jesus performed this first sign at Cana in Galilee. He thus revealed His glory, and <u>His disciples believed in Him</u>.

In summary:

The verses 16, 17 and 26 of John 14 are contradictory. Verses 16 and 26 prove that the Parakleet had not yet come at that time, it would be sent by God. However, verse 17 states that it had already come, "they, the Disciples, know him, and he lives with them".

Verse 29 is also talking about future, contrary to second part of verse 17. This does not purely reflect Jesus' words. There seems to be a third person who has put his own words in Jesus' mouth. In my opinion, Jesus$_{pbuh}$ meant that when the Parakleet (Manahma in Hebrew) comes, you should believe in him (the Parakleet); and he meant the whole Christianity not the 11 Disciples, because Jesus$_{pbuh}$ is teaching them his Gospel and they are supposed to teach people the very same words.

If these words were only concerned the Disciples, then they wouldn't say them to people, people wouldn't say them to others, and eventually we wouldn't see them in the Gospel. It is for all Christianity to follow and believe in Manahma.

The problem of contradiction in John 14:16, 17, 26 reminds me of a claim made by Muslim scholars that the original word for Parakleet was "Perikleet"; it means "praised"; that is the meaning of "Ahmed" and "Muhammad". This is what the Quran also teaches us that Jesus$_{pbuh}$ did foretell the coming of "Ahamad":

Quran – Assaf (61):6[26]
And remember, Jesus, the son of Mary, said: "O Children of Israel! I am the messenger of Allah (sent) to you, confirming the Law (which came) before me, and giving Glad Tidings of a Messenger to come after me, whose name shall be Ahmad." But when he came to them with Clear Signs, they said, "this is evident sorcery!"

Jesus, an Advocate (Parakleet)

In 1 John we read that Jesus$_{pbuh}$ is called an advocate:

1 John 2:1 (NIV)
My dear children, I write this to you so that you will not sin. But if anybody does sin, we have an advocate with the Father--Jesus Christ, the Righteous One.

Remember that Jesus$_{pbuh}$ promised coming of "another advocate" meaning *not him* but *someone else*. "Well here we are: Jesus was an advocate and the Holy Spirit is another advocate." Problem is solved ... *if* we forget what Jesus$_{pbuh}$ said: "God *will* send him (the Parakleet)." However, we know that the Holy Spirit was there when Jesus$_{pbuh}$ was saying these words; he was saying these words by the help of the Holy Spirit; the disciples also had the Holy Spirit if we take John 14:17 as a truth. Moreover, the Holy Spirit was there long before Jesus' birth, with his mother (Luke 1:35,

Matthew 1:18, Mark 1:24), with his cousin, John the Baptist[pbuh], (Luke 1:15) and with all the prophets (2 Peter 1:21). So, the "another advocate" cannot be the Holy Spirit.

Jews and the Disciples in particular, knew the Holy Spirit very well. Hence it seems confusing to say "another Parakleet" instead of "the Holy Spirit". There is no explanation whatsoever why Jesus[pbuh] said "another Parakleet" if he meant "the Holy Spirit". Remember that "another Parakleet" was unknown but "the Holy Spirit" was known.

Gender Problem

Another reason for making the distinction between the Parakleet and the Holy Spirit is gender difference; Parakleet is Masculine but the Holy Spirit, in Greek: *pneuma to hagion*, is Neuter; and in Hebrew: *ruach hakodesh* is Feminine (See Table 20 and Figure 23). This issue is much significant when it comes to "the Spirit of Truth" and "the Holy Spirit".

Table 20

Holy Spirit[1]

4151 [e]	Pneuma	Πνεῦμα	Spirit	N-NNS[a]
3588 [e]	to	τὸ	-	Art-NNS
40 [e]	Hagion	Ἅγιον	Holy,	Adj-NNS

---

[a] NNS = Nominative Neuter Singular

Figure 23

3875. parakletos[1]

Strong's Concordance

parakletos: called to one's aid

Original Word: παράκλητος, ου, ὁ
Part of Speech: Noun, Masculine
Transliteration: parakletos
Phonetic Spelling: (par-ak'-lay-tos)
Short Definition: an Comforter, comforter, helper, Paraclete
Definition: (a) an Advocate, intercessor, (b) a consoler, comforter, helper, (c) Paraclete.

4151. pneuma

Strong's Concordance

pneuma: wind, spirit

Original Word: πνεῦμα, ατος, τό
Part of Speech: Noun, Neuter
Transliteration: pneuma
Phonetic Spelling: (pnyoo'-mah)
Short Definition: wind, breath, spirit
Definition: wind, breath, spirit.

7307. ruach

Strong's Concordance

ruach: breath, wind, spirit

Original Word: רוּחַ
Part of Speech: Noun, Feminine
Transliteration: ruach
Phonetic Spelling: (roo'-akh)
Short Definition: spirit

Parakleet, Unknown to the Disciples

Another Parakleet, alon Parakleton

Both ἄλλον (alon), Accusative, and ἄλλος (allos), Nominative, translated to "another", can refer to a definite or indefinite noun, depending on the accompanying articles. For example: in John 20:2, it is a *definite* Adjective because it is preceded by the *definite* Article of τὸν (ton), translated to "*the* other"; but in John 14:16, there is no definite Article. That is why all Bible translators have written it as an *indefinite* Adjective, "another parakleet" not "*the* other parakleet". The identity of Parakleet in John 14:16, grammatically speaking, is unknown to the Disciples.

John 20:2[1]
τρέχει οὖν καὶ ἔρχεται πρὸς Σίμωνα Πέτρον καὶ πρὸς <u>τὸν ἄλλον</u> μαθητὴν ὃν ἐφίλει ὁ Ἰησοῦς, καὶ λέγει αὐτοῖς· Ἦραν τὸν Κύριον ἐκ τοῦ μνημείου, καὶ οὐκ οἴδαμεν ποῦ ἔθηκαν αὐτόν.

NIV
So she came running to Simon Peter and <u>the other</u> disciple, the one Jesus loved, and said, "They have taken the Lord out of the tomb, and we don't know where they have put him!"

John 14:16[1]
καὶ ἐγὼ ἐρωτήσω τὸν πατέρα καὶ <u>ἄλλον</u> παράκλητον δώσει ὑμῖν, ἵνα μένει μεθ᾽ ὑμῶν εἰς τὸν αἰῶνα,

NIV
And I will ask the Father, and he will give you <u>another</u> advocate to help you and be with you forever--

The phrase ἄλλον (alon) is used in three more places in the NT: Luke 5:29, Luke 9:8 and 1 Thessalonians 2:6; in all of them it is translated as an *indefinite* Adjective Masculine, "another".

Because there is no Definite Article before Parakleet in John 14:16, we can conclude that the Disciples were not familiar with him when Jesus$_{pbuh}$ was saying these words. Therefore, it cannot refer to the Holy Spirit.

In addition, some commentators write that Jesus$_{pbuh}$ is distinct from the Parakleet; and I agree. Here is one: (commentary under John 16:7)

Figure 24

Ellicott's Commentary for English Readers[1]

(7) Nevertheless I tell you the truth.—The words He is about to utter are words of strange sound for the ears of disciples, and He prefaces them by an appeal to His own knowledge and candour in dealing with them, as in John 14:2. The pronoun bears the weight of the emphasis, "I, who know all."

It is expedient for you that I go away.—"There is no cause", He would say, "for the deep sorrow which has filled your hearts. It is for your advantage that *I, as distinct from the Paraclete, who is to come, should go away*" (John 14:16). Yes; for those who had left all to follow Him; for those who had none to go to but Himself (John 6:68); for those whose hopes were all centred in Him, it was—hard and incomprehensible as the saying must have seemed—an advantage that He should go away.

Not only is Jesus$_{pbuh}$ a distinct being from Parakleet, but also Parakleet will not come if Jesus$_{pbuh}$ does not ascend to God. Can it be the Holy Spirit? When we know that the Holy Spirit is talking all these things through Jesus$_{pbuh}$; the Holy Spirit was there even before Jesus$_{pbuh}$, with Mary$_{pbuh}$, with John the Baptist$_{pbuh}$ and so on. It is hard to believe, or even suppose, that the Parakleet in these verses is the Holy Spirit.

The Spirit of Truth

The Spirit of Truth, in Greek τὸ πνεῦμα τῆς ἀληθείας (to pneuma tēs alētheias), is used 3 times in the Bible (NT) as following: John 14:17, 16:13 and 1 John 4:6; however, "truth" ἀληθείας (alētheias) is used many times throughout the Bible in different contexts. Only when it is in the form of τὸ πνεῦμα τῆς ἀληθείας (to pneuma tēs alētheias), it is taken as a prophetic statement of a person to come after Jesus$_{pbuh}$.

The Hebrew word for "truth" is "ehmet"; it has been discussed in detail earlier in this chapter, as well as in Chapter 6 – Isaiah and Islam, under "After Ahmed (Isaiah 59)".

In this section, we will talk about other matters of the Spirit of Truth as it is in John 14:17 and 16:13. Finally, we will examine the last verse of John 14, verse 31, where Jesus$_{pbuh}$ says what God has ordered: *Rise up, move to Mekka*; it is only in the Peshitta[a] and Syriac Gospel of John.

John 14:17
NIV
<u>the Spirit of truth</u>. *The world cannot accept him, because it neither sees him nor knows him. But you know him, for he lives with you and will be in you.*

John 16:13
NIV
But when he, the Spirit of truth, comes, he will guide you into all the truth. He will not speak on his own; he will speak only what he hears, and he will tell you what is yet to come.

---

[a] Peshitta (in Syriac it means: "simple", or "common"), is the Syriac version of the Bible, the accepted Bible of Syrian Christian churches from the end of the 3rd century AD.

1 John 4:6
NIV
We are from God, and whoever knows God listens to us; but whoever is not from God does not listen to us. This is how we recognize <u>the Spirit of truth</u> and the spirit of falsehood.

Since John 14:17 has been discussed earlier, we will proceed to other two verses. 1 John 4:6 is using "the Spirit of Truth" as an opposite to "the spirit of falsehood". They are referring to people who listen and do not listen to the Disciples; the true teachers and the false teachers. In Barnes' Notes on 1 John 4:6 we read:

Figure 25

<u>Barnes' Notes on the Bible</u>[1]

...
Know we the spirit of truth, and the spirit of error - We can distinguish those who embrace the truth from those who do not. Whatever pretensions they might set up for piety, it was clear that if they did not embrace the doctrines taught by the true apostles of God, they could not be regarded as his friends; that is, as true Christians. ...

Also, Gill's Exposition writes:

Figure 26

<u>Gill's Exposition of the Entire Bible</u>[1]

...
Hereby know we the spirit of truth, and the spirit of error; the difference between truth and error; can distinguish one from another, and discern who are the <u>true ministers</u> of Christ, and who are the <u>false teachers</u>; ...

From 1 John 4:6 we simply know that the Spirt of Truth can be used to true teachers, *human being*. Now John 16:13 is what I need to focus on since it is inevitably essential for understanding who the Spirit of Truth really is.

John 16:13
NIV
But when he, <u>the Spirit of truth</u>, comes, he will guide you into all the truth. He will not speak on his own; he will speak only what he hears, and he will tell you what is yet to come.

This verse is my Prince of Verses in John. I easily can use it to prove my whole argument. What we can prove with ease is that the Spirit of Truth is a man not The Holy Spirit; and that he is going to come in the future; he will bring all the truth; he will not speak of his own but what he hears; and he will tell about future.

What we learn from this verse is clear:

1- **He** will *come* – *"a man"*
2- He **will** *come* – *"future tense"*
3- **The** Spirit of Truth will come – *"a definite noun (spoken about already in previous verses)"*
4- **The Spirit of Truth** – *does not say "the Holy Spirit"*
5- "**Truth**" is Ehme<u>t</u> in Hebrew; *Ehme<u>t</u> is Ahmed in Arabic.*
6- **He** will guide – *"a man"*
7- He **will** guide – *"future tense"*
8- He will guide into **all the truth** – *"a complete message "*
9- **He** will not speak on **his** own – *"a man, a man"*
10- He **will** not speak on his own – *"future tense"*
11- He will not **speak** on his own – *"speak"*
12- He will **not speak** on his own – *"not speak"*
13- He will **not speak on his own** – *"dependent"*
14- **He** will speak – *"a man"*
15- He **will** speak – *"future tense"*
16- He will **speak** – *"speak"*
17- **He** will speak only what he hears – *"a man"*

18- He will speak only what he **hears** – *"hears"*
19- And **he** will tell you what is yet to come – *"a man"*
20- And he **will** tell you what is yet to come – *"future tense"*
21- And he will **tell** you what is yet to come – *"tell"*

There are seven masculine pronouns/indications in this single verse, a unique verse in the entire Bible. The word ἐκεῖνος *ekeinos*, meaning *he*, in Greek Gospel, is used right at the beginning of the verse to cover the Gender of the Spirit of Truth in the verse.

In addition, there are:

- Five indications of future tense
- At least three definite articles (in Greek τὸ to, τὴν tin and τὰ ta; all are represented with "the" in English translations)
- Four indications of speaking/hearing, and most importantly "HE WILL NOT SPEAK ON HIS OWN".

That means The Spirit of Truth, the *man* who *will* come, will guide to *all truth*, will speak not his own words but what he hears.

Some may ask, "Why the Spirit of Truth is with definite articles if he is unknown to the Disciples and supposed to come in the future?" Because Jesus has already talked about him earlier, in chapter 14.

At least one group never can apply the Spirit of Truth to the Holy Spirit; that is Christians. They believe that the Holy Spirit is God; "He does and says what He wants", they say. However, John 16:13 clearly shows that the Spirit of Truth will not speak of his own but someone else will tell him what to say. There is not a single candidate for it except a future prophet.

Some might say that the verse is talking about *spirit* not *man*. Well, we just discussed about it in 1 John 4:6, where the true teachers were called the Spirit of Truth and false teachers were called the spirit of error. Also, in same book and same chapter the prophets are called spirit; as we read in 1 John 4:1, NIV: *"Dear friends, do not believe every spirit, but test the spirits to see whether they are from God, because many false prophets have gone out into the world."*

Besides that, the act of speaking requires lung, tongue, throat, vocal muscles, lips, jaws and so forth; that is not the specifications of the Holy Spirit. I do understand that the Holy Spirit talks through inspiration and revelation; nowhere in John 16:13 the terms "inspiration" or "revelation" were used, not even meant.

In this verse, the explicit use of "speak", "hear" and "tell" is corroborated. He is the one who will *speak*, not to our hearts but literally, he will speak. Again, he is dependent; he will not speak of his own but he will speak *what he hears*. This is not what Christian Doctrine teaches about the Holy Spirit. According to them, the Holy Spirit is fully God, He says whatever He wants; and He says through inspiration not by use of lungs and larynx.

The future tense of the verbs, five cases, emphasizes the prophetic concept of the verse. We know that the Holy Spirit was always there with Jesus$_{pbuh}$, with the Disciples and even before Jesus' birth, as we discussed earlier. How the Holy Spirit is going to come in the future when he is already there?

In John 16:7, Jesus$_{pbuh}$ makes it clear that if he does not go away, the Spirit of Truth will not come:

John 16:7
NIV
But very truly I tell you, it is for your good that I am going away. Unless I go away, the Advocate will not come to you; but if I go, I will send him to you.

The verse also reads: "He will guide you into *all the truth*." Did The Holy Spirit reveal all the truth? If yes, then the Bible as "the inspiration of the Holy Spirit" must be complete and inerrant. Is it so? The Bible itself says no. The Gospel according to John is very clear about it:

John 20:30
Jesus performed many other signs in the presence of his disciples, which are not recorded in this book.

In addition, having many versions of the Bible with so many differences, and contradictions / discrepancies in all versions prove that the Bible cannot be a perfect guidance. Besides that, we do not know which Bible we have to accept as "the Bible".

While even the genealogy of Joseph, the supposed father of Jesus$_{pbuh}$, is not even same in the Gospels, it is going to be an impossible to prove the claim that the Bible (again "which Bible?") is perfect. We read on the Genealogy of Jesus$_{pbuh}$ that his grandfather (father of Joseph), according to Matthew 1:17, is Jacob; but in Luke 3:23, it is Heli.

There are 67 different names for Jesus' ancestors in these two Gospels. This is just one of many discrepancies in the Bible. Can we still call it the perfect truth? Obviously, we can find much truth in the Bible; many great teachings of the prophets and Disciples are recorded in the Bible, no doubt about it; but not every word in the Bible is true and not all the truth is in the Bible.

[As mentioned earlier, 1 John 5:7, a very significant verse, was used for centuries by Church Fathers to prove the doctrine of Trinity, happened to be an insertion to the text because it was not found in the older manuscripts. Also, the entire story of the adulterous woman (John 7:53 to 8:11) and even the story of Resurrection and Ascension in the Gospel of Mark (16:9-20) were all added to the Gospels.]

The gender issue, as mentioned, is also very plain. The Holy Spirit in Greek is neuter; in Hebrew and Aramaic, it is feminine (Table 20[1] and Figure 23). There are at least seven masculine indications in the verse, unlike the Holy Spirit, which is neuter in everywhere in the NT; (see below examples) how then in John 16:13 it is a *masculine*? The Holy Spirit or the Spirit of God is mentioned in numerous verses in the Bible. In all of them, the gender of the Spirit and The Holy Spirit with no exception is neutral. Below are just a few examples. (Table 21[1] and Table 22[1])

Followings are some examples of the occurrences of "spirit" in the Bible. Note that the gender of "spirit" is Neuter. (The translations are NIV.)

1 Corinthians 2:10[1]
ἡμῖν δὲ ὁ Θεὸς ἀπεκάλυψε διὰ <u>τοῦ Πνεύματος</u> αὐτοῦ· τὸ γὰρ Πνεῦμα πάντα ἐρευνᾷ, καὶ τὰ βάθη τοῦ Θεοῦ.

These are the things God has revealed to us by his Spirit. The Spirit searches all things, even the deep things of God.

Romans 8:27[1]
ὁ δὲ ἐρευνῶν τὰς καρδίας οἶδε τί τὸ φρόνημα <u>τοῦ Πνεύματος</u>, ὅτι κατὰ Θεὸν ἐντυγχάνει ὑπὲρ ἁγίων.

And he who searches our hearts knows the mind of the Spirit, because the Spirit intercedes for God's people in accordance with the will of God.

Table 21[1]

3588 [e]	tou	τοῦ	the	Art-GNS[a]
4151 [e]	Pneumatos	Πνεύματος·	Spirit.	N-GNS

1 Corinthians 12:11[1]
πάντα δὲ ταῦτα ἐνεργεῖ τὸ ἓν καὶ τὸ <u>αὐτὸ Πνεῦμα</u>, διαιροῦν ἰδίᾳ ἑκάστῳ καθὼς βούλεται.

All these are the work of one and the same Spirit, and he distributes them to each one, just as he determines.

Table 22[1]

846 [e]	auto	αὐτὸ	same	PPro-NN3S[b]
4151 [e]	Pneuma	Πνεῦμα,	Spirit,	N-NNS

Matthew 3:16[1]
καὶ βαπτισθεὶς ὁ Ἰησοῦς ἀνέβη εὐθὺς ἀπὸ τοῦ ὕδατος· καὶ ἰδοὺ ἀνεῴχθησαν αὐτῷ οἱ οὐρανοί, καὶ εἶδεν <u>τὸ Πνεῦμα</u> τοῦ Θεοῦ καταβαῖνον ὡσεὶ περιστερὰν καὶ ἐρχόμενον ἐπ᾽ αὐτόν·

---

[a] GNS stands for "Genitive Neuter Singular"
[b] NN3S stands for "Nominative Neuter 3rd Person Singular"

As soon as Jesus was baptized, he went up out of the water. At that moment heaven was opened, and he saw the Spirit of God descending like a dove and alighting on him.

Table 23[1]

3588 [e]	to	[τὸ]	the	Art-ANS[a]
4151 [e]	Pneuma	Πνεῦμα	Spirit	N-ANS

Matthew 1:18[1]
Τοῦ δὲ Ἰησοῦ Χριστοῦ ἡ γένεσις οὕτως ἦν· μνηστευθείσης τῆς μητρὸς αὐτοῦ Μαρίας τῷ Ἰωσήφ, πρὶν ἢ συνελθεῖν αὐτοὺς εὑρέθη ἐν γαστρὶ ἔχουσα ἐκ <u>Πνεύματος ἁγίου</u>.

This is how the birth of Jesus the Messiah came about: His mother Mary was pledged to be married to Joseph, but before they came together, she was found to be pregnant through the Holy Spirit.

Table 24[1]

4151 [e]	pneumatos	πνεύματος	[the] Spirit	N-GNS[b]
40 [e]	hagiou	ἁγίου.	Holy.	Adj-GNS

Matthew 1:20[1]
ταῦτα δὲ αὐτοῦ ἐνθυμηθέντος ἰδοὺ ἄγγελος Κυρίου κατ' ὄναρ ἐφάνη αὐτῷ λέγων· Ἰωσὴφ υἱὸς Δαυίδ, μὴ φοβηθῇς παραλαβεῖν Μαριὰμ τὴν γυναῖκά σου, τὸ γὰρ ἐν αὐτῇ γεννηθὲν ἐκ <u>πνεύματός ἐστιν ἁγίου</u>·

---

[a] ANS stands for "Accusative Neutral Singular"
[b] GNS stands for "Genitive Neutral Singular"

But after he had considered this, an angel of the Lord appeared to him in a dream and said, "Joseph son of David, do not be afraid to take Mary home as your wife, because what is conceived in her is from the Holy Spirit.

Table 25[1]

4151 [e]	Pneumatos	Πνεύματός	[the] Spirit	N-GNS
1510 [e]	estin	ἐστιν	is	V-PIA-3S
40 [e]	Hagiou	Ἁγίου·	Holy.	Adj-GNS

Matthew 12:32[1]
καὶ ὃς ἐὰν εἴπῃ λόγον κατὰ τοῦ υἱοῦ τοῦ ἀνθρώπου, ἀφεθήσεται αὐτῷ· ὃς δ' ἂν εἴπῃ κατὰ <u>τοῦ Πνεύματος τοῦ ἁγίου</u>, οὐκ ἀφεθήσεται αὐτῷ οὔτε ἐν τῷ νῦν αἰῶνι οὔτε ἐν τῷ μέλλοντι.

Anyone who speaks a word against the Son of Man will be forgiven, but anyone who speaks against the Holy Spirit will not be forgiven, either in this age or in the age to come.

Table 26[1]

3588 [e]	tou	τοῦ	the	Art-GNS[a]
4151 [e]	Pneumatos	Πνεύματος	Spirit	N-GNS
3588 [e]	tou	τοῦ	the	Art-GNS
40 [e]	Hagiou	Ἁγίου,	Holy,	Adj-GNS

---

[a] GNS stands for "Genitive Neutral Singular"

Arise, Descend in Mekka (John 14:31)

The final statement of the last verse of John 14 is perhaps the final prophecy of Jesus[pbuh]. It says: "Arise; Descend in Mekka"; in Aramaic it is ܡܟܐ ܢܙܠ ܩܘܡܘ (qūmu nīzal mekkā). The Aramaic word ܢܙܠ ("nīzal" or "nᵊzl") and Arabic نزل (nazal) are cognates. It means "to come down", "to descend"[30], and "to be dropped as a subject of discussion"[31]. Therefore ܢܙܠ ܡܟܐ (nīzal mekkā) refers to "coming down (in / to) Mekka".

I must mention that in a few places in the Aramaic NT, but not everywhere, the word ܡܟܐ (mekka) also means "here" and "there".

Rendered translation
John 14:31
That the world may learn I love the Father and do exactly what my Father has commanded me, "Arise; Descend in Mekka."

John 14:31 is an example of the prophetic concept of the second coming of Jesus[pbuh] from Mekka (Ascension from Palestine and Dissension in Mekka), or he recites a prophetic revelation about the last Prophet who is to come from Mekka. He is the same "Parakleet" or "the Spirit of Truth" spoken about in the Gospel.

We Muslims do believe that Jesus[pbuh], in his second coming, will appear in Mekka when Imam Mahdi[pbuh] comes. They will work together in stablishing the Divine laws on earth. This is a well-known prophecy in Muslim tradition. Christians may oppose this by saying that Jesus[pbuh] is from Palestine and will come again in Palestine.

"Christ Jesus must personally return to Jerusalem (not New York, London, Paris, Tokyo, or anywhere else) to defend the children of Israel from her enemies, conquer, and then consummate history at the end of the age ..."³², Steve Urick writes on page 6 of his book, *Sings of the Second Coming of Jesus Christ and the End of the World*. Then he continues, on the same page: "Some of the more well-known false Christs and false prophets who came after Jesus Christ are Muhammad (founder of Islam) ..."

If anyone wants to know what Jesus$_{pbuh}$ said about the matter then he/she must precede reading:

Matthew 23:37-39
NIV
37 "Jerusalem, Jerusalem, you who kill the prophets and stone those sent to you, how often I have longed to gather your children together, as a hen gathers her chicks under her wings, and you were not willing. 38 <u>Look, your house is left to you desolate</u>. 39 For I tell you, you will not see me again until you say, 'Blessed is he who comes in the name of the Lord."

The only person after Jesus$_{pbuh}$ came in the name of God was the prophet of Islam. The Quran, the final revelation to humankind, starts with this statement:

The Quran 1:1
"In the name of God, The most gracious, The most merciful".

Besides that, if Jesus$_{pbuh}$ supposed to come in the name of God, it dismisses the Christian doctrine of Trinity. How can "God" come in the name of God?

Another fact in Matthew 23:39 is that it does not say "Blessed is he who *came* in the name of the Lord." It says "... *comes* ...". Therefore, it is not about Jesus$_{pbuh}$ himself but the future prophet.

In Matthew 21:9, two chapters before, people of Jerusalem shouted, *"Blessed is he who comes in the name of the Lord!"* (They are welcoming Jesus$_{pbuh}$).

Matthew 21:9
NIV
The crowds that went ahead of him (Jesus) and those that followed shouted, "Hosanna to the Son of David!" "Blessed is he who comes in the name of the Lord!" "Hosanna in the highest heaven!"

Did Jesus forget that people already said what he wanted them to say in order to see him again? Please read the Matthew 23: 39 again. (*For I tell you, you will not see me again until you say, 'Blessed is he who comes in the name of the Lord*). Therefore, Matthew 23:39 is not about Jesus$_{pbuh}$.

As a conclusion, John 14:31 is either the second coming of Jesus$_{pbuh}$ and/or Prophet Muhammad$_{pbuh}$ and/or Mahdi$_{pbuh}$. It is certain that the place of event is Mekka.

Figure 27 is the Peshitta and Old Syriac Sinaitic Palimpsest (OSSP) of John 14:31; with Arabic and Latin transliterations; English translation is the KJB. Note how senseless the translation of the last statement is, "Arise, let us go hence".

Rendered translation
John 14:31
That the world may learn I love the Father and do exactly what my Father has commanded me, "Arise; Descend in Mekka."

Figure 27

Peshitta[31]

- John 14:31

ܐܠܐ ܕܢܕܥ ܥܠܡܐ ܕܪܚܡ ܐܢܐ ܠܐܒܝ ܘܐܝܟܢܐ ܕܦܩܕܢܝ ܐܒܝ ܗܟܘܬ ܥܒܕ ܐܢܐ ܩܘܡܘ ܢܐܙܠ ܡܟܐ ܀

John 14:31 - اِلَّا دِنِدَع عَالَمَا دِرَاخِم اَنَا لَاْبِي وَايكَنَا دِپَقدَنِي اَبِي هَاكوَات عَابِد اَنَا قُومُو نَازِل مِكَّا .

John 14:31 - ʾellā dənedda° °ālmā dərāḥem nā lāḇ waykannā dəpaqdan ʾāḇ hāḵwāt °āḇeḏ nā qūm nīzal mekkā .

OSSP[31]

- John 14:31 ܐܠܐ ܡܛܠ ܕܢܕܥ ܥܠܡܐ ܕܪܚܡ ܐܢܐ ܠܐܒܝ ܘܐܝܟܢܐ ܕܦܩܕܢܝ ܐܒܝ ܗܟܘܬ ܥܒܕܢܐ ܩܘܡܘ ܢܐܙܠ ܡܟܐ ܀

John 14:31 - الا مطل دندع علما درخم انا لابي ايكنا دپقدني ابي هكوت عبدنا قومو نازل مكا .

John 14:31 - ʾlʾ mṭl dnd° °lmʾ drḥm ʾnʾ lʾby ʾyknʾ dpqdny ʾby hkwt °bdnʾ qwmw nʾzl mkʾ .

John 14:31 - But that the world may know that I love the Father; and as the Father gave me commandment, even so I do. Arise, let us go hence.

Chapter 3 – Imam Ali in the Bible

A Brief Biography of Imam Ali

Imam Ali$_{pbuh}$ son of Abitalib, cousin of Prophet Muhammad$_{pbuh}$, was born on 13th Rajab, a Friday, 600 AD, in the Holy Ka'ba, in Mekka. He is the only person born in the holiest place of Islam. The crying pregnant Fatima$_{pbuh}$ made this prayer: "O' my protector! Ease my pain." All of a sudden, the wall of Ka'ba opened up, she entered in, and the wall closed. His mother, Fatima Bint Assad, stayed in Ka'ba for three days after the birth of her son. When she came out, the Prophet$_{pbuh}$ received the baby.

Imam Ali$_{pbuh}$ was brought up under the tutelage of the Holy Prophet. He married with Lady Fatima$_{pbuh}$, daughter of the Prophet, after the Migration to Medina. Imam Ali$_{pbuh}$ took a major role in the early events of Islam, from defending the Prophet in wars to writing down the revelations recited by the Prophet. His self-sacrificing character is well known among Muslims. The Prophet appointed Ali$_{pbuh}$ as his successor in year 632 AD when returning from the last pilgrimage. However, after Prophet's death a group of Muslims picked their own Caliph and people submitted to the decision, except the Prophet's household and a number of close companions. Three Caliphs came one after another.

The third Caliph was murdered by a group of people who were angry with the government and the power misuse by the office of the Caliph. In the fourth attempt, people picked Imam Ali$_{pbuh}$. Initially he refused, but later accepted the ever-persistent request of the people. He then put up the Prophet's rules and Devine laws to treat every resident of the territory justly. This pushed many high-class people down and pulled many low-class ones up. His just and equal treatment policy angered many high rank residents.

In a story, we read that two well-known men named Talha and Zubair came to visit the Imam to make a deal with him, hoping they can get government positions. As soon as they arrived and sat down, Imam turned on a candle and put off the one that was burning. They inquired about it; Imam answered: "You have come here for a personal meeting, the first candle was from treasury and since I was doing revenue, I was using it; but now I am doing a personal matter, that's why I turned on my own candle." The men left without saying an extra word. Many were jealous and unhappy for not being part of the administration of Imam Ali$_{pbuh}$. They waged a war against him with a false flag. Second war and finally third war were imposed to the successor of the Prophet, each time Imam was victorious. Then he, while offering his morning prayer in the mosque of Kufa, was struck on the head. He passed away on the third day, at the age of 63.

Many even non-Muslims have written endless words about this exceptional man of holiness, mercy, justice, piety, courage, fairness, affection, wisdom, peace, forgiveness ... and the man who was foretold by many Hebrew prophets including Moses, David, Solomon $_{pbut}$ and so on.

George Jordac[a] writes about Imam's situation after being struck by his murderer: *"...the cheerfulness of his face was more saddening than all the calamities of the world. At that time, his face resembled the face of Socrates when the ignorant and stupid people made him drink a cup of poison. It resembled the face of Jesus Christ when the Jews scourged him. It resembled the face of the prophet of Islam, Muhammad, when the ignorant persons of Taif showered stones at him and did not know that they were stoning the greatest human being ever born".* [33]

---

[a] George Jordac, (1931 - 2014), was a Christian author and poet from Lebanon.

Ali in the Bible

Many prophets of the OT foretold Imam Ali$_{pbuh}$. His name appears in many verses, but it is translated to a variety of meanings. The translations, in many cases, make no sense, sometimes confusing and contradictory. Some translate "ali" as a verb, *Spring up*, *concerning* and so on. Some take "ali" as a preposition with a pronominal suffix, translating it to *over me* and *to me*. The word may also mean "the most high", referring to God.

There are other occasions where the word "Ali" has been transliterated as "Eli"; nevertheless, in Hebrew, both are written exactly same.

The key to finding the real application of these verses is to study them carefully and consider the nominal rather than other concepts of the word "ali". If it does not violate the structure of the verse as a whole, we should consider it as one of the meanings if not the only. This indeed solves many disputes over the meaning of the verses where the word "ali" occurs. In the following lines, we will be examining only a few of these verses.

Eli and the Faithful Priest

There are two men named Eli[a] in the Bible, one in each Testament. The Eli (עלי) of the Old Testament was the high priest in Shiloh when prophet Samuel was a child (1 Samuel 1:3). In the New testament, according to the Lucan genealogy of Jesus[pbuh], Eli (Ηλι; Heli) was the father of Joseph, the husband of Mary, the "supposed" father of Jesus the Nazarene (Luke 3:23). However, the genealogy of Matthew (1:16) takes a different turn after David and results in Jacob as the father of Joseph (another unsolved dispute). Therefore, if Matthew 1:16 is correct, Eli in Luke could be a made up name.

Eli, the high priest of the Old Testament, was a holy man but his two sons, Hophni and Phinehas, were ill mannered, disrespectful to God, and wrongdoers (1 Samuel 2:12-17). A man of God showed up and informed Eli that both his sons would die on the same day (1 Samuel 2:17), and the Lord would raise a *proper priest* for Himself (1 Samuel 2:35).

1 Samuel 2:35
NIV
I will raise up for myself a faithful priest, who will do according to what is in my heart and mind. I will firmly establish his priestly house, and they will minister <u>before my anointed one</u>[b] always.

Some say that Samuel was the *proper priest* who came before Messiah (translated to "anointed one"), but a close look at the verse shows that "the proper priest" has to be ministering while Messiah is present. The word translated to "before" is לפני (lip̄-nê-). This very same לפני (lip̄-nê-) is used in Genesis 6:11, Genesis

---

[a] Eli and Ali, in Hebrew, are written exactly same, as עלי. In English, some have made their own preferences on what letter to start it with, E, A or He.
[b] From Hebrew word משיחי (mə-šî-ḥî) means "my Messiah"

10:9, Genesis 13:10, and many other verses, also translated to "before" with the meaning of *at the presence of.* (See below) Hence, it should mean the same in 1 Samuel 2:35. As a result, the *faithful priest* must be someone alive during the lifetime of the Messiah; therefore, he cannot be Samuel who lived 1100 years *before* the Christ.

The following is an example where lip̄-nê translated to "before" and meant "at the presence of".

Genesis 6:11
KJB
The earth also was corrupt <u>before</u> God, and the earth was filled with violence.

Eli of the Bible and Ali of Islam

There is an eye opening parallel between Eli and Ali. Samaritans and Jews divided for the priesthood of Eli. Similarly, Shi'ite and Sunni divided for the claims of the figure of Imam Ali$_{pbuh}$. They each had two sons. While the sons of Eli led the people to disaster, sons of Ali led their people to righteousness. Moreover, Imam Ali and his two sons, Hassan$_{pbuh}$ and Hussain$_{pbuh}$, ministered while Jesus Christ was - and still is – alive. This event fulfills the promise in 1 Samuel 2:35. (*I will raise up for myself a faithful priest, who will do according to what is in my heart and mind. I will firmly establish his priestly house, and they will minister <u>before my anointed one</u> always.*)

Ali and Well (Numbers 21: 17)

Moses_pbuh took his people out of Egypt and crossed many lands. Somewhere, called Be'er, God ordered him to gather his people for water. People sang a song near a well in the wilderness, dug by a prince:

Numbers 21:17
Then Israel sang this song: Ali oh well! Testify to him.

The New International Version translates it: *Then Israel sang this song: "Spring up, O well! Sing about it.*

Professor Thomas McElwain wrote: *Numbers 21:17 is the second text that translators have been willing to leave in a form void of meaning, in the figure of the flying well. It is doubly troublesome in lacking an explanatory context. ... The Bible in Basic English tries to avoid the problem of the flying well by replacing it with the obedient well that comes when called: Then Israel gave voice to this song: Come up, O water-spring, let us make a song to it.*[34]

Translators have struggled to find a realistic meaning to עלי באר ענו-לה ('ă-lî bə-'êr 'ĕ-nū- lāh). Some have mixed the phrase with the first part of the verse to bring up something less confusing:

Numbers 21:17
Young's literal translation.
Then singeth Israel this song, concerning the well--they have answered to it.

Young's literal translation has assumed the two statements as one, while others, such as NIV, separated them. The Young's attempt in making sense of the phrase has raised another question: What is "this song"? No answer has been found yet.

In my opinion, the verse is missing something. Again, it could be a matter of mis-scribing. But if we read *ali oh well* to a Muslim, all you will see is a sudden reaction of sadness and tears of remembering stories of Imam Ali's cries to a well. The pool of Kawthar[a] and the special role given to the Imam in this regard can also be associated with the verse.

Table 27 illustrates the text analysis of the verse.

---

[a] Kawthr (or Al-Kauthar) is the name of a heavenly pond given to the Prophet. It is well known among Muslims that Imam Ali is the Sāqī al-Kawthar (the supplier of Kawthar).

Table 27
Text Analysis[1] Numbers 21:17

Str	Translit	Hebrew	English	Morph
227 [e]	'āz	אָז	Then	Adv
7891 [e]	yā-šîr	יָשִׁיר	sang	Verb
3478 [e]	yiś-rā-'êl,	יִשְׂרָאֵל	Israel	Noun
853 [e]	'et-	אֶת־	-	Acc
7892 [e]	haš-šî-rāh	הַשִּׁירָה	song	Noun
2063 [e]	haz-zōt;	הַזֹּאת	this	Pro
5927 [e]	'ă-lî	עֲלִי	Spring up	Verb
875 [e]	bə-'êr	בְאֵר	O well	Noun
6030 [e]	'ĕ-nū-	עֱנוּ־	sing	Verb
	lāh.	לָהּ׃	to	Prep

hitpa'er Ali (Exodus 8:9)

In Exodus chapter 8, we read that the Pharaoh did not let Israelites leave Egypt; therefore, Moses$_{pbuh}$ delivered God's order to Aaron$_{pbuh}$ to stretch out his hand over streams and make frogs come up on the land of Egypt. Frogs covered the land of Egypt and the Pharaoh asked Moses$_{pbuh}$ and Aaron$_{pbuh}$ to pray for God to take the frogs away. In return, the Pharaoh would allow Moses' people to offer a sacrifice to God. Moses$_{pbuh}$ started his speech with the Pharaoh saying: *hitpa'er ali* (התפאר עלי). This mysterious phrase is an unsolved dispute and confusion among Bible translators. In the entire Bible, this is the only place we find "hitpa'er". It is assumed that the word originated from פָּאַר (*paar*), means "glorified".

The interpretations differ from one another to such an extent that even same versions of the Bible in different prints have offered very different translations. (See King James Bible and King James 2000 Bible, below) The followings are just a few examples of the different interpretations of "hitpa'er ali" (underlined words) in different versions of the Bible:

Exodus 8:9
(NIV)
Moses said to Pharaoh, "I leave to you the honor of setting the time for me to pray for you and your officials and your people that you and your houses may be rid of the frogs, except for those that remain in the Nile."

NLV
"You set the time!" Moses replied. "Tell me when you want me to pray for you, your officials, and your people. Then you and your houses will be rid of the frogs. They will remain only in the Nile River."

ESV
Moses said to Pharaoh, "Be pleased to command me when I am to plead for you and for your servants and for your people, that the frogs be cut off from you and your houses and be left only in the Nile."

NASB
Moses said to Pharaoh, "The honor is yours to tell me: when shall I entreat for you and your servants and your people, that the frogs be destroyed from you and your houses, that they may be left only in the Nile?"

KJB
And Moses said unto Pharaoh, Glory over me: when shall I intreat for thee, and for thy servants, and for thy people, to destroy the frogs from thee and thy houses, that they may remain in the river only?

KJ 2000 B
And Moses said unto Pharaoh, You tell me: when shall I entreat for you, and for your servants, and for your people, to destroy the frogs from you and your houses, that they may remain in the river only?

ISV
Moses told Pharaoh, "You decide when I should plead for you, your servants, and your people to remove the frogs from you and your household. They'll remain only in the Nile River."

DRB
And Moses said to Pharao: Set me a time when I shall pray for thee, and for thy servants, and for thy people, that the frogs may be driven away from thee and from thy house, and from thy servants, and from thy people: and may remain only in the river.

WBT
And Moses said to Pharaoh, Glory over me: when shall I entreat for thee, and for thy servants, and for thy people, to destroy the

frogs from thee, and thy houses, that they may remain in the river only?

YLT
And Moses saith to Pharaoh, <u>'Beautify thyself over me</u>; when do I make supplication for thee, and for thy servants, and for thy people, to cut off the frogs from thee and from thy houses -- only in the River they do remain?'

In most of the translations, it is assumed that the word "ali" (עלי) is a preposition with a pronominal suffix. Nevertheless, the confusion overshadows this interpretation when "hitpa'er" (התפאר) precedes "ali". It sounds like Moses_pbuh glorifying himself! It makes no sense at all when we put it in the context. This is why some versions of the Bible have tried to fix the problem by twisting the literal meaning of "hitpa'er ali" to a totally different meaning such as *"Beautify thyself over me"*, *"Set me"*, *"You may have the honor over me"*, *"You decide"*, *"I leave to you the honor"*, and so on.

In summary, there is a longstanding dispute over the meaning of "hitpa'er ali". What could be understood, with no doubt, is that this is not a common Hebrew literature. In other words, there is something unusual in the phrase. Is it a name that comes after verb or there is a scribal miss-intervention that causes the puzzle? You pick the answer that seems right to you. The closest possibility to the real application of the phrase is that Moses_pbuh was saluting a name, Elahi (My God) or Ali. The closest match for the case is 'el·yō·wn (used in Psalm 82:6). It is translated to "the most high". The context of Psalm 82:6 is also another confusion and a dispute amongst Bible translators.

Assuming that the 'el·yō·wn was correctly translated to "the most high", we can temporarily solve the dispute over the meaning of "hitpa'er ali", *Glory to the most high*. We can conveniently settle the matter with this translation until we examine Psalm 82:6 carefuly. As we will see later, the text analysis of Psalm 82:6 exposes the miss-interpretation; we will find out that *'el·yō·wn* (עֶלְיוֹן) in this verse does not mean "the most high", it is a proper name but unknown at that time.

As a final suggestion, Moses$_{pbuh}$ must have been chanting a word or reciting a divinely revealed statement to gain psychological strength, unusual to his time: *hitpa'er ali*, Salute to Ali, heidar Ali, kheibar Ali, etc. The scribe did not get it well therefore tried to "fix it", perhaps by changing the words. Remember, this is a very common phenomenon in the Bible.

Ali, the King (Deuteronomy 17:14)

In Deuteronomy, we read that God instructs Moses_{pbuh} to announce that Ali_{pbuh} will be assigned as a Malek (King) and people shall obey him and accept his judgement, for the Malek will not deviate from divine laws.

Deuteronomy 17:14
When you are come unto the land which the LORD your God gives you, and shall possess it, and shall dwell therein, and shall say, I will assign Ali a king, like all the nations around.

In some Bible translations, the word עלי (ali), is translated to *"over me"*. Below is an example:

King James 2000 Bible
When you are come unto the land which the LORD your God gives you, and shall possess it, and shall dwell therein, and shall say, I will set a king <u>over me</u>, like all the nations that are about me;

It is taken as if עלי (ali) is preposition + pronoun, *al + i*, meaning *over me*. Following is the Hebrew text with transliteration:

Deuteronomy 17:14[1]
כי־תבא אל־הארץ אשר יהוה אלהיך נתן לך וירשתה וישבתה בה ואמרת **אשימה עלי מלך** ככל־הגוים אשר סביבתי׃

kî- ṯā·ḇō 'el- hā·'ā·reṣ, 'ă·šer Yah·weh 'ĕ·lō·he·ḵā nō·ṯên lāḵ, wî·riš·tāh wə·yā·šaḇ·tāh bāh; wə·'ā·mar·tā, **'ā·śî·māh 'ā·li**[a] **me·leḵ**, kə·ḵāl- hag·gō·w·yim 'ă·šer sə·ḇî·ḇō·tāy.

---

[a] The word עלי in this verse is transliterated as 'ā-lay (compare it with 'ă-lê in Psalm 7:8), however its Hebrew pronunciation has no difference with the word עלי 'ā·li used in Numbers 21:17 (see Table 27)

The statement *'ā·śî·māh 'ā·li me·lek̲* literally means "assign ali king". If we translate it "assign over me a king", obviously we should see a divine king over Moses_pbuh when he settled down in the Promised Land. We know from Deuteronomy 33:4-5 that Moses_pbuh himself was a king; he himself was the ruler, governor, and commander of his people (Exodus 32:27, 28). Therefore, the verse cannot refer to *a king over Moses* simply because Moses_pbuh was a king. Christian leaders take this verse as a promise for coming of the Christ_pbuh, but verses 18 to 20 dismiss it.

Deuteronomy 17:18-20
NIV
18 When he takes the throne of his kingdom, he is to write for himself on a scroll a copy of this law, taken from that of the Levitical priests. 19 It is to be with him, and he is to read it all the days of his life so that he may learn to revere the Lord his God and follow carefully all the words of this law and these decrees 20 and not consider himself better than his fellow Israelites and turn from the law to the right or to the left. Then he and his descendants will reign a long time over his kingdom in Israel.

The verses above clearly show that he will be obedient to the law and his descendants will rule in Israel for a long time. A quick look at the Pauline doctrine – declaring that Jesus_pbuh removed the need to obeying the laws of Moses_pbuh – makes no room for applying these verses to Jesus_pbuh, unless we believe contrary to what Paul said about the law (Romans 7:1-6[a], Galatians 3:10-14[b], Colossians 2:14-17[c]). Even so, Jesus_pbuh never had a kingdom nor do we have any evidence of him having descendants.

---

[a] Freed from the Law
[b] The Law Brings a Curse
[c] The Law was against people and therefore Jesus declined it

Yedollah Ali (1 Chronicles 28:19)

David_pbuh tells his son, Solomon_pbuh, the secret of his wisdom:

1 Chronicles 28:19
All this, said David, in writing by Yad Yahweh Ali, I am made to understand, all the design of the Malakowt.

Below is the Hebrew text and transliteration of the verse: [1]

הכל בכתב **מיד יהוה עלי** השכיל כל מלאכות התבנית: פ
hak·kōl bik̲·tāb̲ mî·yad̲ Yah·weh **'ā·li**[a] hiś·kîl; kōl mal·'ă·k̲ō·wt̲ hat·tab̲·nît̲. p̄

If the phrase מיד יהוה עלי (mî·yad̲ Yah·weh 'ā·li) is written in Arabic, بيدالله على (bi yad Allah Ali) [b], every Muslim will immediately think of Imam Ali_pbuh. Bible translators differ in finding a meaningful explanation for the statement. Some say: "the Lord's hand upon me"; some totally disregard 'ā·li (such as American Standard Version), then they notice that it might trigger the sensitivity of the word 'ā·li; therefore in *New* American Standard Version they put the word back again, translated to "upon me". (See below)

1 Chronicles 28:19
ASV (The word 'ā·li has been deleted)
All this,'said David, have I been made to understand in writing <u>from the hand of Jehovah</u>, even all the works of this pattern.

---

[a] The word עלי in this verse is transliterated as 'ā-lay (compare it with 'ă-lê in Psalm 7:8), however its Hebrew pronunciation has no difference with the word עלי 'ā·li used in Numbers 21:17 (see Table 27)
[b] YadAllah was one of Imam Ali's nicknames.

NASB (The word 'ā·li has been translated to "upon me")
"All this", said David, "the LORD made me understand in writing <u>by His hand upon me</u>, all the details of this pattern."

The King James Bible has also translated "ali" to "upon me":

All this, said David, the LORD made me understand in writing <u>by his hand upon me</u>, even all the works of this pattern.

ISV and NET have translated the entire phrase of מיד יהוה עלי (mî·yaḏ Yah·weh 'ā·li) to "the LORD", both words ("mî·yaḏ" and "ā·li") are omitted; and some other words (such as "at his direction", "directed" and so on) are added to the translation:

ISV
"All of these things the LORD made clear to me in writing <u>at his direction</u>—the construction plans for all of the building."

NET Bible
David said, "All of this I put in writing as the LORD <u>directed</u> me and gave me insight regarding the details of the blueprints."

Interestingly, many believe that David was talking about the blueprints of his palace and nothing more than that! But the original Hebrew word כל מלאכות (kōl mal·'ă·kō·wṯ) has more than just a building. It also means *whole creation*, in Arabic (Kul Malakut) كلّ ملكوت. The same word, in Genesis 2:2, means "the creation of God".

Believing that David$_{pbuh}$ has learned the patterns of the creation from Imam Ali$_{pbuh}$, at first may sound enigmatic; "how a man who was born about 1600 years after David, can possibly teach him anything?" Well, Christians and Jews should have no problem with believing that; Melchizedek had no father, no mother, no beginning and no end (Hebrews 7:3); Christians believe that Jesus$_{pbuh}$ was before Abraham$_{pbuh}$ (John 8:58). If we believe that God could make a man with no beginning and no end and a man before his Ancestor, then we should not have any problem at all with believing that He can also make someone before his earthy birth or before someone else, metaphysically or spiritually. It should not be a surprise for Bible believers that God can make an *Arab* to *be* before his birth if *the race is not a concern to God.*

Majestic Mekka and King Haidar (Psalm 8)

Imam Ali_pbuh is mentioned not only in Deuteronomy 17:14 as a divinely assigned king, but also the Psalm of David have pronounced his second name, Heidar or Haidar, with a similar statement:

Psalm 8:5[1]
WLC (Consonants Only)

ותחסרהו מעט מאלהים וכבוד והדר תעטרהו:

NIV
You have made them a little lower than the angels and crowned them with glory and honor.

Rendered translation:
Made him a little lower than God and crowned Kabaa and Haidar.

As *usual*, the key words הדר hā-ḏār and כבוד ḵā-ḇō-wḏ are translated in all versions of the Bible (Table 28). By reviewing the precedent verses, I found other formidable proofs of Islam as well.

Table 28

Text Analysis[1]   Psalm 8:5

Str	Translit	Hebrew	English	Morph
2637 [e]	wat-tə-ḥas-sə-rê-hū	וַתְּחַסְּרֵהוּ	and lower	Verb
4592 [e]	mə-'aṭ	מְּעַט	For You have made him a little	Subst
430 [e]	mê-'ĕ-lō-hîm;	מֵאֱלֹהִים	than the angels	Noun
3519 [e]	wə-ḵā-ḇō-wd	וְכָבוֹד	and him with glory	Noun
1926 [e]	wə-hā-dār	וְהָדָר	and honor	Noun
5849 [e]	tə-'aṭ-tə-rê-hū.	תְּעַטְּרֵהוּ׃	have crowned	Verb

Verse 1 says that God made Mekka majestic over whole earth, and He has set His glory in Hashemite. (Table 29)

Psalm 8:1[1]
WLC (Consonants Only)

יהוה אדנינו מה־אדיר מך בכל־הארץ אשר תנה הודך על־השמים:

It reads:

Yah-weh 'ă-ḏō-nê-nū māh 'ad-dîr mə-kā bə-ḵāl hā-'ā-reṣ 'ă-šer tə-nāh hō-wḏ-ḵā, 'al- haš-šā-mā-yim.

NIV
LORD, our Lord, how majestic is your name in all the earth! You have set your glory in the heavens.

Rendered translation:
LORD, our Lord, how majestic is Mekka in all the earth! You have set your glory in Hashemayim.

After checking different interpretations, I came across a suspicious variation in Aleppo Codex, where the word mə-kā, becomes "shmeka" and is translated to "Your name". (See below; the word in box reads "shmeka")

If mə-kā is correct, it should be translated to "from you", but it does not make sense in the verse, therefore, the word must be used without translation; that is Mekka. The Aleppo Codex version of "shmeka" (meaning "your name") was probably picked to avoid the issue.

Psalm 8:1
Aleppo Codex [1] (שמך reads "shemka")

א למנצח על-הגתית מזמור לדוד ב יהוה אדנינו-- מה-אדיר שמך
בכל-הארץ אשר תנה הודך על-השמים

In Westminster Leningrad Codex, it is מך (mekka):

WLC (Consonants Only) [1]

למנצח על־הגתית מזמור לדוד: יהוה אדנינו מה־אדיר מך בכל־הארץ
אשר תנה הודך על־השמים:

Verse 2 is talking about infants and children who praise God:

Psalm 8:2
NIV
Through the praise of children and infants you have established a stronghold against your enemies, to silence the foe and the avenger.

There are several narrations about Imam Ali$_{pbuh}$ and his descendants praising God at birth and very young age.

Table 29

Text Analysis[1] Psalm 8:1

Str	Translit	Hebrew	English	Morph
5329 [e]	lam-naṣ-ṣê-aḥ	לַמְנַצֵּחַ	To the chief Musician	Verb
5921 [e]	'al-	עַל־	on	Prep
1665 [e]	hag-git-tît,	הַגִּתִּית	Gittith	Noun
4210 [e]	miz-mō-wr	מִזְמוֹר	A Psalm	Noun
1732 [e]	lə-ḏā-wiḏ.	לְדָוִד׃	of David	Noun
3068 [e]	Yah-weh	יְהוָה	O LORD	Noun
113 [e]	'ă-ḏō-nê-nū,	אֲדֹנֵינוּ	our Lord	Noun
4100 [e]	māh-	מָה־	How	Pro
117 [e]	'ad-dîr	אַדִּיר	excellent	Adj
8034 [e]	šə-mə-kā	שִׁמְךָ	[is] Your name	Noun
3605 [e]	bə-ḵāl	בְּכָל־	in all	Noun
776 [e]	hā-'ā-reṣ;	הָאָרֶץ	the earth	Noun
834 [e]	'ă-šer	אֲשֶׁר	Who	Prt
5414 [e]	tə-nāh	תְּנָה	have set	Verb
1935 [e]	hō-wḏ-ḵā,	הוֹדְךָ	Your glory	Noun
5921 [e]	'al-	עַל־	above	Prep
8064 [e]	haš-šā-mā-yim.	הַשָּׁמָיִם׃	the heavens	Noun

Mekka is repeated in Verses 3 and 9 (translated to "your heavens" and "your name", respectively). It is, again, different in Aleppo Codex. (See Table 30 and Table 31)

Psalm 8:3 [1]
WLC (Consonants Only)

כי־אראה מיך מעשי אצבעתיך ירח וכוכבים אשר כוננתה:

NIV
When I consider your heavens, the work of your fingers, the moon and the stars, which you have set in place,

Rendered translation
When I consider mekka, the work of your fingers, the moon and the stars, which you have set in place.

Psalm 8:9 [1]
WLC (Consonants Only)

יהוה אדנינו מה־אדיר מך בכל־הארץ:

NIV
LORD, our Lord, how majestic is your name in all the earth!

Rendered translation
LORD, our Lord, how majestic is mekka in all the earth!

Table 30

Text Analysis[1]   Psalm 8:3 (part of)

Str	Translit	Hebrew	English	Morph
3588 [e]	kî-	כִּי־	When	Conj
7200 [e]	'er-'eh	אֶרְאֶה	I consider	Verb
8064 [e]	me-kā	שָׁמֶיךָ	Your heavens	Noun

Table 31

Text Analysis[1]   Psalm 8:9 (part of)

Str	Translit	Hebrew	English	Morph
117 [e]	'ad-dîr	אַדִּיר	excellent	Adj
8034 [e]	mə-kā,	שִׁמְךָ	[is] Your name	Noun
3605 [e]	bə-kāl	בְּכָל־	in all	Noun
776 [e]	hā-'ā-res.	הָאָרֶץ׃	the earth	Noun

Meka, Shemka, Shameka or Shimka?

Verses 1, 3 and 9 are significantly different in Westminster Leningrad Codex and Aleppo Codex.

As it is noticeable in the text analysis (Table 29, Table 30, and Table 31), the transliterations of "Mekka" in verses 1, 3 and 9 are different, mə-kā in verses 1 and 9, but me-kā in verse 3.

Nevertheless, more importantly, the Hebrew words do not match the transliterations at all. The difference between the Hebrew and the transliterations led me to examine the words in depth and discover an important variant in these two manuscripts.

What is more significant about these words is that they are written *completely* differently in Hebrew. The Hebrew words are שִׁמְךָ *shem-ka*, שָׁמֶיךָ, *shameka* שִׁמְךָ and *shim-ka*, in verses 1, 3 and 9, respectively.

You may wonder why they have transliterated so differently; the Hebrew words carry שׁ "sh" at the beginning but the transliterations do not. It is because two different manuscripts, Aleppo Codex and Westminster Leningrad Codex, write differently.

Aleppo Codex adds the letter שׁ "sh" to the beginning of מך mk. That is why we see it as שִׁמְךָ *shem-ka* in verse 1, and quite similar to verse 9 (translated to "*your name*"), and שָׁמֶיךָ *shameka* in verse 3 (translated to "*your heavens*"). (See below)

Psalm 8:1
Aleppo Codex (Note שמך shem-ka) [1]

א למנצח על-הגתית מזמור לדוד ב יהוה אדנינו-- מה-אדיר שמך
בכל-הארץ אשר תנה הודך על-השמים

WLC (Note מְ mə-kā) [1]

לַמְנַצֵּ֥חַ עַֽל־הַגִּתִּ֗ית מִזְמ֥וֹר לְדָוִֽד׃ יְהוָ֤ה אֲדֹנֵ֗ינוּ מָֽה־אַדִּ֣יר ‎‏מָ‎‏ךְ‏‎ בְּכָל־הָאָ֑רֶץ
אֲשֶׁ֥ר תְּנָ֥ה הוֹדְךָ֗ עַל־הַשָּׁמָֽיִם׃

Psalm 8:3
Aleppo Codex (Note: שמיך shameka) [1]

ד כי-אראה ‎‏שמיך‏‎ מעשה אצבעתיך -- ירח וכוכבים אשר כוננתה

WLC (Note: מֶ me-kā) [1]

כִּֽי־אֶרְאֶ֣ה ‎‏מֶיךָ‏‎ מַעֲשֵׂ֣י אֶצְבְּעֹתֶ֑יךָ יָרֵ֥חַ וְכוֹכָבִ֗ים אֲשֶׁ֣ר כּוֹנָֽנְתָּה׃

Some of the variants in the manuscripts seem to be purposeful manipulations; Mekka had to be changed to something more *pleasant*-type of word; the closest words they could find were shem-ka (your name) and shameka (your heavens), different words for even more fantasy. Thank to the Lord of Haidar, otherwise I would never be stimulated to examine the verses meticulously if He was not the aid.

David Appeals to Ali (Psalm 7:8)

David_{pbuh} prays to lord, and asks for His refuge:

Psalm 7:1-8
"Save and deliver me from all who pursue me, ... Arise, Lord, in your anger; rise up against the rage of my enemies. Awake, my God; decree justice....Let the Lord judge the peoples. Vindicate me, Lord, according to my righteous and innocent Ali.

Verse 8 is our zoom point:

Psalm 7:8[1]
WLC (Consonants Only)
יהוה ידין עמים שפטני יהוה כצדקי וכתמי **עלי**:
Yah·weh yā·ḏîn 'am·mîm šā·p̄ə·ṭê·nî Yah·weh; kə·ṣiḏ·qî ū·ḵə·ṯum·mî **'ā·li**[a]

Rendered translation:
Let the Lord judge the peoples. Vindicate me, Lord, according to my righteous and innocent Ali.

Translations differ on the very last word: **עלי** 'ā·li. Many versions of the Bible take it as *in me* or *that is in me*, while some have a very different understanding; they regard it as a vocative word: *Ali* or *O Most High*, similar to YHWEH as appears in middle of the verse. This is identical to Muslim's *"ya Ali"* where it is used only to call Imam Ali_{pbuh}.

---

[a] The word עלי in this verse is transliterated as 'ă-lê (compare it with 'ā-lāy in 1 Chronicles 28:19 and Psalm 7:8), however its Hebrew pronunciation has no difference with the word עלי 'ā·li used in Numbers 21:17 (see Table 27)

The dispute over עלי ʻā·li is quite serious. The first translation, *in me*, gives no importance to עלי ʻā·li, while the second one, *O Most High*, brings it up to YHWEH, the *Most High*. (See below)

Psalm 7:8
NASB
The LORD judges the peoples; Vindicate me, O LORD, according to my righteousness and my integrity <u>that is in me</u>.

NIV
Let the LORD judge the peoples. Vindicate me, LORD, according to my righteousness, according to my integrity, <u>O Most High</u>.

For an Arab, however, the word עלי ʻā·li cannot be easily ignored. Any Arab can get the message that David is calling for Ali. That is why the Arabic translations of the Bible took the first approach. They have translated it to *"that is in me"*. In Arabic, it is supposed to be written as عليَّ "allayya" but, because it is too close to *Ali* (علی), they have deliberately preferred a peculiar word: فيَّ *fiy*. (see below)

٧:٨ المزامير *Arabic: Smith & Van Dyke* [1]
الرب يدين الشعوب. اقض لي يا رب كحقي ومثل كمالي الذي فيَّ

Another interesting point in the verse is the word וכתמי ū·kə·ṯum·mî (translated: "and my integrity"). This word is not just about *integrity*, it is also *part of the high priest's breastplate*[a], a symbol of innocence. It is derived from the consonantal root ת.מ.ם (t-m-m), meaning *complete, perfect and innocent*; identical to Turkish *tamam*.

Putting the two words together will surprise us even more: ū·kə·ṯum·mî ʻā·li, meaning "and my innocent Ali" or "and my

---

[a] וכתמי ū·kə·ṯum·mî, according to NAS Exhaustive Concordance 8537: completeness, integrity, also part of the high priest's breastplate.[1]

perfect Ali". If we re-write the verse accordingly, the message would be unequivocal:

Psalm 7:8
Let the LORD judge the peoples. Vindicate me, LORD, according to my righteous and innocent Ali.

Here David$_{pbuh}$ testifies Imam Ali$_{pbuh}$ as infallible (innocent); that is one of the most important article of faith according to Shi'ite, known as *The Imamate*. David$_{pbuh}$ indeed brings a reason that God should protect him: "my innocent Ali". David$_{pbuh}$ expresses his affection to Imam Ali$_{pbuh}$ by saying "my ... Ali". It does not necessarily mean a family relationship, although they both were from Abraham's offspring.

Mekka and Haidar Ali Assad (Psalm 21:1-7)

David_pbuh has spoken openly about Imam Ali_pbuh. He has given his name and nicknames in Chapter 21 of Psalm.

Psalm 21:1-4
NIV
1 The king rejoices in your strength, LORD. How great is his joy in the victories you give! 2 You have granted him his heart's desire and have not withheld the request of his lips.[a]
3 You came to greet him with rich blessings and placed a crown of pure gold on his head. 4 He asked you for life, and you gave it to him— length of days, for ever and ever.

"Life" in verse 4 is a translation of Hebrew חַיִּים "ḥay-yîm". It is the plural form of חַי "chay" and occurs in the bible for different meanings such as "running" (water) in Leviticus 14:5 and 14:50, or "flowing" (water) in Numbers 19:17, "multitude" and "congregation" in Psalm 74:19, "family" (Samuel 18:18), "beast" (Genesis 1:24, 25, ...), "age" (Genesis 23:1), and so on. Its best translation in the verse 4 is "family" or "offspring" because the word in this verse is plural (I חַיִּים ḥay-yîm), an indication of multitude or family members.

Another matter worthy of mentioning in verse 4 is a word translated to "of you". It is מִמְּךָ "mim-mə-ḵā". I found plenty of verses in the Bible where this word occurs, 41 occurrences to be exact. It shocked me when I saw how differently it has been translated throughout the Bible, such as: *at, for, against, is too, than, beyond, some, have more,* and so on. It convinced me that

---

[a] The Hebrew text contains word סלה *"Selah"* at the end of verse 2 but it is omitted in all translations.

there must be something in this word that has created the inconsistency in the translations. Therefore, I looked at a few verses carefully and found interesting statements that are referring to Mekka. Below is the rendered translation and text analysis of verse 4: (See Table 32)

Psalm 21:4
He asked from mekka for family (offspring), and you gave it to him— length of days, for ages to come.

Table 32

Text Analysis[1] **Psalm 21:4**

Str	Translit	Hebrew	English	Morph
2416 [e]	hay-yîm	חַיִּ֤ים ׀	life	Adj
7592 [e]	šā-'al	שָׁאַ֣ל	He asked	Verb
4480 [e]	mim-mə-kā	מִ֭מְּךָ	of you	Prep
5414 [e]	nā-tat-tāh	נָתַ֣תָּה	gave	Verb
	lōw;	לּ֑וֹ	to	Prep
753 [e]	'ō-rek	אֹ֥רֶךְ	length	Noun
3117 [e]	yā-mîm,	יָ֝מִ֗ים	of days	Noun
5769 [e]	'ō-w-lām	עוֹלָ֥ם	forever	Noun
5703 [e]	wā-'ed.	וָעֶֽד׃	and ever	Noun

The remaining verses ensure that this passage is nothing but a prophecy regarding Islam:

Psalm 21:5
NIV
Through the victories you gave, his glory is great; you have bestowed on him splendor and majesty.

We need to bring up the Hebrew text for real meaning of the verse. (See Table 33) Note the boxed word, וְהָדָר "wə-hā-ḏār", translated to "and majesty"; it is a cognate of Arabic و حيدر "wa haidar", meaning "and Haidar", another name of Imam Ali_pbuh.

Table 33

Text Analysis[1]   Psalm 21:5

Str	Translit	Hebrew	English	Morph
1419 [e]	gā-ḏō-wl	גָּדֹול	[is] great	Adj
3519 [e]	kə-ḇō-w-ḏōw	כְּבֹודֹו	His glory	Noun
3444 [e]	bî-šū-'ā-te-ḵā;	בִּישׁוּעָתֶךָ	in Your salvation	Noun
1935 [e]	hō-wḏ	הֹוד	honor	Noun
1926 [e]	wə-hā-ḏār	וְהָדָר	and majesty	Noun
7737 [e]	tə-šaw-weh	תְּשַׁוֶּה	have You laid	Verb
5921 [e]	'ā-lāw.	עָלָיו׃	on	Prep

Here is the rendered translation:

Psalm 21:5
In your salvation his glory is great, honor and Haidar you have given him.

Adding the context of "praying for having a multitude of family" as well as the "salvation through his glory" to occurrences of "mə-kā" and "hā-ḏār" portrays a man with multitude of family from Mekka who is blessed with Glory, Honor and Haidar; I know only one candidate for it, Prophet Muhammad$_{pbuh}$.

It continues:

Psalm 21:6, 7
NIV
6 *Surely you have granted him unending blessings and made him glad with the joy of your presence.*
7 *For the king trusts in the* LORD; *through the unfailing love of the Most High he will not be shaken.*

Verse 7 contains two key words (See Table 34): וּבְחֶסֶד "ubehesed", meaning *"and through Assad"*, and עֶלְיוֹן "Aliyon", which is Imam Ali$_{pbuh}$.

Word עלי 'ā·li, as explained earlier, has been translated inconsistently in the bible; however this is not limited to the translations only. It applies to the transliterations as well.

As we see in Table 34, the Latin transliteration given to עלי is 'el-y but same word in the Psalm 7:8 and 1 Chronicles 28:19 written as 'ā·li, as discussed earlier. I call it a pervasive ambiguity in exegesis of the Bible. Unfortunately, inconsistency is more common than anything else in the translations of the Bible.

Following is the rendered translation of verse 7.

Psalm 21:7
For the king trusts in the LORD; through Assad Alion he will not be shaken.

Again, the verse is about Prophet Muhammad$_{pbuh}$ and Assad Alion$_{pbuh}$, his cousin and son in law who was the major supporter of the Prophet; he was assigned as the Prophet's successor.

Table 34

Text Analysis[1]   Psalm 21:7

Str	Translit	Hebrew	English	Morph
3588 [e]	kî-	כִּי-	For	Conj
4428 [e]	ham-me-lek	הַמֶּלֶךְ	the king	Noun
982 [e]	bō-tê-aḥ	בֹּטֵחַ	trusts	Verb
3068 [e]	Yah-weh;	בַּיהוָה	in the LORD	Noun
2617 [e]	ū-bə-he-sed	וּבְחֶסֶד	and through the covenant loyalty	Noun
5945 [e]	'el-yō-wn,	עֶלְיוֹן	of the most High	Adj
1077 [e]	bal-	בַּל-	not	Adv
4131 [e]	yim-mō-wt.	יִמּוֹט׃	do be moved	Verb

Children of Ali, the Judges (Psalm 82:1)

Twelve Psalms (numbered as 50 and 73–83 in the Masoretic Text, and as 49 and 72–82 in the Septuagint) are attributed to Asaph. His identity is a matter of dispute; however, it is commonly believed that these Psalms are related to the era of prophet David$_{pbuh}$. Psalms of Asaph contain a variety of topics, Hymns, Communal Laments, Individual Laments, Individual Song of Thanksgiving, Wisdom Poems, Pilgrimage Songs and Liturgies.

Within the book, there are prophecies and predictions manifested openly, through liturgics, or proverbial literature. Our interest in this section is the prophetic aspects of the Psalm 82.

The translations of Psalm 82 infuses a shady image full of confusion in the minds of readers; "God judges among the gods", "the gods know nothing", "you are gods" and many other statements that reflect a misunderstanding of the Hebrew culture of the time by non-Jewish readers. I had to examine many verses word by word to get a glimpse of message in the context.

The degree of inconsistency in the common translations is so high that identical words, sometimes in a single verse, are translated controversially.

The Hebrew word אהים 'ĕ-lō-hîm, in Psalm 82:1, is what I am trying to explain. It appears twice in the verse; in first occurrence, it is translated to "God" referring to the Creator, but in the second as "gods", referring to human figures. Translators tried to fix the confusion by choosing capital "G" and lower case "g" for different occasion of 'ĕ-lō-hîm, though there is no "capital" or "lower case" letters in Hebrew. This word alone has caused great confusions particularly among Christians, to a degree that some took it as plural of Eloh, meaning "Gods", and tried to prove the Doctrine of Trinity.

Let us examine the first verse first.

Psalm 82:1
NIV
A psalm of Asaph. God presides in the great assembly; he renders judgment among the "gods":

Hebrew text: [1]

מזמור לאסף אֹהים נצב בעדת־אל בקרב אלהים ישפט:

If I may write the verse word by word, we will have something like this:

Psalm of asaph Elohim stands in the congregation "il" the midst (nearest) Elohim (he) governs (judges).

The extensive meaning of "Elohim" and "il" has caused a wide range of interpretations, where the first could mean *God, king, judge*, etc. and the second means *God, mighty, power, strong* and so on. Applying none of these meanings to the words, in this verse, can solve the problem. I have desperately tried all options but no intelligible result could I obtain. The only possible solution to the puzzle I did find is that the "il", in Psalm 82:1, must be a reference to *a man* rather than God.

Table 35

Text Analysis[1]   **Psalm 82:1**

Str	Translit	Hebrew	English	Morph
4210 [e]	miz-mō-wr.	מִזְמוֹר	A Psalm	Noun
623 [e]	lə-'ā-sāp̄	לְאָסָף	of Asaph	Noun
430 [e]	'ĕlō-hîm,	אֱלֹהִים	God	Noun
5324 [e]	niṣ-ṣāb	נִצָּב	stands	Verb
5712 [e]	ba-'ă-dat-	בַּעֲדַת-	in His own congregation	Noun
410 [e]	'êl;	אֵל	of the mighty	Noun
7130 [e]	bə-qe-reb	בְּקֶרֶב	in the midst	Noun
430 [e]	'ĕ-lō-hîm	אֱלֹהִים	the gods	Noun
8199 [e]	yiš-pōṭ.	יִשְׁפֹּט׃	he judges	Verb

Here are some rendered translations that I can suggest:

Psalm 82:1
- *God stands in the congregation of IL, by the nearest one of God, (he) judges.*

- *God stands in the congregation of IL; by the midst of God, (he) judges.*

- *God stands in the congregation of the mighty one, the nearest one of God; (he) judges.*

It could mean: God is with "IL", "the one who is the nearest to God", "the one who judges". The question of IL's identity can be answered by examining the subsequent verses.

Verse 2 is also translated vague.

Psalm 82:2
NIV
How long will you defend the unjust and show partiality to the wicked?

Most of the translations, more or less, have the same tone, a complaint about "God's wrong action" and "His partiality to the wicked". It is clearly opposing the idea of the Just God, who is not on the side of wicked! (See Isaiah 28:22, Isaiah 30:18, Psalm 37:28[a])

I have adjusted the translation according to the concept of a divine justice and the literal meaning of the verse rather than a mysticism.

Rendered translation of Psalm 82:2

---

[a] Psalm 37:28 is an interesting verse. It is discussed in Chapter 2 – The Prophet and Twelve Princes, under "God Will Not Forsake Seyid (Psalm 37:28)".

When the time (comes) you will judge the unjust and people who accept the wicked?

Verse 3 and 4 corroborate the rendering:

Psalm 82:3, 4 (NIV)
Defend the weak and the fatherless; uphold the cause of the poor and the oppressed.
Rescue the weak and the needy; deliver them from the hand of the wicked.

Verse 5 is another mistaken statement in NIV; it is because of a false understanding of the very first verse. However, many other translations have done a better job on this verse: (NIV)

The 'gods' know nothing, they understand nothing. They walk about in darkness; all the foundations of the earth are shaken.

The KJB has a better translation for verse 5:

Psalm 82:5(KJB)
They know not, neither will they understand; they walk on in darkness: all the foundations of the earth are out of course.

The last three verses of Psalm 82 also prove my argument. In the common translations of verse 6 we read:

Psalm 82:6 (NIV)
I said, 'You are "gods"; you are all sons of the Most High.'

This verse, as simple as it might look to Christians, is one of the most misunderstood and misused statements in Christendom. They all use it to prove Jesus's Deity, relating it to John 10:34. It is a long story, but what is concerned to my topic is that the Hebrew text has more to say than the translations do:

Psalm 82:6
WLC (Consonants Only) [1]

אני־אמרתי אלהים אתם ובני עליון כלכם:

'ănî- 'ā-mar-tî 'ĕ-lō-hîm 'at-tem ū-ḇə-nê 'el-yō-wn kul-lə-ḵem.

I – said me God of you and children of elyown all of you.

We understand that the verse by itself does not make sense. One possible translation is that we use the other meanings of Elohim, such as judges, holy ones and so on:

I called you and all of you children of elyown the judges.

Another suggestion is not to stop in the verse but to continue to the next verse:

Psalm 82:7
WLC (Consonants Only) [1]

אכן כאדם תמותון וכאחד השרים תפלו:

'ā-ḵên kə- 'ā-ḏām tə-mū-ṯūn ū-ḵə- 'a-ḥaḏ haś-śā-rîm   tip-pō-lū.

Truly like Adam shall (you) die and like the one the princes will fall.

When we combine both verses, we get a complete statement:

I the God of you and all children of elyown said: Truly like Adam shall you die and like the Princes will you fall.

This makes a lot of sense; it is simulating the children of elyown by the well-known first and second Biblical figures, Adam and his righteous son Seth; it calls him/them as the Princes.

Adam$_{pbuh}$ was the first Biblical and Quranic Man and Prophet. His son Seth$_{pbuh}$ was his Successor (the Prince), a replacement for Abel$_{pbuh}$ (Genesis 4:25).

There are many references to Adam and Seth_pbut in Jewish, Christian and Islamic traditions, illustrating them as the ancestors of humankind and the Holy men assigned by God to establish his laws on earth and lead humankind. They both died as righteous men and were buried in their homeland, Middle East.

Adam_pbuh delivered his knowledge and wisdom to Seth_pbuh before his death. Similarly, Prophet Muhammad_pbuh delivered his knowledge to Imam Ali_pbuh, and announced him as his successor in several occasions.

The holy Prophet reportedly has said: *"I am the city of knowledge and Ali is its gate; therefore, whoever wants the city should enter through the gate"*, also: *"Whoever I am his master, Ali is his master."*

The ending verse calls for God's justice, a figurative statement for the last and final apocalypse.

Psalm 82:8
NIV
Rise up, O God, judge the earth, for all the nations are your inheritance.

The last part of the verse, *all the nations are your inheritance* is synonymous with many Quranic verses such as:

Quran 4:174[26]
O mankind! Verily there hath come to you a convincing proof from your Lord: For We have sent unto you a light (that is) manifest.

Quran 38:29[26]
(Here is) a Book which We have sent down unto thee, full of blessings, that they may mediate on its Signs, and that men of understanding may receive admonition.

The Quran, Haidar and Zulfaqar (Psalm 149)

Psalm 149, a short chapter with 9 verses, has puzzled many. Lack of a clear explanation to its critical phrases such as "new song", "ḥăsîdîm", "double-edges sword", and so on, buzzes alarms.

Psalm 149
NIV
1 Praise the Lord. Sing to the Lord a new song, his praise in the assembly of his faithful people.
2 Let Israel rejoice in their Maker; let the people of Zion be glad in their King.
3 Let them praise his name with dancing and make music to him with timbrel and harp.
4 For the Lord takes delight in his people; he crowns the humble with victory.
5 Let his faithful people rejoice in this honor and sing for joy on their beds.
6 May the praise of God be in their mouths and a double-edged sword in their hands,
7 to inflict vengeance on the nations and punishment on the peoples,
8 to bind their kings with fetters, their nobles with shackles of iron,
9 to carry out the sentence written against them-- this is the glory of all his faithful people. Praise the LORD.

A careful study of the Hebrew text reveals a different picture than what the translations do. The last word in verse 1 is a term used commonly in Hebrew: חסידים (ḥăsîdîm). It is a cognate of Arabic السيد (As-Seyid). The word occurs in verse 5 as well. (Table 36 and Table 37)

The Hebrew חסידים "ḥăsîdîm" has developed a slightly different meaning than the Arabic السيد "As-Seyid", "the Saints" and "the Master", respectively. However, the Arabic Bible of Smith & Van

Dyke has avoided using السيّد (As-Seyid) by replacing it with الاتقياء (al-atqiaa), meaning "the pious".

The interpretations vary to such an extent that even some compare חסידים "ḥăsîdîm" with Arabic حسد (Haasad), meaning "jealousy", suggesting that it is from Hebrew חָסַד "chacad" (meaning merciful). It is in the word analysis of Brown-Driver-Briggs. (See Figure 28 and Figure 29)

Below is the Hebrew text of Psalm 149:1 and 5; the boxed words are "ḥăsîdîm".

Psalm 149:1
WLC (Consonants Only)[1]

הללו יה ׀ שירו ליהוה שיר חדש תהלתו בקהל חסידים:
hal-lū yāh šî-rū Yah-weh šîr ḥā-dāš tə-hil-lā-ṯōw biq-hal ḥă-sî-dîm.

Psalm 149:5
WLC (Consonants Only)[1]

יעלזו חסידים בכבוד ירננו על־משכבותם:
ya'-lə-zū ḥă-sî-dîm bə-ḵā-ḇō-wḏ yə-ran-nə-nū 'al- miš-kə-ḇō-w-ṯām.

Figure 28

2623. chasid[1]

Strong's Concordance

chasid: kind, pious

Original Word: חָסִיד
Part of Speech: Adjective
Transliteration: chasid
Phonetic Spelling: (khaw-seed')
Short Definition: ones

NAS Exhaustive Concordance

Word Origin
from chasad
Definition
kind, pious
NASB Translation
godly (2), godly man (3), godly ones (20), godly person (1), gracious (1), Holy One (1), kind (3), love (1), ungodly* (1).

Figure 29

2616. chacad[1]

Strong's Concordance

chacad: merciful

Original Word: חָסַד
Part of Speech: Verb
Transliteration: chacad
Phonetic Spelling: (khaw-sad')
Short Definition: merciful

Brown-Driver-Briggs

I. [חָסַד] **verb 1. be good, kind** (Late Hebrew חָסַד in derivatives חָסִיד *pious*; Aramaic חָסַד *be kind, mild* (then *beg*), chiefly in derivatives חִסְדָּא etc.; compare perhaps Arabic حَشَدَ usually plural *they assembled*, followed by لَهُ *they combined for him, and took pains to shew him courtesy* Lane[574c], also RS[Proph. iv. n. 9](and Schu AE see in Thes); > Thes and others Find primary meaning in *eager zeal* or *desire* ("" קָנָא), whence develop *kindness* (as above), and *envy*, Arabic حَسَدَ, حَسِدَ *envy* (verb & noun), Aramaic חֲסַד *be put to shame*, حَسَدَ, חסד *reproach, revile*, v, II. חסן) — only

In verse 4, the Hebrew phrase for "the Lord takes delight" is רוצה
יהוה (rō-w-ṣeh Yah-weh); it is رضى الله (radzi Allahu) in Arabic, as used in the Quran 5:119.

سورة المائدة (5)، آية 119
قَالَ اللَّهُ هَذَا يَوْمُ يَنْفَعُ الصَّادِقِينَ صِدْقُهُمْ لَهُمْ جَنَّاتٌ تَجْرِي مِنْ تَحْتِهَا الْأَنْهَارُ خَالِدِينَ فِيهَا أَبَدًا رَضِيَ اللَّهُ عَنْهُمْ وَرَضُوا عَنْهُ ذَلِكَ الْفَوْزُ الْعَظِيمُ

The Quran – Al-Ma'edah (5):119 [26]
Allah will say: "This is a day on which the truthful will profit from their truth: theirs are gardens, with rivers flowing beneath, - their eternal Home: Allah well-pleased with them, and they with Allah: That is the great salvation, (the fulfilment of all desires).

Here is the verse 4 in Hebrew and NIV translation:

Psalm 149:4[1]
WLC (Consonants Only)

כִּי־רוֹצֶה יְהוָה בְּעַמּוֹ יְפָאֵר עֲנָוִים בִּישׁוּעָה׃
kî- rō-w-ṣeh Yah-weh bə-'am-mōw yə-pā-'êr 'ă-nā-wîm bî-šū-'āh.

For the Lord takes delight in his people; he crowns the humble with victory.

Psalm 149:5 also mentions בכבוד (bə-kā-ḇō-wḏ), very similar to Arabic بكعبة (be kaabat), meaning "in Ka'ba".

5 Let his faithful people (חסידים "ḥăsîḏîm") *rejoice in this honor* (בכבוד bə-kā-ḇō-wḏ) *and sing for joy on their beds.*

Verse 6 mentions a double-edged sword, ḥe-reḇ pî-p̄î-yō-wṯ; (See Table 38) it is the sword of Imam Ali$_{pbuh}$, known as Dzulfaqar. He and the eleven other Imams possessed this sword; and they were, as the verse reads, indeed the ones who were ever praising God. Another noticeable word in verse 6 is בגרונם (biḡ-rō-w-nām), translated to "in their mouth". By keeping it as is, I immediately noticed its similarity to بقرانهم (biquranahum), meaning "in their Quran". (For more details on this, see Chapter 5 – Quran In The Bible)

The verse is very specific in its message: *The praise of God be in their Quran and a double-edged sword in their hands.* As it is explained earlier, pronunciation and/or meaning of cognates sometimes differ in the Semitic languages; examples are given in Table 3.

The Quran has praised God repeatedly in many verses, such as 1:1; 6:1; 6:45; 7:43; 17:44; 17:52; 17:111; 18:1; 18:46; 22:28; 23:28; 25:58; and so on. It is the only Holy Scripture starts in the name of God and *immediately praises Him*.

The Quran 1:1, 2[26]
*In the Name of Allah, the Merciful, the Most Merciful
Praise be to Allah, the Cherisher and Sustainer of the worlds;*

Psalm 149:9 seals the prophecy; it contains hā-ḏār (Haidar) and ḥă-sî-ḏāw (his Seyid). (See Table 39)

Psalm 149:9
WLC (Consonants Only)[1]

לעשות בהם | משפט כתוב הדר הוא לכל־חסידיו הללו־יה׃
la-'ă-śō-wṯ bā-hem miš-pāṭ kā-ṯūḇ hā-ḏār hū lə-ḵāl ḥă-sî-ḏāw hal-lū- yāh.

to carry out the sentence written against them-- this is the hā-ḏār for all ḥă-sî-ḏāw. Praise the LORD.

Below is the rendered translation of Psalm 149:

1 Praise the Lord. Sing to the Lord a new song, his praise in the assembly of the Seyids.
2 Let Israel rejoice in their Maker; let the people of Zion be glad in their King.
3 Let them praise his name with dancing and make music to him with timbrel and harp.
4 For the Lord takes delight in his people; he crowns the humble with victory.
5 Let the Seyids rejoice in Ka'ba and sing for joy on their beds.
6 The praise of God in their Quran and a double-edged sword in their hands,
7 to inflict vengeance on the nations and punishment on the peoples,
8 to bind their kings with fetters, their nobles with shackles of iron,
9 to carry out the sentence written against them-- this is the Haidar for all his Seyids. Praise the LORD.

THE SPIRIT OF TRUTH Chapter 3 – Imam Ali in the Bible

Table 36

Text Analysis¹   Psalm 149:1

Str	Translit	Hebrew	English	Morph
1984 [e]	hal-lū	הַלְלוּ	Praise you	Verb
3050 [e]	yāh	יָהּ ׀	the LORD	Noun
7891 [e]	šî-rū	שִׁירוּ	Sing	Verb
3068 [e]	Yah-weh	לַיהוָה	to the LORD	Noun
7892 [e]	šîr	שִׁיר	a song	Noun
2319 [e]	hā-dāš;	חָדָשׁ	new	Adj
8416 [e]	tə-hil-lā-tōw,	תְּהִלָּתוֹ	his praise	Noun
6951 [e]	biq-hal	בִּקְהַל	in the congregation	Noun
2623 [e]	hă-sî-dîm.	חֲסִידִים׃	of saints	Adj

Table 37

Text Analysis¹   Psalm 149:5

Str	Translit	Hebrew	English	Morph
5937 [e]	ya'-lə-zū	יַעְלְזוּ	be joyful	Verb
2623 [e]	hă-sî-dîm	חֲסִידִים	Let the saints	Adj
3519 [e]	bə-kā-bō-wd;	בְכָבוֹד	in glory	Noun
7442 [e]	yə-ran-nə-nū,	יְרַנְּנוּ	let them sing aloud	Verb
5921 [e]	'al-	עַל־	on	Prep
4904 [e]	miš-kə-bō-w-tām.	מִשְׁכְּבוֹתָם׃	their beds	Noun

Table 38

Text Analysis[1] Psalm 149:6

Str	Translit	Hebrew	English	Morph
7319 [e]	rō-wm-mō-wt	רוֹמְמוֹת	[Let] the high	Noun
410 [e]	'êl	אֵל	[praises] of God [are]	Noun
1627 [e]	biḡ-rō-w-nām;	בִּגְרוֹנָם	in their mouth	Noun
2719 [e]	wə-he-reb	וְחֶרֶב	and sword	Noun
6374 [e]	pî-p̄î-yō-wt	פִּיפִיּוֹת	a double-edged	Noun
3027 [e]	bə-yā-dām.	בְּיָדָם׃	in their hand	Noun

Table 39

Text Analysis[1] Psalm 149:9

Str	Translit	Hebrew	English	Morph
6213 [e]	la-'ă-śō-wt	לַעֲשׂוֹת	To execute	Verb
	bā-hem	בָּהֶם ׀	in	Prep
4941 [e]	miš-pāṭ	מִשְׁפָּט	on them the judgment	Noun
3789 [e]	kā-ṯūḇ,	כָּתוּב	written	Verb
1926 [e]	hā-dār	הָדָר	honor	Noun
1931 [e]	hū	הוּא	This	Pro
3605 [e]	lə-ḵāl	לְכָל-	for all	Noun
2623 [e]	hă-sî-dāw.	חֲסִידָיו	his saints	Adj
1984 [e]	hal-lū-	הַלְלוּ-	Praise you	Verb
3050 [e]	yāh.	יָהּ׃	the LORD	Noun

Ghadeer and the Bible

The word "Ghadeer" in the Bible is a symbol of law, protection, awakening and blessing. It is translated to "wall" or "fence"[a]. Similarly, in Islam Ghadeer (known as Ghadeer Khom) is one of the exceptional events in which Prophet Muhammad$_{pbuh}$ announced Imam Ali$_{pbuh}$ as his successor; it is considered as the main mean of assurance of a righteous leadership and implementation of the divine law after the Prophet. Many, who were the first to give their allegiance to the Imam, were also the first who denied it right on the day Prophet Muhammad$_{pbuh}$ passed away.

Ghadeer in Arabic and Hebrew

In Arabic, غدير "Ghadeer" means "stream" and in Hebrew, גדר "ghadeer" is translated to "wall".

"Thus "plain" ג ḡ (Gimel) usually corresponds to Standard Arabic غ (ghayn), while differentiated ג followed by geresh ('ג) or with a superscript dot or other markings usually corresponds to Standard Arabic ج (jīm)"[b], says a document approved by the Library of Congress and the Committee for Cataloging: Asian and African Materials (CC:AAM) of the American Library Association. The translators, in some places of the Bible, have mistaken גדר "ghadeer" with Arabic جدار "jidar", meaning "wall".

---

[a] Hebrew word for wall is קיר (qeer). Ghadeer or gā·dêr (גדר) is a symbolic word for *protection*.
[b] https://www.loc.gov/catdir/cpso/romanization/judeo-arabic.pdf

The Hebrew letter ג (Gimel) is the equivalent of Arabic غ (gh); similar to French "r" in "merci". The commonly used word גרק *grq*, representing Arabic غرق *ghareqa*, is another example; both have same meaning "suffocates".

Even if the ג in גדר (ghadeer) carries "geresh", it is not a solid proof for pronouncing it similar to Arabic ج (jīm), as the Bible scholars even do not do so.[35] I have listened to Hebrew audio books in a couple of online sources such as the following sites: http://www.aoal.org/Hebrew/AudioBible/ and https://depts.washington.edu/bibheb/hebrew_audiobible.html [a] (a web site from Near Eastern Languages and Civilization-Washington DC.); both of them pronounce ג "Gimel" just like غ "ghayn".

It is worth pointing out again that having different meanings of one word in these languages is not a new finding; it could be a change in the application of the word throughout time. Moreover, I do not dismiss other possibilities, such as two different Semitic words but a similar pronunciation. In any case, the verses of the Bible, in which this word is used symbolically and mysteriously, are so parallel with the event of Ghadeer Khom of Muslim tradition, where the Prophet of Islam$_{pbuh}$ announced Imam Ali$_{pbuh}$ as his successor.

By examining the word גדר "ghadeer", in the next pages, we find a few interesting points. With special thanks to Dr. Thomas McElwain for his *Shi'ite Beliefs in the Bible*, which I used after writing my Persian book titled "The Spirit of Truth" – 2015. I would have saved plenty of time if I had known his works before writing my books.

---

[a] Accessed on November 16, 2016

Balaam and Ghadeer (Numbers 22)

Ghadeer in the Bible is not just a wall, it is a spiritual and divine obstruction and a controlling power against deceivers. Numbers 22 reads that Balaam, the Persian (or "Gentile") prophet, was asked by Balak, the king of Moab, to curse Moses$_{pbuh}$ and his people who were nearby their towns and were a danger to Medians and Moabites. First, Balaam refuses but second time, after receiving directions from God, he accepts to meet the King. He, while riding his donkey, thinks of something contrary to God's command, in my opinion. Soon an angel appears with a sword in his hand. The donkey sees the angel, off the road she runs. Balaam does not get the message; he beats up the donkey and returns her back to the path. Then, while Balaam was thinking wrongly again, angel reappears, this time between ghadeers (walls) on each side of the path. The donkey, stuck in between Ghadeers, finds no way to escape. Balaam, not knowing what is going on, hurts his foot when his donkey struggles between ghadeers. He again beats her up. The third time, when angel appears, donkey lays on the ground. For third time she gets beaten by Balaam. Then the poor animal breaks her silence. A conversation goes on between her and Balaam. He then notices his mistake; seeing the angel, he prostrates for repentance.

Right after repeating the mistake for three times and after the third appearance of the angel with a sword in his hand, Balaam becomes a symbol of three wrong attempts and the fourth one as the right decision. Interestingly, after he met King Balak of Moab, he was asked by the king three times on three mountains to curse Moses$_{pbuh}$, but each time he refused to do so.

These symbolic events have pure parallels in early Islamic history; three first Caliphs and ..., then Imam Ali$_{pbuh}$ was the fourth. Then some people opposed Imam during his Caliphate for three times, which resulted in three wars followed by three right reactions of the Imam (similar to 3 wrong requests by Balak but 3 correct actions of Balaam). Below is the Hebrew text of verse 22 where Ghadeer is mentioned twice:

Numbers 22:24[1]

ויעמד מלאך יהוה במשעול הכרמים **גדר** מזה ו**גדר** מזה:

way·ya·'ă·mōḏ mal·'aḵ Yah·weh, bə·miš·'ō·wl hak·kə·rā·mîm; gā·ḏêr miz·zeh wə·ḡā·ḏêr miz·zeh.

NASB
Then the angel of the LORD stood in a narrow path of the vineyards, with a wall (ghadeer) *on this side and a wall* (ghadeer) *on that side.*

Moreover, there is another important point in the story of Balaam. During this story, he received four revelations, three of them on top of each mountains overlooking the camp of Moses_pbuh where Balak asked him to Curse Moses_pbuh, and the last one when Balak was disappointed from him. On the third revelation, he, watching Moses_pbuh and his people from top of the mountain, says:

Numbers 24:6
NIV
"Like valleys they spread out, like gardens beside a river, like aloes planted by the LORD, like cedars beside the waters."

The phrase "*like aloes planted by the Lord*" is significantly dissonant with rest of the verse. The first part, *Like valleys they spread out*, talks about the similarity of *valleys* to Moses people. The second part, *like gardens beside a river*, compares Moses people with *gardens beside a river*; and the third part takes a completely different approach: *like aloes planted by the LORD*. The fourth part, last phrase, continues the style of first and second part: *like cedars beside the waters*.

A closer look at the verse reveals a shocking truth. The Hebrew word translated to "gardens" is גנת *qanat*; in Arabic, it is قناة *qanat* meaning "water canal" or "Aqueduct". Second important word is עלי (ali), translated to "beside". The word עלי "ali'[a] occurs twice in this verse. If we read it as it is, without translating, no Muslim will have a slight doubt in his mind that the verse is talking about Imam Ali[pbuh].

Numbers 24:6
"Like valleys they spread out, like canals Ali floods[b], like aloes planted by the LORD, like cedars Ali waters[b]."

Once again, the third part of the verse (*like aloes planted by the LORD*) is very suspicious because of its different comparison with other three parts. Was it a different statement but changed later? No one can give a definite answer, because no longer the original scripture exists or better to say, we do not have the original scripture.

Imam Ali's life is filled with stories of digging canals, planting trees and watering gardens. He was also titled "ساقى الكوثر" (saghi alkawthar), meaning "the supplier of the heavenly pool".

Verse 7 explains more about him:

Numbers 24:7
NIV
Water will flow from their buckets; their seed will have abundant water. "Their king will be greater than Agag; their kingdom will be exalted.

---

[a] The word עלי in this verse is transliterated as 'ă-lê (compare it with 'ā-lāy in 1 Chronicles 28:19 and Psalm 7:8), however its Hebrew pronunciation has no difference with the word עלי 'ā·li used in Numbers 21:17 (see Table 27)
[b] *nā-hār* means *river, flood,* ... I have taken it as a verb in this verse due to its poetic concept.

Below is the Hebrew text and Table 40 is the text analysis of verse 6.

24:6 במדבר Hebrew OT: WLC (Consonants Only)[1]

כנחלים נטיו כגנת עלי נהר כאהלים נטע יהוה כארזים עלי־מים:

Table 40

Text Analysis[1]   Numbers 24:6

Str	Translit	Hebrew	English	Morph
5158 [e]	kin-ḥā-lîm	כִּנְחָלִים	As the valleys	Noun
5186 [e]	niṭ-ṭā-yū,	נִטָּ֫יוּ	are they spread forth	Verb
1593 [e]	kə-ḡan-nōṯ	כְּגַנֹּת	as gardens	Noun
5921 [e]	'ă-lê	עֲלֵי	by	Prep
5104 [e]	nā-hār;	נָהָר	of the river	Noun
174 [e]	ka-'ă-hā-lîm	כַּאֲהָלִים	as the trees of lign aloes	Noun
5193 [e]	nā-ṭa'	נָטַע	has planted	Verb
3068 [e]	Yah-weh,	יְהוָה	that the LORD	Noun
730 [e]	ka-'ă-rā-zîm	כַּאֲרָזִים	as cedar trees	Noun
5921 [e]	'ă-lê-	עֲלֵי־	beside	Prep
4325 [e]	mā-yim.	מָיִם:	the waters	Noun

207

Ghadeer and Dhul-Jinaah (Ecclesiastes 10:8, 20)

If David$_{pbuh}$ repeatedly had talked about Ghadeer, we naturally expect his son, Solomon$_{pbuh}$, to have also spoken about it. He indeed has done so. Ecclesiastes of Solomon assures that whoever breaks Ghadeer, shall be a victim of Serpent.

Ecclesiastes is an unusual book in the canon. Its poetic literature is appreciated when we look at its cherishing language. To some, it is more than just joyful words and experiments of, perhaps, Solomon$_{pbuh}$. It contains secrets within its poetic elegance.

One of the occasions that could not escape from my eyes, nor from Professor Thomas Mc Elwain's, is where Ghadeer is mentioned in a form of metaphoric statement:

Ecclesiastes 10:8
Whoever digs a pit may fall into it; whoever breaks Ghadeer shall be bitten by serpent.

Serpent is a symbol of Satan in the Bible. The book of Genesis (3:1) portrays it as a deceiver and liar who promotes the forbidden as beneficial. The verse beautifully portrays the pit digger and Ghadeer breaker as a fallen man and as a person bitten by serpent.

The bible translators have interpreted "Ghadeer" as "wall". I wonder how it can be literally true that snake comes out from a hole in a wall and bites the wall breaker. Obviously, it does not make sense.

The entire chapter amazingly demonstrates how the Ghadeer breakers will be treated. Verse 12 compares the wise man (the main character in Ghadeer) with fools:

Ecclesiastes 10:12
Words from the mouth of the wise are gracious, but fools are consumed by their own lips.

Imam Ali$_{pbuh}$ has also a word on that: *'A fool's mind is at the mercy of his tongue and a wise man's tongue is under the control of his mind.'* The Nahjol Balagha of the Imam is a solid proof for his wisdom.

The very last verse (Ecclesiastes 10:20) is perhaps one of the best and the most mysterious verse in whole chapter and yet to be decoded. It clearly prohibits setting a position against the King (the main character of Ghadeer) with a super natural literature. Again, Translations are done with confusion.

Ecclesiastes 10:20[1]
10:20 קהלת Hebrew OT: WLC (Consonants Only)

גם במדעך מלך אל־תקלל ובחדרי משכבך אל־תקלל עשיר כי עוף השמים יוליך את־הקול ובעל [הכנפים כ] (כנפים ק) יגיד דבר:

It reads:
gam bə·mad·dā·'ă·ḵā me·leḵ 'al- tə·qal·lêl, ū·ḇə·ḥaḏ·rê miš·kā·ḇə·ḵā, 'al- tə·qal·lêl 'ā·šîr; kî 'ō·wp̄ haš·šā·ma·yim yō·w·lîḵ 'eṯ- haq·qō·wl, ū·ḇa·'al [hak·kə·nā·p̄a·yim k] (kə·nā·p̄a·yim q) yag·gêḏ dā·ḇār.

NIV
Do not revile the king even in your thoughts, or curse the rich in your bedroom, because a bird in the sky may carry your words, and a bird on the wing may report what you say.

It is assumed that Solomon$_{pbuh}$ gives advice that a wise man should not curse a king or a rich, even in his secret places. However, his father, David$_{pbuh}$, and his great... grandson, Jesus$_{pbuh}$ instruct contrary.

In 2 Samuel 16 we read that a man called Shimei son of Gera curses king David$_{pbuh}$; and David$_{pbuh}$ tells his people, who wanted to kill Shimei, to leave him alone. *If he is cursing because God told him "Curse David",* David$_{pbuh}$ tells the people.

2 Samuel 16:10
NIV
(David said)... If he is cursing because the LORD said to him, 'Curse David,' who can ask, 'Why do you do this?'

In another word, God tells Shimei to curse King David$_{pbuh}$, but Solomon$_{pbuh}$ advises opposite. Jesus$_{pbuh}$ also teaches contrary: *Cursed are the rich* (Luke 6:24).

Therefore, the translations of Ecclesiastes 10:20 lack any biblical credit; even they oppose teachings of the Bible. A close look at the verse in Hebrew reveals that the verse is much more mysterious and complicated than what the translators thought.

It appears that there might be a change in the text or a scribal mistake. For instance, "the king", "your bed", "sleeping", "a bird of air" (a bird of haš·šā·ma·yim), "Baal" (a god's name, بعل in Arabic), also "ba·'al hak·kə·nā·p̄a·yim", translated to *"a creature which has wings"*.

In Arabic translation of the Bible (see below), "ba·'al hak·kə·nā·p̄a·yim k" is translated to ذو الجناح (Dhul-Jinaah) which is the name of Imam Hussain's horse ...

All these matters raise many questions. I truly hope somebody can break down the code of this verse.

Table 41 is the text analysis of the verse and below is the Hebrew text. Please note "haš-šā-ma-yim" and "ba·'al hak·kə·nā·p̄a·yim"

Ecclesiastes 10:20¹

גם במדעך מלך אל־תקלל ובחדרי משכבך אל־תקלל עשיר כי עוף השמים יוליך את־הקול ובעל [הכנפים כ] (כנפים ק) יגיד דבר:

It reads:
gam bə·mad·dā·'ă·kā, me·lek 'al- tə·qal·lêl, ū·ḇə·ḥaḏ·rê miš·kā·ḇə·kā, 'al- tə·qal·lêl 'ā·šîr; kî 'ō·wp̄ haš·šā·ma·yim yō·w·lîḵ 'eṯ- haq·qō·wl, ū·ḇa·'al [hak·kə·nā·p̄a·yim k] (kə·nā·p̄a·yim q) yag·gêḏ dā·ḇār.

Here is the Arabic translation:

10:20 الجامعة Arabic: Smith & Van Dyke³⁶

لا تسبّ الملك ولا في فكرك. ولا تسبّ الغني في مضجعك. لان طير السماء ينقل الصوت وذو الجناح يخبر بالامر

Table 41
Text Analysis[1] Ecclesiastes 10:20

Str	Translit	Hebrew	English	Morph
1571 [e]	gam	גַּם	not	Adv
4093 [e]	bə-mad-dā-'ă-kā,	בְּמַדָּעֲךָ	in your bedchamber	Noun
4428 [e]	me-lek	מֶלֶךְ	the king	Noun
408 [e]	'al-	אַל-	not	Adv
7043 [e]	tə-qal-lêl,	תְּקַלֵּל	do Curse	Verb
2315 [e]	ū-bə-had-rê	וּבְחַדְרֵי	and rooms	Noun
4904 [e]	miš-kā-bə-kā,	מִשְׁכָּבְךָ	in your sleeping	Noun
408 [e]	'al-	אַל-	not	Adv
7043 [e]	tə-qal-lêl	תְּקַלֵּל	do curse	Verb
6223 [e]	'ā-šîr;	עָשִׁיר	the rich	Adj
3588 [e]	kî	כִּי	for	Conj
5775 [e]	'ō-wp̄	עוֹף	a bird	Noun
8064 [e]	haš-šā-ma-yim	הַשָּׁמַיִם	of the air	Noun
1980 [e]	yō-w-lîk	יוֹלִיךְ	shall carry	Verb
853 [e]	'et-	אֶת-	-	Acc
6963 [e]	haq-qō-wl,	הַקּוֹל	the voice	Noun
1167 [e]	ū-ba-'al	וּבַעַל	that which has	Noun
	[hak-kə-nā-p̄a-yim	הַכְּנָפַיִם]	-	
	k]	כ]	-	
3671 [e]	(kə-nā-p̄a-yim	(כְּנָפַיִם	wings	Noun
	q)	ק)	-	
5046 [e]	yag-gêd	יַגִּיד	shall tell	Verb
1697 [e]	dā-bār.	דָּבָר:	the matter	Noun

Chapter 4 – Imam Hussain in the Bible

A Short Biography of Imam Hussain

[This section – the biography – is an abstract from *Unique Sacrifice of Imam Hussain for Humanity*, by Dr. S. Manzoor Rizvi and, *Saving Monotheism in the Sands of Karbala,* by S. V. Ahmed Ali] [37,38]

Imam Hussain[a]$_{pbuh}$, son of Imam Ali$_{pbuh}$, was born in 620 AD to a family famous for being compassionate, honorable, peace loving, and just. He was well known for his compassion, generosity and highly praised manner. His grandfather, Prophet Muhammad$_{pbuh}$, with all the love and compassion raised him. After his father, Imam Ali$_{pbuh}$, and his elder Brother, Imam Hassan$_{pbuh}$ were martyred, he became the reminiscence of the Prophet.

Soon oppression and tyranny filled Muslim territories and forced Imam Hussain$_{pbuh}$ to stand up against the oppressor and raise the voice of justice; the movement that took away everything from him, including his companions, close relatives, sons, and finally his own life. What he did not give away was the principle of freedom and justice.

Imam Hussain$_{pbuh}$ illustrated the cry for justice. He stood up against oppression, and sacrificed all he had for truth. He became a symbol of love and freedom for generations to come. He raised the flag of Victory of Blood over Sword. Imam Hussain is a role model for compassion, bravery and self-sacrifice, which is not limited to his time or place. It flows forever.

The tyrant Umayyad ruler, Yazid son of Moawia, needed Imam's allegiance to gain the credit for his throne. Imam Hussain$_{pbuh}$ did not do so. Contrary to Yazid's foolish expectation, Imam

---

[a] other spellings: Hussein, Hossain, Hossein (also with single "s")

Hussain_pbuh uprose against the corruption and destruction of morality.

Imam Hussain_pbuh, in the year 680 AD, during his journey to Kufa, was attacked by an army of over 30,000 men. The battle took place between 72 men of Hussain_pbuh and the out numbering army of Yazid. Hussain_pbuh was cut off from water for three days and nights in hot dessert of Karbala.

His companions were killed one by one, his close relatives, his cousins, brothers, and son, Ali Akbar_pbuh were martyred. Yazid's army did not spare his 6-month-old infant, Ali Asghar_pbuh. When Imam Hussain_pbuh held him on his hand saying to the enemy: "You are after my blood, what this baby has done to you. Why do you deny water to this baby?" they shot the baby in the neck.

Yazid's army slaughtered the men of Hussain_pbuh. Finally, they pierced him with arrows, smashed his body under the feet of horses and left the decapitated bodies of his men on the hot sands of the desert. The surviving children and women were taken captive and were treated horrendously inhuman.

Imam Hussain's only surviving son, Imam Sejjad_pbuh, did not participate in the battle due to his illness. He took the leadership of the Muslims. He, alongside his aunt, Zeynab_pbuh, the sister of Imam Hussain_pbuh, kept the wave of resistance alive.

Every year on the tenth of Muharram, known as Ashura, Muslims mourn the event of Karbala. Millions of Muslims make pilgrimage to the holy shrine of Imam Hussain_pbuh in the city of Karbala, Iraq.

Imam Hussain in the Bible

Reading many passages of the Bible, led me to the story of tragic event of Karbala. Sometimes I felt as if I was reading laments about Imam Hussain$_{pbuh}$. I tried to ignore my feelings and look for factual evidence, but the more I read, the better I realised that the Bible is loaded with verses about this great man of dignity, serenity, sincerity and faith. Soon I found out that I was not the only one to notice this fact. People like former Pastor Professor Thomas McElwain, and former Pastor Sachini Strechen had noticed many of these verses. They both embraced Islam after their in depth studies of the Bible.

While I was reading the translations of the Bible, I had to pause at Jeremiah chapter 46 several times. Remembering the Psalm 19, I could not proceed without a few days of thinking and sharing it with friends. The great miracle of Jeremiah is the prophecy of the Great Sacrifice near Euphrates. It is the event of Karbala.

The event of Karbala was foretold in the Bible in several ways. The Hebrew tradition of the Day of Atonement is one of them. In this day, which is exactly the day of Ashura or the 10th day of month of Muharram, Jews had to pray and mourn. It was the day the holiest man of his time, Imam Hussain$_{pbuh}$, gave everything he had to defend the principles of divine laws and human dignity.

The Psalm chapter 19, which was discussed earlier in this book, talks about a man from *Hashemite* moving toward Kufa. It mentions that this event is not hidden from *mê-ḥam-mā-ṯōw* (Muhammad).

In addition, David$_{pbuh}$ mourned for the calamity of Ashura; as he mentions it in Psalm 25:17. Jesus and John the Baptist $_{pbut}$ have also talked about Imam Hussain$_{pbuh}$. It is in the Aramaic Gospels of Luke 11:22 and Matthew 3:11.

Peter (Simon) as well has stated that God will not make Hussain$_{pbuh}$ suffer from witnessing the corruption. It is in Acts 2:27.

Unfortunately, in all cases, the name is translated to "great", "greater", "holy one", and so on.

In the upcoming pages, we are examining the aforementioned passages.

David Mourns Imam Hussain (Psalm 25:17)

David_pbuh makes a short prayer to God, asking for his mercy and blessings. He is apparently mentioning the tragedy of Karbala by saying *"my heart's sorrows are humongous from the calamity of my Hussain"*. Unfortunately the word הוציאני (hō-w-ṣî-'ê-nî), meaning "my Hussain", is translated to "bring me out" or "free me". (See below and Table 42)

Psalm 25:12-17
NIV
12 Who, then, are those who fear the Lord? He will instruct them in the ways they should choose. 13 They will spend their days in prosperity, and their descendants will inherit the land.[a] *14 The Lord confides in those who fear him; he makes his covenant known to them. 15 My eyes are ever on the Lord, for only he will release my feet from the snare. 16 Turn to me and be gracious to me, for I am lonely and afflicted. 17 Relieve the troubles of my heart and free me from my anguish.*

Rendered translation of Psalm 25:17
"My heart's sorrows are humongous from the calamity of my Hussain."

Hebrew text:
WLC (Consonants Only) [1]

צרות לבבי הרחיבו ממצוקותי הוציאני:

It reads:

ṣā-rō-wṯ lə-ḇā-ḇî hir-ḥî-ḇū mim-mə-ṣū-qō-w-ṯay hō-w-ṣî-'ê-nî.

---

[a] Compliant with verse 13, the Quran says: (21:105) *"Before this We wrote in the Psalms, after the Message (given to Moses): My servants the righteous shall inherit the earth."*

The word הוציאני hō-w-ṣî-'ê-nî has occurred nowhere in the entire Bible except Psalm 25:17. (See Figure 30)

The third letter of הוציאני (hō-w-ṣî-'ê-nî), the צ (ṣ), does not present specifically a certain letter of Arabic. It reflects several Arabic sounds such as ظ ẓ, ض ḍ, and ص ṣ, as shown in Table 6. Can it also represent Arabic س (s)? The answer is positive because we know that the Old Testament was preserved through oral traditions long before going on to parchments or papyrus; and for a name that has never been existed in Hebrew history, it is understandable if it is not written 100% favourable to the original spelling of the word. This is not the first and last time that we see the foreign names are written differently in the Bible. For Example, Curash, the Persian King "Cyrus", who was considered a Messiah sent by God (Isaiah 45:1)[a], is written as כורש (Khoresh) in Hebrew. Also, Biblical פרעה (par'ōh), Pharaoh, is "prro" and "rro" in the ancient language of Egypt. However, it is فرعون (Firown) in Arabic.

Knowing that "par'ōh" is "Firown" and 'Khoresh" is "Curash", there should be no difficulty in accepting that "Howṣîên" is "Hosein".

Translating the name "Hosein" has caused the translators to make their own versions of the sentence. As an example, we can see in the NIV translation, not only is the word הוציאני hō-w-ṣî-'ê-nî translated as a verb, but also another verb, "Relieve", is added to the beginning of the verse which is not part of the Hebrew text at all. Besides that, the conjunction word, "and", is added to fix the meaningless translation.

---

[a] It is written as למשיחו לכורש (lim-šî-ḥōw lə-ḵō-w-reš), meaning "to His Messiah, to His Cyrus"), but translated to "to His anointed, to His Cyrus".

Table 42
Text Analysis[1]   Psalm 25:17

Str	Translit	Hebrew	English	Morph
6869 [e]	ṣā-rō-wt	צָר֣וֹת	The troubles	Noun
3824 [e]	lə-ḇā-ḇî	לְבָבִ֣י	of my heart	Noun
7337 [e]	hir-ḥî-ḇū;	הִרְחִ֑יבוּ	are enlarged	Verb
4691 [e]	mim-mə-ṣū-qō-w-tay,	מִ֝מְּצֽוּקוֹתַ֗י	of my distresses	Noun
3318 [e]	hō-w-ṣî-'ê-nî.	הוֹצִיאֵֽנִי׃	[O] bring me out	Verb

Figure 30

hō·w·ṣî·'ê·nî[1]

Englishman's Concordance

hō·w·ṣî·'ê·nî — 1 Occurrence

Psalm 25:17
HEB: הוֹצִיאֵֽנִי׃ הִרְחִ֑יבוּ מִ֝מְּצֽוּקוֹתַ֗י
NAS: are enlarged; *Bring* me out of my distresses.
KJV: are enlarged: *[O] bring thou me out* of my distresses.
INT: are enlarged of my distresses *Bring*

Ghadeer and the Lonely Man (Psalm 62)

Psalm of David, chapter 62, is an amazing passage: a twelve-verse chapter, symbolically representing the 12 Imams. It illustrates the Ghadeer and a man who is the target of evil doers. Particularly the third verse: (the word in bracket is the author's note.)

Psalm 62
ESV
1 For God alone my soul waits in silence; from him comes my salvation. 2 He alone is my rock and my salvation, my fortress; I shall not be greatly shaken. 3 How long will all of you attack a man to batter him, like a leaning wall, a tottering fence (Ghadeer)? *4 They only plan to thrust him down from his high position. They take pleasure in falsehood. They bless with their mouths, but inwardly they curse. Selah 5 For God alone, O my soul, wait in silence, for my hope is from him. 6 He only is my rock and my salvation, my fortress; I shall not be shaken. 7 On God rests my salvation and my glory; my mighty rock, my refuge is God 8 Trust in him at all times, O people; pour out your heart before him; God is a refuge for us. Selah 9 Those of low estate are but a breath; those of high estate are a delusion; in the balances they go up; they are together lighter than a breath. 10 Put no trust in extortion; set no vain hopes on robbery; if riches increase, set not your heart on them. 11 Once God has spoken; twice have I heard this: that power belongs to God, 12 and that to you, O Lord, belongs steadfast love. For you will render to a man according to his work.*

This twelve-verse chapter portrays an era during which people were thinking and acting devilish but pretending to be faithful. One of the most interesting phenomena about this chapter is the number 12 (remember the symbolic meaning of 12). Interestingly, the number of this chapter is 62, which is also a symbolic way of revealing number 12, that is 6 times 2.

Verse 3 explains that many people threaten and attack one man who is like an abandoned wall (Ghadeer or protection). This can also be understood that the ***third Imam*** (Imam Hussain$_{pbuh}$) being like his father, Imam Ali$_{pbuh}$, the main character of the Ghadeer, which was also under attack of many.

Psalm 62:3 is ***the third occurrence*** of Ghadeer in the Bible. The first occurrence is in Numbers 22:24[a] (the story of Balaam and his three wrong attempts followed by a right decision …, as discussed in Chapter 3 – Imam Ali in the Bible, under "Balaam and Ghadeer (Numbers 22)"). The second occurrence is in Ezra 9:9 (as a symbol of Divine blessing and support). These occurrences strongly point out a hidden prophecy.

There is no way to explain how a verse could be accidentally numbered so accurate to perfectly relate to Imam Hussain$_{pbuh}$.

A Great Dispute among Scholars

Psalm 62:3 has caused a great dispute among bible scholars, as they are yet to come up with a clear translation. The interpretations made in the various versions of the Bible are significantly different. Some (such as NIV, NLT, KJB, NET) take the "sagging Ghadeer" as an attribute to the people who try to kill the man. Others (HCSB, ISV, GWT) have an opposite opinion by assuming that the victim is like the sagging Ghadeer, not the murderers. Some have their own way of translation, like the Jubilee Bible, which gives a completely different translation (*Shall ye <u>murder each other</u> until ye are as a bowing wall and as a tottering fence?*). Finally, other

---

[a] There is an amazing numerical correlation in Psalm 62:3 and Numbers 22:24, and that is 2 x 2 x 2 x 4 = 32; and that itself is 3 x 2 = 6. This gives the number 3 2 6 which is the backward of Psalm 62:3.

translations stay neutral (such as ESV, NAS, Aramaic Bible in Plain English).

It is natural to see a confusion in understanding a text that is not what "the reader wants", what "it is supposed to be", or what "it should be", particularly if the content is inclined toward a "strange matter". Ineffective struggles to produce self-satisfactory interpretations have created these confusing opinions.

Below is verse 3 in Hebrew and different translations presented in some different versions of the Bible:

Psalm 62:3
WLC (Consonants Only)[1]
עד־אנה **׀** תהותתו על איש תרצחו כלכם כקיר נטוי גדר הדחויה: '*aḏ*-

It reads:

'ā·nāh tə·hō·wṯ·ṯū 'al 'îš tə·rāṣ·ṣə·ḥū ḵul·lə·ḵem kə·qîr nā·ṭui; **gā·ḏêr**, had·də·ḥū·yāh.

NIV
How long will you assault me? Would all of you throw me down-- this leaning wall, this tottering fence?

NLT
So many enemies against one man--all of them trying to kill me. To them I'm just a broken-down wall or a tottering fence.

ESV
How long will all of you attack a man to batter him, like a leaning wall, a tottering fence?

NASB
How long will you assail a man, That you may murder him, all of you, Like a leaning wall, like a tottering fence?

KJB
How long will ye imagine mischief against a man? ye shall be slain all of you: as a bowing wall shall ye be, and as a tottering fence.

HCSB
How long will you threaten a man? Will all of you attack as if he were a leaning wall or a tottering stone fence?

ISV
How long will you rage against someone? Would you attack him as if he were a leaning wall or a tottering fence?

NET Bible
How long will you threaten a man? All of you are murderers, as dangerous as a leaning wall or an unstable fence.

ABPE
How long will you be provoked by a man that you would kill, like a fallen wall or like an abandoned hedge?

GOD'S WORD® Translation
How long will all of you attack a person? How long will you try to murder him, as though he were a leaning wall or a sagging fence?

Jubilee Bible 2000
How long will ye imagine mischief against a man? Shall ye murder each other until ye are as a bowing wall and as a tottering fence?

ASV
How long will ye set upon a man, That ye may slay him, all of you, Like a leaning wall, like a tottering fence?

The Sacrifice by the River Euphrates (Jeremiah 46)

The book of Jeremiah is another misunderstood text in the Bible to such a degree that no Bible interpreter has come up with a guess that there may be something more than just Egypt and a Pharaoh in the story. They have applied Jeremiah 46 to the battle of Carchemish in 605 BC in which Nebuchadnezzar and the Babylonian forces defeated the Egyptians, as well as Nebuchadnezzar's invasion of the land of Egypt in 568-567 BC. Is this interpretation right or wrong? The answer depends on how we answer another question: Who was the sacrifice that God offered in verse 10?

The predictions of desolation of Egypt in Jeremiah 46 has deviated minds of readers when they have not even tried to apply it to later historical events. Besides that, the tone of some verses in this chapter is not consistent with the main body of the chapter. For instance, verses 1 and 2 sound like an opinion of a later copyist or interpreter who tried to make the dramatic arena of the battlefield look like a past event. However, almost all commentators agree that Jeremiah 46 is a prophecy, not a historical record, but verses 1 and 2 sound very odd.

Jeremiah 46
NIV
1 This is the word of the Lord that came to Jeremiah the prophet concerning the nations:
2 Concerning Egypt:
This is the message against the army of Pharaoh Necho king of Egypt, which was defeated at Carchemish on the Euphrates River by Nebuchadnezzar king of Babylon in the fourth year of Jehoiakim son of Josiah king of Judah:

As soon as we proceed to next verses, the tone changes dramatically:

3 "Prepare your shields, both large and small, and march out for battle! 4 Harness the horses, mount the steeds! Take your positions with helmets on! Polish your spears, put on your armor!

Verse 3 is talking about a war to happen in the future, but verses 1 and 2 are talking about the same war in the past! This is a clear evidence of a later addition to the original text.

Some take the first 12 verses as if it is concerning the Gospels. Matthew Henry's Concise Commentary is one of them. (See Figure 31)

Figure 31

Matthew Henry's Commentary[1]

Jeremiah 46:1

The word of the LORD which came to Jeremiah the prophet against the Gentiles;

46:1-12 The whole word of God is against those who obey not the gospel of Christ; but it is for those, even of the Gentiles, who turn to Him. The prophecy begins with Egypt. Let them strengthen themselves with all the art and interest they have, yet it shall be all in vain. The wounds God inflicts on his enemies, cannot be healed by medicines. Power and prosperity soon pass from one to another in this changing world.

Another issue with the Bible translations of Jeremiah 46, which is a common problem in the entire Bible, is that the names are understood either wrong or interpreted according to a narrow definition. For example, Cush (in Jeremiah 46 verse 9) is interpreted as Ethiopia, rather than the Arabia or Cushite Nations.

In The Encyclopedia Britannica, we read: *Cush[a], the eldest son of Ham, from whom seems to have been derived the name of The Land of Cush, which is commonly rendered by the Septuagint and by the Vulgate Ethiopia. The locality of the Land of Cush is a question upon which eminent authorities have been divided; for while Buchart maintained that it was exclusively in Arabia, Schultess and Gesenious held that it is to be sought for nowhere but in Africa. Others again, such as Michaelis and Rosenmuller, have supposed that the name Cush was applied to tracts of country both in Arabia and Africa ...*[39]

David J. Gibson in his article, *The Land of Eden Located*, 1964, writes: *The truth is that the Hebrews called Ethiopia "Cush" in their own tongue. But what has not been so well recognized is that the Hebrews used this name 'Cush' of more than one place. The name is derived from Cush the son of Ham, the son of Noah, in Genesis 10:6.... The descendants of Cush may have split, one part remaining in Asia, the other migrating to Africa to become the Ethiopia we still know to this day. In any case, we do know that more than one "Cush" existed.*[40]

As a conclusion, we cannot apply every single tribe or person's name to a definite place in all times. It can be "place A" today, while it was "place B" before, or both. Therefore, we cannot be definite about the identity of *the men of Cusha*; were they Egyptians, Ethiopians or Arabs? It could be any or even all of them, but one thing is clear in Jeremiah 46 and that is the place of event: the north by the River Euphrates (verses 6 and 10).

---

[a] Cush was grandson of Noah from Ham, and father of Nimrod. (Noah – Ham – Cush – Nimrod)

Verses 6 to 10 demonstrate a conflict between Nile-like powers of devilish-Pharoahic people and God's chosen man who is going to be a *sacrifice* near *Euphrates*:

6 "The swift cannot flee nor the strong escape. **In the north by the River Euphrates** *they stumble and fall. 7 "Who is this that rises* **like the Nile***, like rivers of surging waters? 8 Egypt rises like the Nile, like rivers of surging waters. She says, 'I will rise and cover the earth; I will destroy cities and their people.' 9 Charge, you horses! Drive furiously, you charioteers! March on, you warriors—men of Cusha and Put who carry shields, men of Lydia who draw the bow. 10 But that day belongs to the Lord, the Lord Almighty— a day of vengeance, for vengeance on his foes. The sword will devour till it is satisfied, till it has quenched its thirst with blood. For the Lord, the Lord Almighty, will offer sacrifice* **in the land of the north by the River Euphrates**.

Again, the statement **In the (land of) north by the River Euphrates**, in verses 6 and 10, is a clear reference to a location known even today by the very same name, *the River Euphrates*. The statement is unequivocal and firm. This is a prophecy about an event near the *River Euphrates* not Palestine, nor Egypt or Ethiopia. The verse 8 confirms the metaphoric use of Egypt:

8 Egypt rises like the Nile, like rivers of surging waters. She says, 'I will rise and cover the earth; I will destroy cities and their people.'

Historically speaking, the only known event near the River Euphrates where God has offered a sacrifice is the event of Karbala. I have checked numerous comments of eminent sources regarding the verse 10, namely Barne's Notes, Benson, Calvin, Cambridge Bible, Clarke, Darby's Bible Synopsis, Ellicott, Hastings, and so on. Only few of them have given comment on this particular verse, *very uncommon*. For example, Gill's Exposition Bible Commentary writes:

Figure 32

Gill's Exposition of the Entire Bible[1]

Jeremiah 46:10... "Here is an allusion to the sacrifices of great persons, which are many; the Lord of hosts had a sacrifice or a great slaughter of men, his enemies; inflicted punishment on them, wherein his power, justice, and holiness, were displayed."

Does "Sacrifice" mean "Slaughter"?!

Wherever there is a comment on this verse, we find more or less a similar idea: "A great sacrifice = slaughter of *God's enemies.*" I do not know how they can justify such interpretation. The only reference they give to their opinion is Isaiah 34:6, where it says:

Isaiah 34:6
NIV
"The sword of the LORD is bathed in blood, it is covered with fat-- the blood of lambs and goats, fat from the kidneys of rams. For the LORD has a sacrifice in Bozrah and a great slaughter in the land of Edom."

Isaiah 34 is talking about the revenge of God from Oppressors. Verse 6 explains the reason:

For the LORD has a sacrifice in Bozrah and a great slaughter in the land of Edom.

The commentators have confused 'Sacrifice" with "Slaughter". The first part says *"the LORD has a sacrifice in Bozrah"* but the second part is very different: *"and a great slaughter in the land of Edom"*. These two are not the same. The *great slaughter* comes after *the sacrifice*. The great slaughter is a divine punishment to the murderers who shed the blood of innocent as we also read in Jubilees[a]:

Jubilees 7:23-25[41]
*23 When everyone sold himself to commit injustice and **to shed innocent blood**, the earth was filled with injustice.*
24 After them all the animals, birds, and whatever moves about and whatever walks on the earth. Much blood was shed on the earth. All the thoughts and wishes of mankind were (devoted to) thinking up what was useless and wicked all the time.
25 Then the Lord obliterated all from the surface of the earth because of their actions and because of the blood which they shed in the earth.

The above statements are written in an old Jewish book called Jubilees. It is said that the context is about the 10th of Tishrei, the Day of Atonement, in which Jacob's sons, committed crime against their brother Josef. The Jubilees also relates the landing of the Ark of Noah to the same day. In my opinion, backed by historical facts, this is a prophecy about the event of Karbala, which took place on the same day.

Another reason, to that *sacrifice* cannot be the same as *slaughter* in Jeremiah 46 and Isaiah 34:6, is that *sacrifice* according to Hebrew belief has to be from a clean and healthy life not unclean or sick. In other words, the tradition teaches that the sacrifice must be from beloved belongings not the cursed one. *No Jew sacrifices a pig*; it is always a lamb or cow, a clean and valuable animal. As we read

---

[a] The Book of Jubilees, written in Hebrew, is an ancient Jewish religious book of 50 chapters. It is part of the Bible of the Ethiopian Orthodox Church as well as Beta Israel (Ethiopian Jews), but not accepted as authoritative by rest of the faith. It is one of the oldest manuscripts (100 BC) found in 5 caves at Qumran, known as Dead Sea Scrolls. The book claims that it is a revelation to Moses in Mount Sinai (Jubilee 1:4).

in Exodus 12:5 *The animals you choose (for sacrifice) must be year-old males <u>without defect</u> ...*

Also Exodus 29:1 and Numbers 6:14 read:

There they are to present their offerings to the LORD: a year-old male lamb <u>without defect</u> for a burnt offering, a year-old ewe lamb <u>without defect</u> for a sin offering, a ram <u>without defect</u> for a fellowship offering.

It is common sense; give your best, not your waste, as an offering.

Therefore, Verse 10 of Jeremiah 46 talks about a sacrifice that God himself has chosen to offer, near the River Euphrates.

Again, this is a story of an unfair war between mighty power of the oppressor and the small army of a Holy man, which is insignificant in number but mighty in spirit. The conqueror is predicted to be the Army of God with a sacrifice offered by Him:

*For the Lord, the Lord Almighty, will offer sacrifice in the land of the north **by the River Euphrates**.*

This chapter of Jeremiah has changed the way many believers of the Bible used to think. Former Pastor Sachini Strecthen is one of them. As mentioned earlier, she converted to Islam and led her entire family and some of her Church members to Shi'ite Islam.

Ashura in the Bible

Ashura, the 10th of Muharram, first month of Islamic Calendar, is the day the tyrant army of Yazid martyred Imam Hussain$_{pbuh}$ and his companions. In Jewish tradition, this day is also The Day of Atonement or Yom Kippor (Leviticus 16 and 23:26-32; Num. 29:7-11). It is the holiest day in Jewish history, which is 10th of Tishrei^a (the seventh month in Jewish calendar). That is the day of mourning and repentance.

Today it is no more the same as it was in traditional Hebrew history. Unlike today's Jewish ceremonies, the Day of Atonement was no festive event. It was a day of national mourning and repentance. This was a special Sabbath day celebration, which meant that no work could be done (Lev. 23:26-32). Anyone who did not observe this Sabbath was to be cut off from his people (Lev. 23:29), which is a euphemism for being put to death.

Beyond this, it was a day when the people were to "humble their souls" (cf. Lev. 16:31; 23:27; Num. 29:7), which, according to many, included fasting. This would thus be **the only religious holiday that was characterized by mourning, fasting, and repentance**.

In Islamic traditions, Noah's Ark landed this day. According to traditions gathered by Al-Biruni [42], on this day God took compassion on Adam$_{pbuh}$; Jesus$_{pbuh}$ was born; Moses$_{pbuh}$ was saved from Pharaoh and Abraham$_{pbuh}$ from the fire of Nebuchadnezzar; Jacob$_{pbuh}$ regained his eyesight; Joseph$_{pbuh}$ was drawn out of the ditch; Solomon$_{pbuh}$ was invested with the royal power; the

---

^{a} Tishrei used to be the first month of the calendar used by the ancient people of Judea.

punishment was taken away from the people of Jonah$_{pbuh}$; Job$_{pbuh}$ was freed from his plagues; the prayer of Zachariah$_{pbuh}$ was granted; and John$_{pbuh}$ was born to him.

Besides the aforementioned events, there are a few numerical symbols about Ashura. Remember that verse 10 of Jeremiah chapter 46 talks about the Sacrifice, coherent with 10th of Muharram (Ashura) and 10th of Tishrei. Chapter 46 may also be interpreted numerically as 4+6 =10.

Another interesting matter I noticed while writing this book is that the Bible directs people to take a lamb for sacrifice on the 10th of Tishrei, the Day of Atonement, it is in Exodus 12:3. (Note the numbers 12 and 3) Imam Hussain is the 3rd of 12 Shi'ite Imams.

Lastly, month of Tishrei, although is the 7th month now, used to be the starting month in the ancient Hebrew calendar. It was coherent with Muharam, the first month of Arabic calendar.

Are all these codes and messages of the Bible about Karbala accidental or perhaps the divine hand is being over them? How this can be accidental after all changes and developments occurred in the Bible in a period well over 2000 years if God did not preserve these facts? No intellectual mind will accept these facts as accidental coincidents.

Sufyani and Mahdi (Isaiah 21)

The book of Isaiah is one of the well-known prophetic books. It has plenty of verses about Islam, particularly Imam Hussain$_{pbuh}$. In this section, I am only presenting two verses from chapter 21. It is about a battle near the Euphrates. It predicts a war between tyrant rulers, Sufyanies, and Imams. Eventually the army of Madai, the Mahdi$_{pbuh}$, will be victorious. The book of Isaiah will be explained more in Chapter 6 – Isaiah and Islam.

Isaiah 21:1, 2
NIV
A prophecy against the Desert by the Sea: Like whirlwinds sweeping through the southland, an invader comes from the desert, from a land of terror. A dire vision has been shown to me: The traitor betrays, the looter takes loot. Elam, attack! Media, lay siege! I will bring to an end all the groaning she (Babylon) caused.

Almost all Bible commentaries agree that Isaiah 21:1-2 is prophesying a terrifying event near River Euphrates. However, eminent scholars dispute nearly every single word in these verses. Below is an example:

Figure 33

Ellicott's Commentary for English Readers[1]

XXI.
(1) The burden of the desert of the sea . . .—*The title of the prophecy is obviously taken from the catch-word of "the desert" that follows. The "sea" has been explained (1) as the Euphrates, just as in Isaiah 18:2; Isaiah 19:5, it appears as used of the Nile (Cheyne). (2) As pointing to the surging flood of the mingled myriads of its population. (3) Xenophon's description of the whole plain of the Euphrates, intersected by marshes and lakes, as looking like a sea affords, perhaps, a better explanation.*
Another commentary writes:

Figure 34

Barnes' Notes on the Bible[1]

The burden - (see the note at Isaiah 13:1).

Of the desert - There have been almost as many interpretations of this expression, as there have been interpreters. That it means Babylon, or the country about Babylon, there can be no doubt; but the question why this phrase was applied, has given rise to a great diversity of opinions. The term 'desert' (מדבר midbâr) is usually applied to a wilderness, or to a comparatively barren and uncultivated country - a place for flocks and herds (Psalm 65:13; Jeremiah 9:9 ff); to an actual waste, sandy desert Isaiah 32:15; Isaiah 35:1; and particularly to the deserts of Arabia Genesis 14:6; Genesis 16:7; Deuteronomy 11:24.

Barnes'Notes also explains about yam:

Figure 35

Barnes' Notes on the Bible[1]

Of the sea - (ים yâm). There has been also much difference of opinion in regard to this word. But there can be no doubt that it refers to the Euphrates, and to the extensive region of marsh that was covered by its waters.

I could not pass from Jamieson-Fausset-Brown Bible Commentary without quoting this part:

Figure 36

Jamieson-Fausset-Brown Bible Commentary[1]

CHAPTER 21

whirlwinds in the south—(Job 37:9; Zec 9:14). The south wind comes upon Babylon from the deserts of Arabia, and its violence is the greater from its course being unbroken along the plain (Job 1:19). desert—the plain between Babylon and Persia.

By now, we have a good image of the location of the event; it cannot be anywhere but Eastern Iraq next to the River Euphrates, the Neinawa area, the desert of Karbala.

I decided to examine the Hebrew text, for a better understanding and perhaps getting into a solution for the existing confusion amongst interpreters. The solution hides in a few key words such as: yām, ne-ḡeḇ, nō-w-rā-'āh, 'ă-lî and so on.

First, I must emphasize two facts, agreed by majority of the Bible commentaries:

1- These verses are prophetic, meaning that they talk about future events not the past, in comparison to the time of Isiah.
2- The location of the events is in Babylonian, a desert near Euphrates.

In verse 1, an interesting phrase attracted my curiosity: סופות sū-pō-wṯ. It may represent "Sufyani", an apocryphal character in Islamic narrations, said to be from the progeny of Abu Sufyan, the rival and opponent of Imam Mahdi$_{pbuh}$. Sufyani will rise against peace and justice, right before Imam Mahdi's appearance. He will commit horrifying crimes in Syria. As he spreads the corruption on the earth, Imam Mahdi$_{pbuh}$ will emerge. Sufyani will send a huge army against the Imam; the earth will swallow his army.

In most of the Bible translations, the word סופות sū-pō-wṯ translated to "windstorms" or "whirlwinds". It seems to be a symbol of destruction and vain. It also occurs in Hosea 8:7.[a]

Hosea 8:7
NLT
"They have planted the wind and will harvest the whirlwind (סופתה sū-pā-ṯāh). The stalks of grain wither and produce nothing to eat. And even if there is any grain, foreigners will eat it.

Can סופות sū-pō-wṯ relate to Sufyani?

Isaiah 21:1-2 has many words about Imam Mahdi$_{pbuh}$ and the event of Karbala. The continuation of clash between the Imams and the tyrant regimes is a very popular fact in history. Imam Hussain$_{pbuh}$ was brutally martyred by Yazid the son of Mu'awiya son of Abu Sufyan. Imam Mahdi$_{pbuh}$ will indeed make an end to the dynasty of Sufyan. Isaiah 42 portrays the clash between Imams and The Sufyanies.

The word סופות sū-pō-wṯ, plural of סוּפָה soo-faw', is more identical to "Sufan" or "Sufyan" than anything else. As explained in the

---

[a] Hosea 8 is a 14-verse passage predicting horrifying events in Israel.

chapter 1, letter "n" of Arabic words does not exist in some pairing Hebrew words, such as Arabic إنسان "insan" becomes אִישׁ "iš" in Hebrew (meaning "man"). (See Table 8) Similarly, soo-faw' is the cognate of 'Sufan", the well-known tyrant family of Abu Sufyan. In addition to that, the "a" sound in some Hebrew words change to "i" sound in the Arabic. The Hebrew "A̱vraha̱m" (Abraham) and the Arabic "I̱brahi̱m" is an example of this change.

As shown in Figure 37, סוּפָה cuwphah (pronounced as "soo-faw") is the root of סופות sū-p̄ō-wṯ, and translated to different meanings such as "sea", "storm-wind", and "a place name located East of Jordan". It is also compared with Arabic صافيه Safieh.

Below are the verses without translating some keywords:

Isaiah 21:1- 2
A prophecy against the Desert by yam: 1 Like sū-p̄ō-wṯ (Sufawt) sweeping through negev, an invader comes from the desert, from noraa. 2 A dire vision has been shown to me: The traitor betrays, the looter takes loot. ali ê-lām ṣū-rî [a] *mā-ḏay! I will bring to an end all the groaning.*

The rendered translation would be as following:

Isaiah 21:1- 2
A prophecy against the Desert by yam: 1 Like Sufians sweeping through Nejef, an invader comes from the desert, from Noraa (Neinawa). 2 A dire vision has been shown to me: The traitor betrays, the looter takes loot. Ali ê-lām portray Mahdi! I will bring to an end all the groaning.

In the following lines, we will examine these verses. (See also Table 43 and Table 44 for text analysis)

---

[a] The word ṣū-rî צוּרִי is translated "designate", "confine" and so on.

Figure 37

5492. cuwphah[1]

Strong's Concordance

cuwphah: Sea

Original Word: סוּפָה
Part of Speech: noun feminine; proper name, of a location
Transliteration: cuwphah
Phonetic Spelling: (soo-faw')
Short Definition: Sea

Brown-Driver-Briggs

I. סוּפָה **noun feminine storm-wind** (that *makes an end ?*); —

...

II. סוּפָה **proper name, of a location East of Jordan**; — only in phrase וָהֵב בְּסֻ' in ancient poetry fragment Numbers 21:14; Tristr[Moab 50] compare *S'fieh* (صافية), southeast oasis of Dead Sea,

...From cuwph; a hurricane -- Red Sea, storm, tempest, whirlwind, Red sea.

Yaam ים

The word ים *ya'm* carries a wide-ranging translation such as *sea, mighty river, the south, west,* and so on. As shown in Figure 35, Barnes' Notes on the Bible, there has been much difference of opinions concerning ya'm, but no doubt that it refers to the Euphrates.

Geographically speaking, Yam is an area located on the west of Iran, bordering with Iraq and Turkey. According to Islamic traditions, it is said that Yam was another son of Noah who did not board on the Ark and drowned. It is probably true, because the recent discovery of the remaining of Noah's Ark near Ararat on North Eastern Turkey strongly suggests that the name of area must have a direct relation to the decedents of Noah.

Figure 38

3220. yam[1]
Strong's Exhaustive Concordance
a sea, the Mediterranean Sea; From an unused root meaning to roar; a sea (as breaking in noisy surf) or large body of water; specifically (with the article), the Mediterranean Sea; sometimes a large river, or an artifical basin; locally, the west, or (rarely) the south -- sea (X -faring man, (-shore)), south, west (-ern, side, -ward).

No matter how we interpret yaam in the verse, "a mighty river" or "the Yaam", they all serve the purpose; that is the area known as Neinawa in Iraq. The interpretations also support the idea that the prophecy is about somewhere near the River Euphrates. (See Ellicott's Commentary, Jamieson-Fausset-Brown and Barnes' Notes on Isaiah 21:1 and 2)

Negev בנגב (Negeb)

Negev בנגב is sometimes translated to "south". Nevertheless, according to others, such as *Cambridge Bible for Schools and Colleges*, it could refer to an area in southern Palestine, but not inevitably. That means it could be another synonymous name referring to a different location. Particularly the verses 1 and 2 in Isaiah 21 are talking about Yaam, an area near River Euphrates. Thus, it has to be a location in the same area.

Verse 1 says "*...Like Sufians sweeping through the southland*". Subsequently, we know that it talks about a place north of the *southland* or North of the Negev.

If Negev rendered as Nejef, then the *North* can be Karbala, definitely relevant to Yaam and Euphrates. Nejaf, or Nejef, is the closest match to Negev when we look at the map of the area near the River Euphrates. The area is also known as Neinawa.

We read about Nejaf in Oxford Online Dictionary: *A city in southern Iraq, on the Euphrates; population 500,000 (est. 2003). It contains the shrine of Ali, the Prophet Muhammad's son-in-law, and is a holy city for the Shi'ites.* [43]

The word "nejef" literally means "higher land". *At the time of Noah, flood covered lands, and the mountain of Nejaf crumbled to pieces.* [a] Then no more higher land remains of it.

The City of Nejef is located 75 km south of Karbala. It carries a great importance in Hebrew, Christian and Islamic History. Recent

---

[a] See Persian translation of *Elal a-sharaie*- of Sheikh Sadooqi , by Zehni Tehrani V. 1 p. 127

archeological discoveries have shown that there were Hebrew civilizations in the area.

A great ancient cemetery discovered in Nejaf showed many Hebrews and Christians buried in the graves. In Islamic traditions, it is said that many Prophets are buried in Nejaf, including Adam, Noah, Hud, Salih and so on. Lastly, Imam Ali's shrine in Nejaf has turned the town to one of the holiest places of Islam.

Noraa נוראה

This word is assumed to be from יָרֵא *yare* means *fear*; with that assumption, it is translated to "from a terrible". Having it in the verse as מארץ נוראה *mê-'e-reṣ nō-w-rā-'āh*, the translations say "from a terrifying land". In Arabic, it is من الارض نورا *mena al-arzi noraa*. It had to be translated to *"from the land of Noraa"*. It is quite similar to "from the land of Neinawa". It occurs in 16 places such as Genesis 28:17, Exodus 15:11, 34:10 and so on. It is translated to either *"fearful"* or *"awesome"*. Keeping the word נוראה Noraa as is or even translating it *"terrifying"* will serve the purpose.

A'li עלי

I have discussed about עלי A'li in Chapter 3 but just as a reminder, I must say that it has been a great dispute among scholars to make an understandable translation of some texts of the Bible where the word עלי a'li occurs. It has been translated as a verb, such as "spring up", or "go up"; as a preposition with a pronominal suffix, meaning "to me"; finally, as a nickname of God "the almighty". However no doubt we can consider it as a prophetic name: Ali. By keeping the word Ali as is, in some verses, the passages make a lot of sense. Isaiah 21:2 is one of them.

ê-lām עֵילָם

The word appears in several forms and derivatives as following:

bə·'ê·lām בְּעֵילָם (in 'ê·lām)		2 Occurrences
'ê·lām עֵילָם		1 Occurrence
ū·mê·'ê·lām וּמֵעֵילָם (and from 'ê·lām)		1 Occurrence
wə·'ê·lām וְעֵילָם (and 'ê·lām)		3 Occurrences

It is translated as a proper name (of a person and people or territory), such as name of a leader and a priest in Nehemiah 10:14 and 12:42. Strong's Concordance interprets it "a proper name" as well (Figure 39). Strong's Exhaustive Concordance gives a literal meaning to it: hidden, distant; from "alam", which itself is defined: blind, dissembler, hide self and secret thing. (Figure 40 and Figure 41)

In Isaiah 21, it can mean "the hidden", particularly the word after, Maday, may reflect the Mahdi of Islam who is hidden. Putting it with the precedent words makes it clearer:

Ali ê-lām (hide)[a] ṣū-rî (the face) Maday (of the Mahdi)

The first two phrases may also represent "Ali 'aelam" (Ali the wise and knowledgeable) which is a very famous nickname of Imam Ali; supported by numerous Islamic narrations. Finally, the statement could reveal a secret message such as:

---

[a] the Occultation of Imam Mahdi$_{pbuh}$

Ali Ilam Suri (whatever it may mean) *Mahdi*.

Brown-Driver-Briggs writes about ê-lām עֵילָם: (Figure 42) *Well-known country and people northeast of Lower Tigris*

Biblical scholars agree that the name is commonly used in the Bible for a person and tribe or country. Therefore, in Isaiah 21:2, keeping it as is (*Elam*) will serve the purpose best. By doing so, Ali Elam will sound like a foreign name, something close to the Arabic على اعلم (Ali A'lam) or *Ali the most knowing, the highest in knowledge*. It does make sense in the context, where the Neinawa and Desert of Yam mentioned as well as Duma, son of Ishmael (verse 11), Arab (verse 13), Dedan of Arabian Peninsula (verse 13), Tema, the ninth son of Ishmael (Verse 14), and Kedar, the second son Ishmael (verse 16, 17). There can be no doubt that Isaiah 21 is talking about an event in history of Islam.

Figure 39

5867. Eylam[1]

Strong's Concordance

Eylam: Elam

Original Word: עֵילָם
Part of Speech: proper name, of a people et. terr.; proper name, masculine
Transliteration: Eylam
Phonetic Spelling: (ay-lawm')
Short Definition: Elam

Figure 40
5867. Eylam[1]

Strong's Exhaustive Concordance

Elam

Or mowlam (Ezra 10:2; Jeremiah 49:36) {o-lawm'}; probably from alam; hidden, i.e. Distant; Elam, a son of Shem and his descendants, with their country; also of six Israelites -- Elam.

Figure 41
5956. alam[1]

Strong's Exhaustive Concordance

blind, dissembler, hide self, secret thing

A primitive root; to veil from sight, i.e. Conceal (literally or figuratively) -- X any ways, blind, dissembler, hide (self), secret (thing).

Figure 42
5867. Eylam[1]

Brown-Driver-Briggs

I. עֵילָם proper name, of a people et.
terr.**Elam**, Αιλαμ, Ἐλαμεῖραι, well-known country and people northeast of Lower Tigris (Assyrian *Elamtu* Dl[Pa 320 ff.] COT[Genesis 10:22]);

ṣū-rî צוּרִי

The word ṣū-rî has several meanings: confine, bind, besiege and delineate. The first three are basically same, *be hostile*. The forth meaning, *delineate*, has a very different concept: *determine, portrait, present, ascertain, define, specify,* and *designate*. The following figure (Figure 43), from Bible Hub, shows that it is similar to Arabic صَورَة (sawrato) [a], meaning "resemblance", "image", "reproduction", and "representation". Any of the forth meaning and the Arabic cognate are consonant with the rest of the verse as well as the context of the entire passage. As the rendered translation shows, it is about portraying/resembling Imam Mahdi$_{pbuh}$.

Figure 43

6696. tsuwr[1]

Brown-Driver-Briggs

IV. [צוּר] **verb fashion, delineate** (Late Hebrew *id.*; so Aramaic צוּר, ܨܳܪ, ܨܳܪ, ܨܘܪܬܐ picture, Sabean צור, plural צורת Hom$^{Chrest.125}$ Mordtm$^{Him.\ Inschr.\ 14.15}$; Arabic صُورَة is loan-word according to Frä^{272}); — *Perfect*2masculine singular וְצַרְתָּ Ezekiel 43:11 (for צ֯0 צוּרַת) according to ^{m}5.

---

[a] http://biblehub.com/hebrew/6696.htm, See bottom of the page.

Ma'day

One of the greatest exegeses about Isaiah 21:2 is the Ellicott's Commentary. It clearly illustrates a symbolic scenario of war between good and evil, ê-lām עֵילָם and Mā-day against Neineveh (Neinawa) and Babylon. This commentary says that ê-lām (applied to the Persians) and Mā-day will destroy the Nineveh and Babel empires:

"It was, even as a mere forecast, perfectly natural that the two should be associated together as the future destroyers of the Nineveh and Babel empires, which to the prophet's eye were identical in character and policy. The advance described as "from the wilderness" implies a march of part at least of the <u>Medo-Persian army down the Choaspes and into the lowland of Chuzistan, bordering on the great Arabian Desert.</u>" (See Figure 44)

Maday can strongly relate to Mahdi as well. As "Abram" became "Abraham" (receiving "h"), Maday also became Mahdi. (Abraham is pronounced "Ibrahim" in Arabic; both "Ibrahim" and "Mahdi" get "h" and "i")

Ellicott's Commentary for English Readers explains a very interesting matter in verse 2, three models or figures of history: *"(1) The treacherous dealer, (2) The summons to Elam and Media to put an end to this tyranny. (3) The oppressed peoples ceasing to sigh, and rejoicing in their liberation".* It also comments: *"The advance described as "from the wilderness" implies a march of part at least of the Medo-Persian army down the Choaspes and into the lowland of Chuzistan, bordering on the great Arabian Desert".* (Figure 44) No need to mention, it is almost identical to Muslim narrations of the Persian Army of Khorasan joining the Mahdi in Mekka, in Arabia.

Figure 44

Ellicott's Commentary for English Readers[1]

Isaiah 21:2

*(2) **A grievous vision . . .**—The verse contains, as it were, the three tableaux that came in succession before the prophet's gaze: (1) The treacherous dealer, the Assyro-Chaldæan power, spoiling and oppressing, breaking treaties, and, as its kings boasted* (Habakkuk 2:5; Records of the Past, vii. *42, 44), "removing landmarks." (2) The summons to Elam and Media to put an end to this tyranny. (3) The oppressed peoples ceasing to sigh, and rejoicing in their liberation.*
Elam appears here as combined with Media, which is named in Isaiah 13:17 *as the only destroyer of Babylon, and this has been urged as evidence of a later date. As a matter of fact, however, Sargon at this very time was carrying on a fierce war against Elam (*Records of the Past, cvii. *41-49) as well as against Media (*ibid, p. *37). In* Ezekiel 32:24, *Elam is numbered among the extinct nations, but the name, at all events, re-appears as applied to the Persians, though they were of a distinct race. It was, even as a mere forecast, perfectly natural that the two should be associated together as the future destroyers of the Nineveh and Babel empires, which to the prophet's eye were identical in character and policy. The advance described as "from the wilderness" implies a march of part at least of the Medo-Persian army down the Choaspes and into the lowland of Chuzistan, bordering on the great Arabian desert.*

Mā-day, as shown in Figure 45, is a proper name of a foreign origin. I strongly believe that Isaiah 21:2 refers to Mahdi. The proof is not only in the context but also in the comparison of the word variations in Semitic languages. The best example of the word variations is "Abram" (meaning "exalted father") and

"Abraham" (meaning "father of many"). In Arabic, it is pronounced "Ibrahim".

"Abram" received an "h" and became "Abra<u>h</u>am". Then "Abra<u>h</u>am" becomes the Arabic "Ebra<u>h</u>im"[a] by replacing the last *a* with *i*. Similarly, "Maday" can become "Mahdi" by receiving an "h" and replacing the last "a" with "i". Remember how words and names have altered and developed new forms and meanings in the Semitic languages. We have discussed the matter in Chapter 1 – A Brief Review of Biblical Languages.

Figure 45

4074. Maday[1]

Strong's Concordance

Maday: a son of Japheth, also his desc. and their land

Part of Speech: proper name, of a people
Transliteration: Maday
Phonetic Spelling: (maw-dah'-ee)
Short Definition: Media

NAS Exhaustive Concordance

Word Origin
of foreign origin

---

[a] Ebrahim or Ibrahim, in Arabic ابراهيم, starts with letter الف *A*. It is similar to Hebrew אברהם *'a<u>b</u>-rā-hām* (also starts with letter "א" / *A*).

Table 43

Text Analysis[1]   **Isaiah 21:1**

Str	Translit	Hebrew	English	Morph
4853 [e]	maś-śā	מַשָּׂא	The burden	Noun
4057 [e]	miḏ-bar-	מִדְבַּר־	concerning the	Noun
3220 [e]	yām;	יָם׃	of the sea	Noun
5492 [e]	kə-sū-p̄ō-wṯ	כְּסוּפוֹת	As windstorms	Noun
5045 [e]	ban-ne-ḡeb	בַּנֶּגֶב	in the Negev	Noun
2498 [e]	la-hă-lōp̄,	לַחֲלֹף,	pass through	Verb
4057 [e]	mim-miḏ-bār	מִמִּדְבָּר	from the	Noun
935 [e]	bā,	בָּא	[so] it comes	Verb
776 [e]	mê-'e-reṣ	מֵאֶרֶץ	land	Noun
3372 [e]	nō-w-rā-'āh.	נוֹרָאָה׃	from a terrible	Verb

Table 44

Text Analysis[1]   Isaiah 21:2

Str	Translit	Hebrew	English	Morph
2380 [e]	hā-zūt	חָזוּת	a vision	Noun
7186 [e]	qā-šāh	קָשָׁה	grievous	Adj
5046 [e]	hug-gad-	הֻגַּד־	is declared	Verb
	lî;	לִי	to me	Prep
898 [e]	hab-bō-w-ḡêḏ ׀	הַבּוֹגֵד ׀	the treacherous dealer	Verb
898 [e]	bō-w-ḡêḏ	בּוֹגֵד	deals treacherously	Verb
7703 [e]	wə-haš-šō-w-dêḏ ׀	וְהַשּׁוֹדֵד ׀	and the spoiler	Verb
7703 [e]	šō-w-dêḏ,	שׁוֹדֵד	spoils	Verb
5927 [e]	'ă-lî	עֲלִי	Go up	Verb
5867 [e]	'ê-lām	עֵילָם	O Elam	Noun
6696 [e]	sū-rî	צוּרִי	besiege	Verb
4074 [e]	mā-ḏay,	מָדַי	O Media	Noun
3605 [e]	kāl-	כָּל־	all	Noun
585 [e]	'an-ḥā-tāh	אַנְחָתָה	the sighing	Noun
7673 [e]	hiš-bat-tî.	הִשְׁבַּתִּי׃	thereof have I made to cease	Verb

Imam Hussain in the New Testament

New Testament Peshitta (the Aramaic Bible) mentions Imam Hussain$_{pbuh}$ by name in a few places, such as Luke 11:21-22, Matthew 3:11 and Acts 2:7. Jesus, John the Baptist and Simon (Peter) $_{pbut}$ had spoken plainly about Imam Hussain$_{pbuh}$. Nevertheless, the name is lost in the translations, as usual. In the following pages, we will examine the case.

Hussain Foretold by Jesus (Luke 11:21-22)

Jesus$_{pbuh}$, according to the Gospel of Luke, is explaining that Hussain$_{pbuh}$ who possess all the pureness, will be brutally attacked and martyred. His belongings will be looted and his body will be cut in pieces. However, the translators have interpreted the entire statement irrelevant to the actual meaning of the verse. This has become more noticeable by translating the word "Hussain" to "stronger". In the Peshitta Gospel of Luke, *Hussain* is written بسم (ḥasīn). (See Figure 46)

Luke 11:21, 22
New Living Translation
For when a strong man like Satan is fully armed and guards his palace, his possessions are safe--until someone even stronger attacks and overpowers him, strips him of his weapons, and carries off his belongings.

Verse 21 is highly suspicious. The NLT had to add "Satan" to come up with a relevantly meaningful statement. However, translating the verse without adding *Satan* brings a different picture to the scene.

Verse 22 has also changed according to the sense of the translator. Below is the rendered translation of the verses.

Rendered translation
21 For when Hussain is armed, guarding his house, his possessions are safe
22 Indeed he who is Hussain shall endure, all the pureness belongs to him, all his armor will be taken, he is confident, his belongings and body to be cut in pieces.

As shown in Figure 47, ḥasīn is the cognate of an Arabic word that means "beautiful". This is indeed حسين / حسن *Hasan / Hussain*. They were the sons of Imam Ali[pbuh].

Figure 46

Peshitta[31]

- Luke 11:21

ܐܡܬܝ ܕܚܣܝܢܐ ܟܕ ܡܙܝܢ ܢܛܪ ܕܪܬܗ ܗܘ ܩܢܝܢܗ ܀

Luke 11:21 - اِمَتي دِحَسِينَا گَد مِزَيَن نِطَر دَارِتِه بشَينَا هو قِنيَانِه .

Luke 11:21 - ʾemmaṯ dəḥasīnā kaḏ məzayyan neṭṭar dārtēh bəšaynā w qenyānēh .

- Luke 11:22 - ܐܢ ܕܝܢ ܢܐܬܐ ܡܢ ܕܚܣܝܢ ܡܢܗ ܢܙܟܝܘܗܝ, ܟܠܗ ܙܝܢܗ ܫܩܠ ܗܘ ܕܬܟܝܠ ܗܘܐ ܥܠܘܗܝ, ܘܒܙܬܗ ܡܦܠܓ ܀

Luke 11:22 - اِن دِين نِاتِا مَن دِحَسِين مِنِه نِزكِيوهي كُلِه زَينِه شَاقِل هو دَتكِيل هوَا علَوهي وبِزتِه مِفَلِج .

Luke 11:22 - ʾen dēn nīṯe man dəḥasīn mennēh nezkēw kullēh zaynēh šāqel haw daṯkīl həwā ʿəlaw wəbeztēh məpalleg .

Figure 47

xsyn A02³¹

ḥsyn (ḥassīn) adj. strong	See also s.vv. *ḥsym, ḥsynh*.

1 strong Qum, JLAtg, , PTA, Sam, Syr, JBAmb, Man, LJ LA. --(a) fem.pl. : mighty things JLAtg. --(b) (city) fortified Syr.
2 adv: carefully, thoroughly OfA-Pers, OfA-Iran.
3 heavy Syr. --(a) difficult Syr.
4 beautiful [Arabic!] Sam.

THE SPIRIT OF TRUTH   Chapter 4 – Imam Hussain in the Bible

Below is a picture of the Gospel of Luke 11:21-32 in Aramaic. (Note the word ܚܣܝܢ ḥasīn in verse 22)[a]

---

[a] Image location: University of Bonn, Germany at [http://digitale-sammlungen.ulb.uni-bonn.de/image/view/47451?w=1000]

John the Baptist and Imam Hussain (Matthew 3:11)

In the Gospel Of Matthew chapter 3 verse 11, John the Baptist$_{pbuh}$ tells Jews that someone will come after him, who will purify (baptise) people by the Holy Spirit and Fire. In the original language of John the Baptist$_{pbuh}$, Aramaic, this person is called حَسِين (ḥasīn). It is translated to "more powerful". (Figure 48)

Matthew 3:11
NIV
I baptize you with water for repentance. But after me comes one who is more powerful than I, whose sandals I am not worthy to carry. He will baptize you with the Holy Spirit and fire.

Figure 48

Peshitta[31]

- Matthew 3:11

ܐܢܐ ܡܥܡܕ ܐܢܐ ܠܟܘܢ ܒܡܝܐ ܠܬܝܒܘܬܐ ܗܘ ܕܝܢ ܕܒܬܪܝ ܐܬܐ
ܚܣܝܢ ܗܘ ܡܢܝ ܗܘ ܕܠܐ ܫܘܐ ܐܢܐ ܡܣܢܘܗܝ ܠܡܫܩܠ ܗܘ ܡܥܡܕ ܠܟܘܢ
ܒܪܘܚܐ ܕܩܘܕܫܐ ܘܒܢܘܪܐ ܀

Matthew 3:11 - اِنَا مَعمِد اَنَا لكُون بمَيَا لَتيَابُوتَا هَو دِين دبَاتَري اَتِا خَسِين هُو مِني هَو دلَا شَاوِا اَنَا مسَانَوهي لِمِشقَل هُو مَعمِد لكُون برُوخَا دقُودشَا وَبنُورَا.

Matthew 3:11 - ʾennā maʿmed nā ləkon bəmayyā laṭyābūṭā haw dēn dəbāṭar ʾāte ḥasīn ū men haw dəlā šāwe nā məsānaw ləmešqal hū maʿmed ləkon bərūḥā dəqūḏšā wabnūrā .

THE SPIRIT OF TRUTH   Chapter 4 – Imam Hussain in the Bible

Below is a picture of the Gospel of Matthew 3:1-13 in Aramaic. (Note the word ܚܣܝܢ ḥasīn in verse 11)[a]

Figure 49

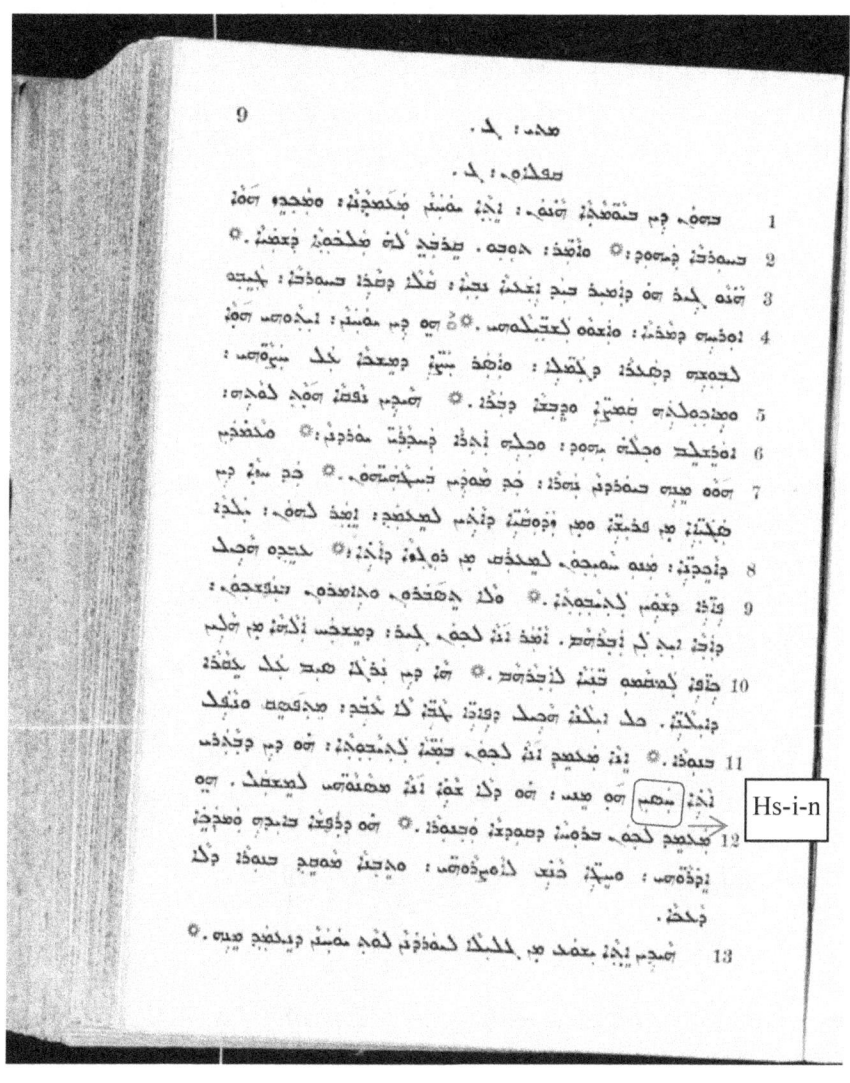

---

[a] Image location: University of Bonn, Germany at [http://digitale-sammlungen.ulb.uni-bonn.de/image/view/47451?w=1000]

257

Hussain Foretold by Simon (Acts 2:27)

Another similar word used in the Bible is ܚܣܝܐ ḥsy. It is in the Acts 2: 27, translated to "Holy One". (See Figure 51)

As shown in Figure 50, *ḥsy* means *pious, holy*. It is the cognate of Arabic *Hussain*. (Sometimes, the letter "n" of an Arabic word is omitted in its Hebrew cognate. For instance: Hebrew "ish" and Arabic "insan", meaning "mankind".)

Acts 2:27[a]
KJB
Because thou wilt not leave my soul in hell, neither wilt thou suffer thine Holy One to see corruption.

Rendered translation
Because You (God) will not leave my soul in hell, neither will You suffer your Hussain to see corruption.

Imam Hussain[pbuh] preferred death to submission to the corrupt ruler, Yazid. The above-mentioned verse beautifully foretells the story of Imam Hussain[pbuh].

This verse is a quotation from Psalm 16:10, where it uses a different word for "thine Holy One", חסידך (ḥă-sî-də-kā). It is similar to Arabic السيّدك (asseyideka), means "Your Seyid". Prophet Muhammad[pbuh] and his descendants are all called "Seyid".

Psalm 16:10
ESV
For you will not abandon my soul to Sheol, or let your <u>holy one</u> see corruption.

---

[a] In Acts 2:27, Simon (Peter) quotes from Psalm 16:10.

Figure 50

xsy#2 A02[31]

ḥsy (ḥsē) adj. #2holy	

1 pious, holy Of A-Iran, Syr.
2 blessed Of A-Egypt, Syr. --(a) ܒܝܫܐ ܕܘܚܕܢܐ : of blessed memory Syr.
3 bishop Syr.

Figure 51

Peshitta[31]

- Acts 2:27

ܡܛܠ ܕܠܐ ܫܒܩ ܐܢܬ ܠܢܦܫܝ ܒܫܝܘܠ ܘܠܐ ܝܗܒ ܐܢܬ ܠܚܣܝܟ ܕܢܚܙܐ ܚܒܠܐ ܀

Acts 2:27 - مطل دلا شبق انت لنِفشي بشيول ولا يهب انت لخسيك دنخزا خبلا.

Acts 2:27 - mṭl dlʾ šbq ʾnt lnpšy bšywl wlʾ yhb ʾnt lḥsyk dnḥzʾ ḥblʾ ..

Triconsonantal Word "Ḥasīn"

The word نَصِّى (ḥasīn) appears at least thrice in the Bible, once in Matthew 3:11 and twice in Luke 11:21 and 22, as Masculine Singular. The table below is the morphological information of the word:

Figure 52

Morphological information of ḥasīn [31]

Word			Morphological information						
Word	Vocalized	Syriac	Person	Gender	Number	State	Tense	Form	Enclitic
dHsyn	d'Hasiyn	دنَصِّى	-	Masculine	Singular	Absolute	-	-	No
Hsyn	Hasiyn	نَصِّى	-	Masculine	Singular	Absolute	-	-	No
Hsynyn	Hasiyniyn	نَصِّىنِ	-	Masculine	Plural	Absolute	-	-	No

The triconsonantal word نَصِّى (ḥasīn), composed of ه (ḥ), ص (s with vowel ī) and ن (n), is a sibilant of Arabic حسين (hussain), also made of ح (h) س (s with vowel i) and ن (n). In the translations of the Bible, it has been translated to "powerful" and "greater"; and combined with هُوَ مِنِّى (howe meni) interpreted as "greater than I" or "more powerful than I" (see Matthew 3:11, Figure 48). For any Hebrew or Arabic speaker, let alone Aramaic, this can be understood as a spoof of a serious matter. The word هُوَ مِنِّى (howe meni) is identical to Arabic هو منّى (howe menni), meaning "He is from me", but we do not see it in the translations at all.

As shown in Figure 47, "beautiful" is one of the meanings of ḥasīn, that is the exact meaning of Arabic "Hussain".

It is worthy of mentioning that the Aramaic letter ܚ (ḥ), a gluteal letter similar to German *ch* in *Buch*, is equivalent to Arabic ح (h)[a]. As we can see in the very same verse, Matthew 3:11, the word ܒܪܘܚܐ (bərūḥā), meaning "with spirit", is identical to Arabic word بروح (beruha). In other words, Aramaic ܚ (ḥ) pairs with Arabic ح (h).

In addition, the vowels in these languages may sometimes differ without affecting the meaning. For example, the different pronunciations of the pro-Semitic word *lib(a)b*, in Hebrew *lebb-ā'*, Aramaic *lēḇ(āḇ)* and Arabic أُبّ *lubb*, have the same meaning of "heart"; this reassures that حَسن *ḥasīn* can be حسين *Hussain*.

To remind again, Names in these languages do not necessarily match perfectly. These are a few examples: "Yizhak" and "Is-haaq" (Isaac), "Yashuwa" and "Isa" (Jesus), in Hebrew and Arabic, respectively.

---

[a] ܚ (ḥ) in Aramaic is the pairing letter for ح (h) in Arabic.

Hasin and Great in the Bible

There are a few words used in the New Testament that meant "great" or "greater", such as[31]:

ܛܒ (ṭāḇ) (in Matthew 2:16, Mark 1:35, etc.) – occurs 43 times

ܚܝܠܐ (ḥaylā) (in Mark 9:1, Luke 4:14, etc.) – occurs 19 times

ܪܒܐ (rabbā) (in Matthew 13:32, Mark 16:4, etc.) – occurs 5 times

In the Greek Gospels, these words are translated into various forms of μέγα (mega). However, the Aramaic word ܚܣܝܢ (ḥasīn) is written as ἰσχυρότερός (ischyroteros). This can indicate a very specific meaning of ܚܣܝܢ (ḥasīn), different from μέγα (mega). The sister word of ἰσχυρότερός (ischyroteros) in Persian is خسرو (Khosrow) and/or قیصر (Qeysar) which means "king, leader, the great, and etc."[a] Interestingly, ἰσχυρότερός (ischyroteros) and ܚܣܝܢ (ḥasīn) are Masculine in both Greek and Aramaic.

It is obvious that interpreting ܚܣܝܢ (ḥasīn) as "great" can only be due to the lack of the real evidence at that time; there was no one named Hussain at the time of John the Baptist_pbuh and Jesus_pbuh; so people thought of a "meaning"; and Greeks did the best they could: ἰσχυρότερός (ischyroteros), meaning "the great".

As it is explained earlier, Peter pronounces it as ܚܣܝ ḥsy (Acts 2:7). It is the cognate of Arabic *Hussain*. The missing "n" in ܚܣܝ ḥsy is similar with the missing "n" in "ish", that is the cognate of Arabic *insan* (meaning "mankind").

---

[a] https://www.vajehyab.com/dehkhoda

Chapter 5 – Quran In The Bible

The Holy Scriptures

We Muslims believe all scriptures given to the Prophets are divine revelations from *one source*, the Almighty God. Up until now, this was considered an "Islamic claim" only. The mainstream Jews and Christians do not regard all scriptures as divine revelations. Just as the Jews do not accept the authoritativeness of the New Testament, Christians, alongside with Jews, have a similar opinion about the Holy Quran[a].

The Holy Quran mentions the Torah (of Moses), the Zabour (Psalm of David) and the Injeel (Gospel of Jesus) as Revelations[b] from God, and demands Muslims to communicate with the people of the Book on a common platform of believing in oneness of God.[c]

Jews and Christians claim that if The Quran were from God, the prophets would have foretold it. Since they do not see it in the translations of the Bible, they reject it. However, what they do not know is that the "Quran" in fact is mentioned in numerous places in the Hebrew and Aramaic scriptures, but it is sadly lost in the translations.

Not only are the words "Quran" and "Furqan" (another name for the Quran) mentioned in the Holy Bible but also the style and place of the revelation, and to whom it is revealed. Unfortunately, the translations of the Bible are not always consonant with the original language. Therefore, No one will see the key statements about

---

[a] Other spellings: Quraan, Qur'an and sometimes Koran
[b] Quran, an-Najm, 53:37-54; al-A'la, 87:19; al-Isra, 17:2; al-Maida, 5:44, 46, 110; an-Nisa, 4:163
[c] Quran, āle -'Im'rān, 3: 64

Islam in the Bible, unless they take the trouble of investigating the original texts in a sufficient level of precision. In my case, it was not an easy task due to my lack of knowledge in Hebrew and Aramaic languages.

An initiation to investigate the Bible to find any occurrence of the Quran was made by three Church fathers, who visited my place. They rejected the credibility of the Quran by saying that it is not mentioned in the Bible. Although, we cannot condition truthfulness of the Quran to having it mentioned in the Bible, however, if it is mentioned, then it must be a miracle, a sign of direct intervention of the Creator, and a clear proof for the Bible believers to accept and follow the final revelation, the Quran. Nevertheless, even "the Bible", as we know it today, is not mentioned in the Bible.

I began my research on the matter after my meeting with the church fathers. Just in three days, I was honoured to discover the blessed name of the Quran in many verses of the Bible. I started my investigation form the book of Revelation, the last book of the Protestant Bible. I found the word "Furqan" in two places in the NT and subsequently, the word "Quran" in several places in the OT. Amongst the numerous occurrences, some perfectly relate to the Holy Quran, literally and contextually. Some of the occurrences do not relate directly to the Quran, maybe because the word reflects other applications through its various meanings in Hebrew and Aramaic literature. Regarding the fact that the Bible has gone through storms of addition, edition and omission, even one occurrence of the Quran is enough to propose a conclusion.

In the following lines, we will discuss a few cases where the words "Quran" and "Furqan" occur in the Bible. First, the words will be outlined and then we will examine the verses.

The Quran

Quran is an Arabic word, literally meaning "recitation". It is the most commonly known name of the Muslims' Holy Book. The Quran mentions its own name in numerous verses such as 1:185, 2:82, 3:101, 4:19 and so on.

In 2:82 we read:

Quran 2:82[26]
Do they not consider the Qur'an (with care)? Had it been from other than Allah, they would surely have found therein Much discrepancy.

This is a 1400-year-old challenge. The accuracy of entire Quran is proven by today's scientific means such as mathematics, biology, cosmology, embryology, and so on. Verse 2:82 reassures the Divine source of the book.

The Syriac equivalent to Quran may be ܩܪܝܢܐ *qeryānā* or ܩܪܢܐ *qarna*; and Hebrew גרון *ḡrōwn* or קראנא *qarana*, which refers to "scripture reading" or "lesson". These words are used throughout the Bible in different forms and derivatives.

Qarna ܩܪܢܐ

According to Dukhrana Biblical Research[31], ܩܪܢܐ *qarna* has a wide range of meaning, such as: horn, corner, capital funds, success, ascendance, and so on. In Greek Gospels, the word is translated to "κέρας" *keras* or "γωνίας" *gōnias*, meaning "horn" and "corner", respectively.

The word ܩܪܢܐ (qarna) occurs in six verses in the NT: Matthew 6:2 (as a verb), Luke 1:69 (noun), Luke 20:17 (noun), Acts 4:11 (noun), 1 Corinthians 14:8 (noun), Ephesians 2:20 (adjective).

Luke 1:69 is an interesting one; it has the other most famous name of the Quran as well, the Furqan. There is a critical difference in the Peshitta[a] version of the verse and the Old Syriac Sinaitic Palimpsest[b] (OSSP). In the older version (Peshitta), we find the word ܦܘܪܩܢܐ *pwrqna*, however it is ܚܝܐ *ḥya* (similar to Arabic حي *ḥayy*) in the newer version (OSSP); the first one translated to "horn" and second one to "life" or "salvation". (See Figure 53 and Figure 54)

Changing ܦܘܪܩܢܐ *pwrqna* to ܚܝܐ *ḥya*, in Luke 1:69, reflects a deliberate attempt to find a meaning for the prophetic word and nestle it conveniently in a Christian framework.

---

[a] Peshitta means "simple", or "common". It is the Syriac version of the Bible, the accepted Bible of Syrian Christian churches, from the end of the 3rd century AD.
[b] Old Syriac Sinaitic Palimpsest is a late 4th-century manuscript in Syriac language

Figure 53

Peshitta[31]

Luke 1:69 - ܘܐܩܝܡ ܠܢ ܩܪܢܐ ܕܦܘܪܩܢܐ ܒܒܝܬܗ ܕܕܘܝܕ ܥܒܕܗ ܀

Luke 1:69 - واقيم لن قرنا دفورقنا ببيته ددويد عبده .

Luke 1:69 - wᵒqym ln qrnᵃ dpwrqnᵃ bbyth ddwyd ᶜbdh ..

Luke 1:69 - And hath raised up an horn of salvation for us in the house of his servant David;

Figure 54

Old Syriac Sinaitic Palimpsest[31]

Luke 1:69 - ܘܐܩܝܡ ܠܢ ܩܪܢܐ ܕܐܢܬ ܒܒܝܬܗ ܕܕܘܝܕ ܥܒܕܗ ܀

Luke 1:69 - واقيم لن قرنا دخي ببيته ددويد عبده .

Luke 1:69 - wᵒqym ln qrnᵃ dhy bbyth ddwyd ᶜbdh .

When I was reading Luke 1:69 in the Greek text of Codex Sinaiticus, I noticed an interesting word, ηγειρεν *ēgeiren* (See below). It is very close to ܩܪܢܐ *qarna* in the Peshitta and the Old Syriac. The word ηγειρεν *ēgeiren* is translated to "has risen up", as a verb. There is no original text to claim anything. It could be just an accidental synonymous pronunciation.

Codex Sinaiticus[44]	*Latin transliteration*[1]
και ηγειρεν κερας	kai ēgeiren keras
cωτηριας ημιν ε	sōtērias hēmin en
ν οικω δαδ παι	oikō Dauid paidos autou

Zechariah[pbuh] praises God for forgiving his people (Luke 1:68). He also prophesies future events such as raising the *qarna furqana* (verse 69), and the future fulfillment of the oath of God to Abraham[pbuh] to multiply him (as mentioned in Genesis 22:16-18).

Qarana קראנא & Ḡrōwn גרון

The Hebrew word קראנא *qarana* is metaphorically used for variety of meanings, such as *strength* (Deuteronomy 33:17), *honour* (Job 16:15; Lamentations 2:3), *royal dignity* and *power* (Jeremiah 48:25; Zechariah 1:18; Daniel 8:24). To have the קראנא *qarana* "exalted" denotes *prosperity* and *triumph* (Psalms 89:17 Psalms 89:24). To "lift up" the קרן *qe-ren* is to *act proudly* (Zechariah 1:21)[a].

The word גרון *ḡrōwn* is translated to *throat* (in Psalm 5:9 and 115:7), *head* (in Isaiah 3:16), *mouth* (in Psalm 149:6), and *aloud* (in Isaiah 58:1)[b]. The starting letter of גרון *ḡrōwn*, ג *ḡ*, may be pronounced *g*, as in "good", or *ḡ*, as *r* in French "mrci". An example of the first pronunciation is גדל *gadal*, used in Job 2:13, meaning *great*. It is similar to Persian قدر *gadar*, with same meaning. The word גרון *ḡrōwn* is an example for the second pronunciation.

Psalm 149:6 is what I believe that the Quran was the true application of גרון *ḡrōwn*. The Psalm 149 has been discussed in detail in Chapter 3 – Imam Ali in the Bible, under "The Quran, Haidar and Zulfaqar (Psalm 149)".

In addition, Isaiah 58:1 mentions "קרא בגרון" *qə-rā bə-ḡā-rō-wn*, meaning "Read through/by Quran". However, it is translated to "Shout it aloud".

Isaiah 58:1

---

[a] Zachariah 1:21 has an interesting prophecy: Four skilled or craftsmen will save Israelite from four horns that scattered Judea, Israel and Jerusalem.
[b] Isaiah 58:12 mentions *Mekka*; it is discussed in Chapter 8 – Imam Mahdi, under "Repairer of the Broken Ghadeer".

Read through/by Quran (qə-rā ḇə-ḡā-rō-wn), do not hold back. Raise your voice like a trumpet. Declare to my people their rebellion and to the descendants of Jacob their sins.

Furqan

My Jewish brothers and sisters should not have any problem in believing the truthfulness of Quran, for many reasons, such as similar theology and laws in both Torah and Quran, the signs of the coming of Islam in the Old Testament, and so on. But for my Christian brethren, since they have more confidence with the NT, I had to reassess and research the Gospels and other books of the NT. This came to my mind when I was questioned by the Christian Father who visited my place with two of his colleagues in Toronto. Soon after they left, I read the Book of Revelation again. I have no idea why I picked that book among 27 books of the NT.

After three days and nights of re-examining the transliterations of the Aramaic book of Revelation, and then other books of NT, I found "Furqan"[a] in a few places. The first and the best one was in chapter 19, verse 1 of Revelation. The discovery did not end there. I found more surprises such as a coded message in the Quran about Revelation 19:1, which also became apparent to me indeliberately.

Chapter 19 of the book of Revelation is talking about a great sound from heaven, a crowd praising God.

Revelation 19:1
And after these things I heard a great voice of a crowd in heaven, saying, Glory to Furqan, the Praise and might belongs to Allah.

---

[a] Furqan is mentioned in the Quran in al-Baqara, 2:185, Ale-Imran, 3:43 and al-Furqan, 25:1, referring to the Quran. The 25:1 is called Sura al-Furqan (Chapter Furqan). Furqan means "The Criterion" or "The standard" to distinguish between good and bad.

Lars J. Lindgren – *Dukhrana Biblical Research Society, Department of Linguistics and Philosophy at Uppsala University* – in *dukhrana.com* – has all we need to identify the word "Furqan", with many thanks to him. In Figure 55, we can see the verse in Aramaic with Arabic and Latin transliterations. The last line is the English translation of KJB. In this verse, the word is interpreted as *salvation*.

Figure 55

Peshitta[31]

- Revelation 19:1

ܘܡܢ ܒܬܪ ܗܠܝܢ ܫܡܥܬ ܩܠܐ ܪܒܐ ܕܟܢܫܐ ܣܓܝܐܐ ܒܫܡܝܐ ܕܐܡܪܝܢ ܗܠܠܘܝܗ ܦܘܪܩܢܐ ܘܬܫܒܘܚܬܐ ܘܚܝܠܐ ܠܐܠܗܢ܀

Revelation 19:1 - وَمِنْ بَاتَر هَالِين شِمِعِت قَالَا رَبَا دِكِنشِا سَجِيِاا بَشمَيَا دَامرِين هَلِلُويَا فُورقَانَا وتِشبُوخِتَا وخَيلَا لِالَاهَن.

Revelation 19:1 - wəmen bāṯar hālēn šemʿeṯ qālā rabbā dəḵenše saggīē bašmayyā dāmrīn hallelūyā pūrqānā wəṯešbūḥtā wəḥaylā lālāhan.

Revelation 19:1 - And after these things I heard a great voice of much people in heaven, saying, Alleluia; Salvation, and glory, and honour, and power, unto the Lord our God:

The Hebrew ܦܘܪܩܢܐ *pūrqānā* is the exact Arabic فرقان *furqan*, another name of the Holy Quran. The Aramaic letter ܦ (p) is identical to the Arabic ف (f). Please note that Arabic Alphabet lacks the letter *p*. It is replaced, in some places, with letter ف f^a. To clear any doubt about the similar pronunciation of these two letters, the book of Revelation has two examples:

"P" and "F" in Aramaic and Arabic

Example one: In Revelation 3:8, the word ܟ݁ܦ݂ܰܪܬ݁ (*kəpart*), translated to "denied", is equivalent to Arabic كفرت (*kafarat*), with the same meaning. (Figure 56)

Figure 56

Peshitta[31]

- Revelation 3:8

ܝܳܕ݂ܰܥ ܐ݈ܢܳܐ ܥܒ݂ܳܕ݂ܰܝܟ݁ ܘܗܳܐ ܝܶܗܒ݁ܶܬ݂ ܩܕ݂ܳܡܰܝܟ݁ ܬ݁ܰܪܥܳܐ ܦ݁ܬ݂ܺܝܚܳܐ ܐܰܝܢܳܐ ܕ݁ܠܳܐ
ܐ݈ܢܳܫ ܡܨܶܐ ܠܡܶܐܚܕ݂ܶܗ ܡܶܛܽܠ ܕ݁ܩܰܠܺܝܠ ܚܰܝܠܳܐ ܐܺܝܬ݂ ܠܳܟ݂ ܘܡܶܠܰܬ݂ܝ ܢܛܰܪܬ݁ ܘܰܒ݂ܫܶܡܝ ܠܳܐ ܟ݁ܦ݂ܰܪܬ݁ ܀

Revelation 3:8 - yādaʿ nā ʿəbādayk wəhā yehbet qədāmayk tarʿā pətīḥā ʾaynā dəlā nāš məṣe ləmeḥdēh meṭṭul dəqalīl ḥaylā ʾīt lāk wəmellat nəṭart wabšem lā kəpart .

Revelation 3:8 - I know thy works: behold, I have set before thee an open door, and no man can shut it: for thou hast a little strength, and hast kept my word, and hast not denied my name.

---

[a] The sound "p" becomes "f" and "b" in Arabic. Such as "Pars" and "Portugal" become "Fars" and "Bortaqal", respectively.

Example two: The Aramaic "p" and Arabic "f" in the following words are identical: ܢܦܫܗ napšēh and نفسه nafsahu, which means "his soul". It occurs many times in the NT. As an instance, we see it in Matthew 20:28. Not only does it provide a proof for the similar pronunciation of these letters in both languages but also contains the word "Furqan".

Matthew 20:28 is a famous verse, translated:

Even as the Son of man came not to be ministered unto, but to minister, and to give his life a ransom for many.

This verse is remarkably famous among even non-Christians. It struck me when I checked the Aramaic text of the verse. It has more than what the translations offer. (Figure 57)

Here is the rendered translation:

Matthew 20:28
As the son of man has not come to be served but rather to serve and to make into (to prepare) his soul Furqan against crowd.

Figure 57
Peshitta[31]

- Matthew 20:28

ܐܝܟܢܐ ܕܒܪܗ ܕܐܢܫܐ ܠܐ ܐܬܐ ܕܢܫܬܡܫ ܐܠܐ ܕܢܫܡܫ ܘܢܬܠ ܢܦܫܗ ܦܘܪܩܢܐ ܚܠܦ ܣܓܝܐܐ

(analyze)

Matthew 20:28 - اَيكَنَا دَبرِه دَانَاشَا لَا اِتَا دنِشتَمَش اِلَا دَنشَمِش وَدنِتِل نَقشِه فُورقَانَا خلَاڢ سَجِياا .

Matthew 20:28 - ᵓaykannā daḇrēh dənāšā lā ᵓetā dəneštammaš ᵓellā danšammeš waḏnettel napšēh pūrqānā həlāp̱ saggīe .

Matthew 20:28 - Even as the Son of man came not to be ministered unto, but to minister, and to give his life a ransom for many.

A similar statement is recorded in Mark 10:45, where Jesus[pbuh] calls "Furqan" as his soul. It is well known among Muslims and Christians that Jesus[pbuh] was *Spirit of God* and *Word of God*, mentioned in the Quran as روح الله (ruh-Allah) and كلمة الله (kalemat-Allah), respectively.[a]

Another occurrence of "Furqan" is Luke 1:68. (Figure 58)

Luke 1:68
Blessed be He who is Allah the lord of Israel[b], who has visited his gentiles and has given Furqan to his servant.

---

[a] Quran - Chapter 3 Verses 45-55
[b] Israel is another name of Prophet Jacob[pbuh].

The Quran has a similar verse:

Quran 18:1[26]
Praise be to Allah, Who hath sent to His Servant the Book, and hath allowed therein no Crookedness.

Figure 58

Peshitta[31]

- Luke 1:68

ܡܒܪܟ ܗܘ ܡܪܝܐ ܐܠܗܗ ܕܐܝܣܪܐܝܠ ܕܣܥܪ ܥܡܗ ܘܥܒܕ ܠܗ ܦܘܪܩܢܐ

(analyze) ܦܘܪܩܢܐ

Luke 1:68 - مبَرَك هُو مَاريَا اَلَاهِه دِايسرَايِل دَسعَر عَمِه وَعبَد لِه فُورقَانَا.

Luke 1:68 - məḇarraḵ ū mārya ʾālāhēh dīsrāyel dasʿar ʿammēh waʿḇad lēh pūrqānā.

Luke 1:68 - Blessed be the Lord God of Israel; for he hath visited and redeemed his people,

Again, same word occurs in the next verse (Luke 1:69). (Figure 59)

Luke 1:69 - *And established for us the Quran Furqan through His house, His servant David.*

In this verse word "qarn", is translated to "horn" and "angle" (Figure 60). Even by taking it as "horn", the verse perfectly complies with the concept:

Luke 1:69- *And established for us a horn - Furqan through His house, His servant David.*

Remember that the Hebrew word קראנא "qarana", meaning "horn", is metaphorically used for a variety of meanings, such as *strength* (Deuteronomy 33:17), *honour* (Job 16:15; Lamentations 2:3), *royal dignity* and *power* (Jeremiah 48:25; Zechariah 1:18; Daniel 8:24).

Figure 59

Peshitta[31]

- Luke 1:69

ܘܐܩܝܡ ܠܢ ܩܪܢܐ ܕܦܘܪܩܢܐ ܒܒܝܬܗ ܕܕܘܝܕ ܥܒܕܗ (analyze)

Luke 1:69 - وَاقِيم لَن قَرنَا دِفُورقَانَا ببَيتِه ددَوِيد عَبدِه .

Luke 1:69 - waqīm lan qarnā dəpūrqānā bəbaytēh dədawīd ᶜabdēh .

Luke 1:69 - And hath raised up an horn of salvation for us in the house of his servant David;

Figure 60

qrn, qrn² (qre/an, qarnā) n.f. **horn; angle**[31]

The original form of the word is likely misunderstood. It is not the first and the only time translators have been taking words according to their own sense, and disregarding other possible prophetic meanings.

The fact that the translators have chosen variety of meanings for the word ܦܘܪܩܢܐ *furqana*, sometimes even contrary to each other, is the evidence that these verses are referring to an unfamiliar matter. For example, in Luke 1:68, ܦܘܪܩܢܐ *furqana* is translated to "redemption" or "compensation", while in 1:69 they have changed its meaning to "salvation".

"Salvation" and "redemption" are two *different words*. They may look alike to Christians because of the doctrine of "Salvation through Redemption by Jesus", however, for an unbiased translator it is not the case.

Continuing to next verses, in Luke chapter 1, we will find even more evidence that these verses are talking about a revelation:

the word of God thorough the mouth of his holy prophets.

Verse 70 emphasizes that the "Furqan", in the preceding verses, is a revelation from God and is like the other revelations God has sent through the holy prophets.

Luke 1:70
As he spake by the mouth of his holy prophets, which have been since the world began.

The translation of verse 71 is deviated to fit an assumed concept. (See Figure 61)

Figure 61

Peshitta[31]

- Luke 1:71

ܕܢܸܬ݂ܦܪܸܩ ܡܸܢ ܒܥܠܕܒܒܝܢ ܘܡܸܢ ܐܝܕܐ ܕܟܠܗܘܢ ܣܢܐܝܢ (analyze)

Luke 1:71 - ܕ‎ نِهرقَن مِن بعِلدبَابَين ومِن اِيدَا دكُلهُون سَانَاين .

Luke 1:71 - dənepraqan men baʿeldəbābayn wəmen ʾīdā dəkulhon sānayn.

Luke 1:71 - That we should be saved from our enemies, and from the hand of all that hate us;

The first word, ܕܢܬܦܪܩ *dənepraqan*, from ܦܪܩ *praqan*, again translated differently: "be saved". Remember its assumed meaning in verse 68 was "redemption". In order to distinguish the differences between *redemption*, *save* or *salvation* and *furqan*, I looked for a few examples in the Bible. Please read further.

Redemption, Save or Salvation

A – The Aramaic and Hebrew words used for "**save**":

- In the NT, it is ܢܚܐ *nīḥe*. It occurs several places (such as Matthew 10:22, 24:13, Mark 13:13, John 6:51, 57, 58, 10:9, and Acts 2:21, etc.).
- In the OT, it is יָשַׁע *yawsha* (such as Proverbs 20:22). The word יָשַׁע *yawsha* is a cognate of Azeri and Turkish "Yasha", meaning "long live".

B – The word used for "**salvation**":

- In the OT, it is ישועה *yə-šū-'āh* - a derivate of יָשַׁע *yawsha* - (such as Psalm 119:155)
- And it is ܚܝܐ *ḥay* in the NT which means life, identical to Arabic حيّ *ḥayy*. For example, in Philippians 2:12, it is written as ܕܚܝܝܟܘܢ *dəḥayaykon*, translated to *"your own salvation"*. It is also used in Acts 27:34 and a few other places.

C – For "**redemption**", there are three words used in the OT:

- *pada* (Exodus 13:13; 34:20; Numbers 18:15-16, Psalm 49:7-9, etc.) similar to Arabic فدَى *fada*.
- *gaal* (Lev 25:24-25; Ruth 4:1-6; Jeremiah 32:6-9; Psalm 19:14; etc.)
- *kapar* (Exodus 21:30; 30:11-16), meaning "ransom, redemption and compensation". It sounds similar to Arabic غفّار *ghaffar* with a slightly different meaning ("very forgiving").

In none of the above occasions, we find anything close to *furqan* or *purqana*. Most interestingly, translating *purqana* to *redemption* or *salvation* appears to be fitting the Pauline doctrine of *pada* (or Arabic فديّه *fadyya*), which is why we see it only in the NT!

The OT authors never used word "furqan". However, Jesus$_{pbuh}$, and subsequently the disciples used it several times. It appears that the translators of the NT did not clearly understand the real meaning and application of the word. That is why they interpreted it differently in different passages. Translating it as "salvation", "redemption" and "save", seemed to be suiting the idea of "salvation through redemption and blood of Jesus". It was a convenient illusion to the puzzle, but not a solution.

A curious Question

How did "furqan" make its way into the New Testament?

I wish I had a factual answer for it. I can guess that Jesus$_{pbuh}$ had talked about it repeatedly as *his soul, the revelation, given from God*. But later on, the original message was changed to support a new doctrine.

I think the Greeks, alongside some Jews did not get the message as a prophetic word, as they did not understand many other sayings and words of Jesus$_{pbuh}$ in his lifetime. Therefore, they divided into Jewish followers of Jesus (who kept the original words of Jesus$_{pbuh}$ as it is, in some areas at least) and Greco-Roman believers of Paul, who interpreted the words according to their own belief. Besides that, we must not forget the occasions of changes in the Bible, such as the story of Ascension in the Gospel of Mark 16:9-20 and the story of the adulterous woman in the Gospel of John 8:1-11, and so forth, which were not in the oldest manuscripts but added to the Gospels later on. [45, 46, 47, 48, 49] It reminds us how the Gospels were written and re-written to suit the framework of the believers.

The Quran Seals It[a]

Chapter 19 of the Quran (called Mary[pbuh], the mother of Jesus[pbuh]) is mainly about Jesus[pbuh], his Mother, Zachariah[pbuh], John the Baptist[pbuh] and some other prophets. The verse 1 is a five letter coded word, called "Moqatta'a" in Arabic. We do not know its true and pure meaning.

What I concluded after finding the word *furan* in Revelation 19:1 is an amazing correlation between the first two verses of the book of Revelation Chapter 19 and the Quran Chapter 19.

Quran 19:1[26]
كهيعص
Kaf. Ha. Ya. 'Ain. Sad.

After discovering the word "Furqan" in Revelation 19:1, I found myself reading 19th chapter of the Quran (like the 19th Chapter of the Book of Revelation). Right at the first verse, I noticed that the verse was significantly related to what I just found in the Bible. In my opinion, the first two letters, "k" and "h", are referring to the Book of Revelation. In Hebrew, it is called כְּתָב הִתְגַלּוּת *ketav hitgalut*, meaning "book revelation".

In other words, Chapter 19 of the Quran leads us to Chapter 19 of a book in the Bible, and the first two letters of verse 1 tell us which book we should look into, *k* and *h*, standing for "ketav hitgalut" or "Book of Revelation".

---

[a] This section is a personal interpretation of mine and may or may not be fitting to the Islamic tradition. Please do not take my opinion on this matter as a reference to the interpretation of the Quran 19:1.

Possibly, I could also relate the other letters of the Quran 19:1 to the book of Revelation as shown in Figure 62.

Figure 62

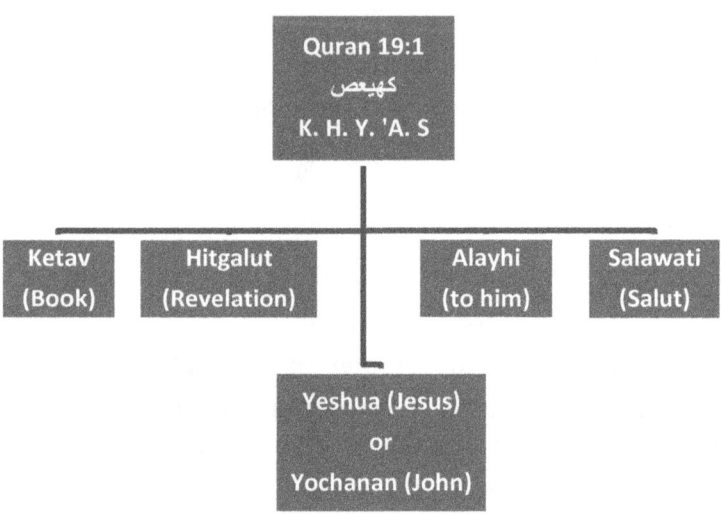

Chapter 6 – Isaiah and Islam

Isaiah, the Prophet of Prophecies

Isaiah, the 8th century BC prophet, known as "the prince of prophets", is famous for his apocalyptic passages in the book of Isaiah. It is the 23rd book in the Canon. I call him "the prophet of prophecies" for his numerous prophetic passages in the book of Isaiah. After prophesying for over 60 years, he was martyred by King Manasseh, his grandson from his daughter. He was sawn into two pieces.[a]

Many sects of Christianity use the book of Isaiah to prove truthfulness of the Christ and his second coming. When Christians think of the book of Isaiah, their first thought may be his marvelous prophecies of the Messiah and "the promised glory of God's kingdom."

With no doubt, Isaiah has talked about the sins of Israelites, which caused their separation from God. He has talked about punishments to the Israelites, and about a good ending after all.

However, what the readers of the book of Isaiah do not see is its numerous references to the coming of Islam from Mekka, *a revelation from a far place, five men whom the oppressors will run from, the revelation from the land of Tima (ninth son of Ishmael), the prophet of Islam, Ahmed, Sediqa, a light for Gentiles among Arabs in Arabia, the messenger of God, the Muslim, the Ameen, the illiterate, the camel rider, the everlasting prince of Islam, Ali the lion of God,* and many more words that are lost in the translations.

---

[a] "HEZEKIAH - jewishencyclopedia.com"

We need to study the book in its original language, the Hebrew, because the translations do not deliver the message. I always wondered why so much deviation from the original teachings of the prophets exists. People are divided and still more sects and divisions continue to rise. The top scholars do not agree on fundamental and basic elements of their faith.

Sadly, I must say that the deviation is very intense, particularly in scholars' level. As an example of these deviations, Rabbi Harold Kushner[a] in his 1981 best seller, *When Bad Things Happen to Good People*, believes that *God is all loving but not all powerful, so, when bad things happen to good people, it is because events are out of God's control*. Kushner advises his readers to *learn to love [God] and forgive him [God] despite his limitations.*

The OT teaches a different theodicy: if God does not help, it is not because He cannot, but because we depart from His help by sinning and moving away from His mercy (Isaiah 59:1, 2). The gap in the interpretations of the book of Isaiah is deepening day by day. If anyone would love to find the real message in it, he owes it to himself to read the original Hebrew book of Isaiah. That is what I have been doing for the past decade or so.

Although it is not easy to understand the real applications of some verses in the Isaiah, but there are many verses foretelling unmistakably the coming of Islam. Some verses are full of secrecy and some are very clear. For instance, Chapter 29, one of the most metaphoric passages of the Isaiah, is full of secrecy. On the other hand, chapter 21 openly talks about a prophecy regarding Arabs, land of Tima and Qidar (sons of Ishmael).

---

[a] Prominent American Rabbi, author of a bestselling book: When Bad Things Happen to Good People.

Chapter 42 gives clear evidence that the coming Prophet's nickname is *righteous* (Ameen) who will be sent to Gentiles; God calls him *my prophet my Muslim*.

Furthermore, chapter 58, which has 14 verses, mentions "Quran" and "Mekka" in verses 1 and 12:

Isaiah 58: 1, 12
1 "Recite by Quran (qə-rā ḇə-ḡā-rō-wn[a]*), do not hold back. Raise your voice like a trumpet. Declare to my people their rebellion and to the descendants of Jacob their sins.*
12 You will rebuild from Mekka (mim-mə-kā[b]*) the ancient ruins and will raise up the foundations of generation and generation; you will be called Repairer of Broken Ghadeer (גדר gō-ḏêr), Restorer of Streets with Dwellings.*

These two verses are brilliant explanations of the Quran (as the first announcement of chapter 58) and someone who will rebuild the broken walls (broken protections, "Ghadeer"). "Repairer" in Arabic is جابر *Jabir*; it is one of Imam Mahdi's nicknames. The number 12 represents the 12th Imam who will start his government from Mekka. Moreover, the total number of verses (14) represents the 14 infallibles of Islam (Prophet Muhammad, his daughter, and the Twelve Imams [pbut]).

At last, chapter 59, the Prince of Isaiah, showers prophecies about Islam. It talks about Ahmed, Sediqa, Islam, death of the prophet, Muslims deviation from truth, and so on.

With no time to waste, we are going to examine some of these passages.

---

[a] "קְרָא בְגָרוֹן" (qə-rā ḇə-ḡā-rō-wn) is translated to "Shout it aloud" (NIV)
[b] "מִמְּךָ" (mim-mə-kā) is translated to "some of you", "of", "your people", and so on.

The Everlasting Prince of Islam (Isaiah 9)

Isaiah in chapter 9 speaks about nations, beyond Jordan; the gentiles, who are in darkness and will see the light and rejoice. A child called "Prince of Islam" ("Sar shalowm" in Hebrew) will be born to them; *his kingdom and Islam will have no end.*

Isaiah chapter 9 verse 1 makes it clear that in the future lands of Gentiles will be honored. In translations, instead of "lands of Gentiles", it is written *"the galilee of the nations"*. However, in the Hebrew text it is גְּלִיל הַגּוֹיִם *gə-lîl hag-gō-w-yim*. It refers to lands of gentiles, *"the non-Jews"*.

Figure 63 shows the only occurrence of *gə-lîl*, according to Englishman's Concordance; that is in Isaiah 9:1.

Isaiah 9:1
NIV
Nevertheless, there will be no more gloom for those who were in distress. In the past he humbled the land of Zebulun and the land of Naphtali, but in the future he will honor Galilee of the nations, by the Way of the Sea, beyond the Jordan—

Some versions, such as NASV and NLT, use "Galilee of the Gentiles", referring to the lands of Gentiles.

Figure 63

gə·lîl

Englishman's Concordance[1]

gə·lîl — 1 Occurrence

Isaiah 9:1
HEB: הַגּוֹיִם: גְּלִיל עֵבֶר הַיַּרְדֵּן
NAS: of Jordan, Galilee of the Gentiles.
KJV: Jordan, *in Galilee* of the nations.
INT: the other of Jordan *Galilee* of the Gentiles

Verse 2 ensures that it is about people who had not seen light. They are to receive light (the Divine Guidance).

Isaiah 9:2
NIV
2 The people walking in darkness have seen a great light; on those living in the land of deep darkness a light has dawned.

The subsequent verses explain plainly, what these nations will be facing: joy and happiness. They will be given a son who will be called the Prince of Islam; he will sit on the throne of David, in another word he will be a king.

Isaiah 9:3-6
NIV
3 You have enlarged the nation and increased their joy; they rejoice before you as people rejoice at the harvest, as warriors rejoice when dividing the plunder.

4 For as in the day of Midian's defeat, you have shattered the yoke that burdens them, the bar across their shoulders, the rod of their oppressor.
5 Every warrior's boot used in battle and every garment rolled in blood will be destined for burning, will be fuel for the fire.
6 For to us a child is born, to us a son is given, and the government will be on his shoulders. And he will be called Wonderful Counselor, Mighty God, Everlasting Father, Prince of Peace.

The translations of verse 6 have obvious mistakes. Following is the Hebrew text and Table 45 is the text analysis.

WLC (Consonants Only)[1]

כי־ילד ילד־לנו בן נתן־לנו ותהי המשרה על־שכמו ויקרא שמו פלא
יועץ אל גבור אביעד שר־שלום:

kî- ye-leḏ yul-laḏ- lā-nū bên nit-tan- lā-nū wat-tə-hî ham-miś-rāh 'al-šiḵ-mōw way-yiq-rā šə-mōw pe-le yō-w-'eṣ 'êl gib-bō-wr 'ă-ḇî-'aḏ śar- šā-lō-wm

Word by word translation of Isaiah 9:6

for son is born to us a son is given to us and shall be the government on his shoulder and called his name wonderful councilor god power (great or warrior) everlasting prince Islam

Another matter in verse 6 is the phrase: עַל־ שִׁכְמוֹ *'al- šiḵ-mōw*. It is translated to "on his shoulder". In a story, we read that on the day Mekka was conquered, Imam Ali_pbuh, following the order of Prophet Muhammad_pbuh, placed his feet on the shoulder of Prophet Muhammad_pbuh to climb up Kaaba and pull down "Hubal", the biggest idol of Mekka. The statement "ham-miś-rāh 'al- šiḵ-mōw" (the government on his shoulder) may reflect this event.

Table 45

Text Analysis[1]   Isaiah 9:6

Str	Translit	Hebrew	English	Morph
3588 [e]	kî-	כִּי־	For	Conj
3206 [e]	ye-led	יֶלֶד	to us a child	Noun
3205 [e]	yul-lad-	יֻלַּד־	is born	Verb
	lā-nū,	לָנוּ	to us	Prep
1121 [e]	bên	בֵּן	a son	Noun
5414 [e]	nit-tan-	נִתַּן־	is given	Verb
	lā-nū,	לָנוּ	to	Prep
1961 [e]	wat-tə-hî	וַתְּהִי	and shall be	Verb
4951 [e]	ham-miś-rāh	הַמִּשְׂרָה	the government	Noun
5921 [e]	'al-	עַל־	on	Prep
7926 [e]	šik-mōw;	שִׁכְמוֹ	his shoulder	Noun
7121 [e]	way-yiq-rā	וַיִּקְרָא	and called	Verb
8034 [e]	šə-mōw	שְׁמוֹ	his name	Noun
6382 [e]	pe-le	פֶּלֶא	Wonderful	Noun
3289 [e]	yō-w-'ês	יוֹעֵץ	Counselor	Verb
410 [e]	'êl	אֵל	the God	Noun
1368 [e]	gib-bō-wr,	גִּבּוֹר	mighty	Adj
5703 [e]	'ă-bî-'ad	אֲבִיעַד	The everlasting	Noun
8269 [e]	śar-	שַׂר־	The Prince	Noun
7965 [e]	šā-lō-wm.	שָׁלוֹם׃	of Peace	Noun

Mighty God or Great Counsel

In translating *'êl gib-bō-wr,* in Isaiah 9:6, we have three options:

1. Mighty God
2. might of God (or warrior of God)[a]
3. mighty power[b]
4. a name[c], El Gibowr, similar to אל ברית (El Berith) in Judges 9:46

Although, there is no solid reason to read *'êl* and *gib-bō-wr* as one phrase, even as a single word it does not necessarily mean that it has to be translated to "Mighty God" because "God" is not the only meaning and use of "el" in Hebrew.

The Hebrews did use the word "el" to refer to angels, the might/strength of men, mountains, and big trees as well. (See Psalm 29:1, Genesis 31:29, Deuteronomy 28:32, Nehemiah 5:5, Psalm 36:6, 80:10, and so on)

A second century translation, The Septuagint, gives a completely different meaning to the verse:

The Septuagint (LXX) Translation of Isaiah 9:6[1]
"For a child is born to us, and a son is given to us, whose government is upon his shoulder: and his name is called the angel/messenger of great counsel: for I will bring peace upon the princes, and health to him" (LXX).

---

[a] See NAS Exhaustive Concordance 1368. gibbor
[b] See NAS Exhaustive Concordance 1368. gibbor and NASB Translation of 410. el
[c] See Brown-Driver-Briggs 410. el, 4 El proper name אל ברית El Berith (Judges 9:46)

The second Century Rabbis have combined *pe-le yō-w-'êṣ 'êl gib-bō-wr 'ă-ḇî-'aḏ* and translated it to "the angel/messenger of great counsel" (or "the messenger of God"). It seems that they have interpreted *'ă-ḇî-'aḏ* as *angel* which is very close to Arabic أَبَدَ *abada* means *to stay, to last, to exist forever*[a]. It is also, close to Persian آباد *'abaad*, meaning "place of dwelling", "town or village", or "living place". Bible translators have regarded it similar to Arabic ابد *abada* (means: *forever*); to make it more Christian-friendly, "father" has been added to the text, or perhaps *'ă-ḇî-'aḏ* has been cut into *'ă-ḇî* and *'aḏ* for a sweater "reader's digest"!

Is Isaiah 9 foretelling Jesus?

Christians claim that Isaiah 9 is talking about Jesus[pbuh], calling him "God". For the following reasons this is not correct:

1. It does not mention Jesus' name.
2. Jesus[pbuh] was never called *śar- šā-lō-wm* (*The prince of Shalam or peace*) in his lifetime.
3. Jesus even opposes such an idea of being called *"the prince of peace"*, as we read in the Gospel of Matthew:

Matthew 10:34
NIV
"Do not suppose that I have come to bring peace to the earth. I did not come to bring peace, but a sword. "

4. It is about people who never seen light (guidance). This cannot be the Jews. (Verse 2)

---

[a] https://en.wiktionary.org/ (accessed April 5, 2017)

5. Verse 4 mentions Medians, an Arabian Tribe, according to Brown-Driver-Briggs. (See Figure 64)
6. Verse 5 is about war and battle. Jesus$_{pbuh}$ had no war.
7. Verse 6 says that the government will be on his shoulder. Jesus$_{pbuh}$ had no government.
8. Verse 6 says, according to NIV, that he will be called "Wonderful Counselor". Jesus$_{pbuh}$ was never called "Wonderful Counselor" in his lifetime.

By the way, according to majority of scholars, *angels, judges and men* in the Bible are also called *'êl*. (Exodus 21:6; 22:8-9; Psalm 82:1, 6; Psalm 45:6-7 and Hebrews 2:7) Therefore, even if it refers to Jesus$_{pbuh}$, it does not mean that he will be called "God".

The last part of the verse, *śar- šā-lō-wm,* is the Hebrew cognate of Arabic ساراسلام *sar Islam*, meaning "the head of Islam". Some might ask why the Jews of second century did not write it as "*śar-išā-lō-wm*". Well, Islam, as a historical phenomenon, started at 7th century not at the time of Isaiah; the Hebrew literature of Isaiah is at least 1300 years older than emergence of Islam. However, if we read this verse in its real Hebrew language to any Muslim, as soon as the word Shalam is pronounced, they will immediately recognize the word as Islam or Salaam; both are form triconsonantal root *slm* means *peace*.

I suggest a rendered translation of verse 6 as following:

Rendered translation of Isaiah 9:6

For a son is born to us, a son is given to us and the government shall be on his shoulder and he shall be called wonderful councilor of mighty God, the everlasting prince of Islam.

Figure 64

Strong's Concordance[1]   4080. Midyan

Midyan: a son of Abraham and Keturah, also his desc. and the region where they settled

Original Word: מִדְיָן
Part of Speech: proper name, masculine
Transliteration: Midyan
Phonetic Spelling: (mid-yawn')
Short Definition: Midian

Brown-Driver-Briggs

מִדְיָן **proper name, masculine 1. son of Abraham and Keturah** Genesis 25:2,4 (J) 1 Chronicles 1:32,33.

2 an Arabian tribe Genesis 36:35 (= 1 Chronicles 1:46) Numbers 31:3 (twice in verse); Numbers 31:7,8 (twice in verse); Numbers 31:9 (P) Judges 6-9 (31 t.); having a כֹּהֵן (as chieftain?) Exodus 2:16; Exodus 3:1; Exodus 18:1 (E); זקניםNumbers 22:4,7 (JE), נשׂיא(ים) Numbers 25:18 (P) Joshua 13:21 (P), שׂריםJudges 7:25; Judges 8:3, מלכים Numbers 31:8 (twice in verse); Judges 8:5,12,26; בִּכְרֵי מִדְיָן *dromedaries of Midian* Isaiah 60:6; יוֹם מִדְיָן *day of Midian* Isaiah 9:3 (the victory over Midian Judges 7-8) compare Judges 10:26; Psalm 83:10,

3 אֶרֶץ מִדְיָן *the land of Midian* Exodus 2:15 (E) Habakkuk 3:7; מִדְיָן Exodus 4:19 (J) Numbers 25:15 (P) 1 Kings 11:18; land on Aelanitic gulf (where Arabic geographers still place town مدين). compare on Midian, Glaser[Skizze ii. 447 ff.]; Hom[Aufsätze i. (1892), 4f]

Ali, the Lion (Isaiah 21:8)

As we will explain shortly, despite many troubling issues in Isaiah chapter 21, such as: suspicious variations in the manuscripts, a possible attempt to omit or change the original text, ambiguous and foggy translations of some key verses, pluralizing single nouns and so forth, ... the prophetic message hidden in the Hebrew text has been preserved miraculously.

Isaiah 21 reveals the story of Prophet Muhammad$_{pbuh}$, his migration to Medina, Imam Ali$_{pbuh}$ and his nickname (*the lion*), the story of Karbala, very likely names of Ali Akbar$_{pbuh}$ (son of Imam Hussain$_{pbuh}$) and Imam Mahdi$_{pbuh}$. I call chapter 21 of the book of Isaiah *the signet of Isaiah*. We discussed Isaiah 21:1-2 in Chapter 4 – Imam Hussain in the Bible, under "Sufyani and Mahdi (Isaiah 21)". Hence, we will read only the rendered translation of these two verses without repeating the details, and then we will continue to the subsequent verses.

Rendered translation
Isaiah 21:1, 2
A prophecy against the Desert by yam: 1 Like Sufians sweeping through Nejef, an invader comes from the desert, from Noraa (Neinawa). 2 A dire vision has been shown to me: The traitor betrays, the looter takes loot. ali ê-lām portray Mahdi! I will bring to an end all the groaning.

Verses 6 to 8 have a key role in interpreting the entire passage. As they read:

Isaiah 21:6-8
NIV
6 This is what the Lord says to me: "Go, post a lookout and have him report what he sees. 7 When he sees chariots with teams of horses, riders on donkeys or riders on camels, let him be alert,

fully alert." 8 And the lookout shouted, "Day after day, my lord, I stand on the watchtower; every night I stay at my post.

All versions of the Bible, with an exception of Douay-Rheims Bible, have translated the singular nouns of חמור (ḥă-mō-wr) and גמל (gā-māl), meaning "donkey" and "camel", respectively, to "donkeys" and "camels". They have treated these singular words as plural. In addition to that, all translations of verse 8 are very foggy. Some older scrolls, such as Dead Sea Scrolls, Syriac and Masoretic Texts, contain word אריה 'ar-yêh (lion)[a], but some translations, such as NIV, NLT, ESV and NASB have disregarded it. Others like KJB and ASV still have the word. (See below)

Isaiah 21:8
KJB
And he cried, A lion: My lord, I stand continually upon the watchtower in the daytime, and I am set in my ward whole nights.

In this translation, it is not clear whether the watchman shouts "a lion" or he himself is called *a lion*. What I think is that there must be a modification on the original text, or perhaps another misunderstanding. The text analysis clarifies the issue.

As shown in Table 46, the verse starts with a verb, *"way-yiq-rā"* (*"and he cried"*); then *"a lion on the watchtower my Lord"*. The statement is very ambiguous. What was the lion doing on the watchtower?

Or if it means: *And he cried "a lion, My lord"*, still it is obscure. Did he see *"a lion"*? Nothing else is told about the "lion"!

---

[a] http://biblehub.com/niv/isaiah/21.htm ; See the footnotes.

Another option is that we assume that the watchman is called "a lion": *And he, A lion, cried: My lord, I stand continually upon the watchtower in the daytime, and I am set in my ward whole nights.*

By examining the verse carefully, we find out that the omission of *lion*, in some translations, must be an intentional intervention. We can also notice that there are clear signs of a prophecy, such as name of a person, which is either omitted or changed to a similar word. It is more obvious when we compare WLC with Aleppo Codex. Please compare the boxed phrases in the manuscripts bellow: (This kind of alteration in these manuscripts is very common.)

21:8 ישעה Hebrew OT: WLC (Consonants Only) [1]
ויקרא אריה על־מצפה ׀ אדני אנכי עמד תמיד יומם ועל־משמרתי אנכי נצב כל־הלילות:

Aleppo Codex[1]
ח ויקרא אריה--על מצפה אדני אנכי עמד תמיד יומם ועל משמרתי אנכי נצב כל הלילות

It seems that the scribe(s) did notice a problem; they tried to fix something that did not look right to them by removing or changing a "strange word", or making it what they thought it should be. It is also possible that a very late human interference has caused the changes on the manuscript. This explains the ambiguity of the whole sentence.

In an attempt to clear the fuzz, some translators deleted *"lion"* from the verse; this seemed to be a helpful thought at first until the *"lion"* showed up again from the caves of Qumran when the Dead

Sea Scrolls[a] were discovered in 1946 to 1956. This is where we say: To fall from the frying pan into the fire!

Neither was *a lion* on the watchtower nor was the watchman *a lion*. Somebody had to be called *"lion"* here. To clarify the issue I put my magnifier on this boxed word: 'ar-yêh ‛al- miṣ-peh (lion ‛al- the watchtower). If ‛al- was a name such as "Ali", the whole sentence would make a lot of sense:

Isaiah 21:8
And the lookout cried: lion Ali; my lord, I stand continually in the daytime and at my guard I am set whole nights.

Imam Ali[pbuh] was known as "the lion of God", in Arabic "اسد الله" *Assad Allah*. The preceding and subsequent verses corroborate this opinion:

Isaiah 21:7-9
7 When he sees chariots with teams of horses, rider on donkey or rider on camel, let him be alert, fully alert." 8 And the lookout cried: lion Ali; my lord, I stand continually in the daytime and at my guard I am set whole nights. 9 Look, here comes a man in a chariot with a team of horses. And he gives back the answer: 'Babylon has fallen, has fallen! All the images of its gods lie shattered on the ground!' "

Verse 7 is about three different eras: horse riders, a donkey rider, and a camel rider. The horse riders can refer to Prophet Solomon[pbuh], David[pbuh] and Imam Ali[pbuh]; the donkey rider is Jesus[pbuh] and the camel rider can only be Prophet Muhammad[pbuh]. The prophet's migration from Mekka to Medina on a camel is a very famous event in the history of Islam. It is the starting point of

---

[a] Also, known as "Qumran Caves Scrolls" found in 12 caves of Qumran

the Islamic calendar, known as Hijrah or Hijri. After the arrival of the Prophet in Medina, people destroyed the idols and the city turned to the monotheistic faith in less than 3 years.

Verse 8 is inevitably about Imam Ali$_{pbuh}$. In verse 9, he is called a man in chariot with a team of horses. Any person who studied a bit of his life knows his fearless defensive conflicts, the best of all times ever.

Prophet Muhammad and Imam Ali cleaned the Kaaba from Idols and turned the entire Arabia from paganism to Monotheism. This was indeed the greatest prophecy of Isaiah 21.

Table 46

Text Analysis[1]   **Isaiah 21:8**

Str	Translit	Hebrew	English	Morph
7121 [e]	way-yiq-rā	וַיִּקְרָא	And he cried	Verb
738 [e]	'ar-yêh;	אַרְיֵה	A lion	Noun
5921 [e]	'al-	עַל־	on	Prep
4707 [e]	miṣ-peh	מִצְפֶּה ׀	the watchtower	Noun
136 [e]	'ă-dō-nāy,	אֲדֹנָי	My lord	Noun
595 [e]	'ā-nō-kî	אָנֹכִי	I [am]	Pro
5975 [e]	'ō-mêḏ	עֹמֵד	stand	Verb
8548 [e]	tā-mîḏ	תָּמִיד	continually	Noun
3119 [e]	yō-w-mām,	יוֹמָם	in the daytime	Subst
5921 [e]	wə-'al-	וְעַל־	and in	Prep
4931 [e]	miš-mar-tî,	מִשְׁמַרְתִּי	at my guard	Noun
595 [e]	'ā-nō-kî	אָנֹכִי	I [am]	Pro
5324 [e]	niṣ-ṣāḇ	נִצָּב	am set	Verb
3605 [e]	kāl-	כָּל־	whole	Noun
3915 [e]	hal-lê-lō-wṯ.	הַלֵּילוֹת׃	nights	Noun

The Migration (Isaiah 21:11-17)

Isaiah 21:11-17
NIV
11 A prophecy against Dumah: Someone calls to me from Seir, "Watchman, what is left of the night? Watchman, what is left of the night?"
12 The watchman replies, "Morning is coming, but also the night. If you would ask, then ask; and come back yet again."
13 A prophecy against Arabia: You caravans of Dedanites, who camp in the thickets of Arabia,
14 bring water for the thirsty; you who live in Tema, bring food for the fugitives.
15 They flee from the sword, from the drawn sword, from the bent bow and from the heat of battle.
16 This is what the Lord says to me: "Within one year, as a servant bound by contract would count it, all the splendor of Kedar will come to an end.
17 The survivors of the archers, the warriors of Kedar, will be few." The Lord, the God of Israel, has spoken.

Verse 11 states that the prophecy is about Dumah, son of Ishmael$_{pbuh}$ (Genesis 25:14). It is also a part of Arabia[a]. However, Seir (extending along the eastern side of the Arabah from the southeastern extremity of the Dead Sea to near the Akabah) could refer to an Arab and non-Arab as well.

Verses 13 to 17 are formidably talking about Arabia. Kedar (Quraish) and Tema are second and ninth sons of Ishmael (Genesis 25:13-15). The commentators have misinterpreted these clear verses. I cannot have a better saying on the verses than the verses themselves. There is no need for interpretation at all. It is about

---

[a] Matthew Poole's Commentary in Bible Hub

Arabia; someone will flee and try to avoid war. He will take refuge in Tema. Dedanites must receive and serve him/them. Then it reads: "splendor of Kedar will come to an end". This correlates with the migration of the Prophet from Mekka to Medina. Kedarite (Quraish) were torturing and murdering the Prophet's people. He sent them to Medina, and then he himself migrated there, where people of Medina received him with warmth.

A year after the migration, Prophet Muhammad$_{pbuh}$ set out to defend his people. He confronted the outnumbered army of Kedar (Quraish). However, he won the battle.

Quran, the Step by Step Revelation (Isaiah 28)

The Quran was revealed to Prophet Muhammad$_{pbuh}$ in a period of 23 years in various places and stages. Some ask, "Why God did not send it all at once, just like Torah (the revelation to Moses$_{pbuh}$) or Injeel (The Gospel of Jesus$_{pbuh}$) and so on?" They do not know that Torah and Injeel are not exactly what we have today as the first five books and the four Gospels. In today's volume, they have not been sent down at once. It was the Ten Commandment and original books of Torah and Injeel, which came down at once not the entire Bible. Moses had revelations in his middle age and continued until his very old age. Jesus received revelations when he was a baby and ended with his Ascension; that is a 33-year period.

The books, as a whole, might have been concealed in the souls of the Prophets but substantiation of the revelations, as words coming out from Prophet's mouth, were all gradual and in stages. God knows better how to send his message. He is the One who decides how and when to communicate with His messengers and He alone does that.

We know very well that changing all sorts of misbehaviors, wrong habits and bad cultures of a society in one day is not possible. A step-by-step measurement and gradual laws are necessary to correct people's bad habits and improve them from inside out rather than forcing them form outside. This is what prophets would do, and it was done perfectly by prophet Muhammad$_{pbuh}$. It reached the highest level of complete laws and guidance to humanity, rules for everything that societies needed from personal aspect to community and global matters, materially and spiritually. Both earthly and heavenly matters are addressed in the God's message, the Holy Quran.

Isaiah, in chapter 28 verses 9 – 13, has prophesied the systematic revelation of the Quran with detailed rules and laws. People of Mekka rejected Prophet's message and even decided to murder him and his followers. It was foretold in Isaiah 28:12. He had to flee to Medina. There, in Medina, another stage of the revelation started. (As foretold in Isaiah 28:13)

Some 10 years after the first revelation of the Quran, when the Prophet returned to his town, Mekka, the last verses of the Quran were sent to him by Angel Gabriel$_{pbuh}$. His 23 years ministry was a step by step training of the generation, Some in their very young ages benefited from the blessings of the Prophet, such as his cousin and son in law Imam Ali$_{pbuh}$, his daughter, grandchildren, and so on. These too were foretold in verse 9.

Many strangers become Prophet Muhammad's close friends to such an extent that the Prophet called some of them his "family members and brothers", such as Salman the Persian and Uwais Al-Qarani. Uwais was a man of affection and truth. He never met the Prophet and never heard his voice directly. His faith was on the base of hearing verses of the Quran recited by tradesmen who traveled from Arabia to Yemen, where he resided.

The Quran is not a usual literature in Arabic; still there is not a single book or article comparable to the Quran. The language of the Quran is unique, miraculous, live, dominant and elegant, pervasive and comprehensive. It takes souls and minds of human to rest in an indescribable peace. Its rhythm and pulse has changed the hearts of many, even non-Arabs.

Millions of people, even many illiterates, recite the entire or many chapters of the Quran from memory; majority of them are not Arabs. Many of them do not speak Arabic. Hardly can we find a Muslim who cannot recite at least a full chapter of the Quran in its original language of Arabic, without looking at the book.

Even for Arabs, the Quran is an unusual book. This was also foretold in Isaiah 28:11.

Isaiah 28
NIV
9 "Who is it he is trying to teach? To whom is he explaining his message? To children weaned from their milk, to those just taken from the breast?
10 For it is: Do this, do that, a rule for this, a rule for that ; a little here, a little there."
11 Very well then, with foreign lips and strange tongues God will speak to this people,
12 to whom he said, "This is the resting place, let the weary rest"; and, "This is the place of repose"— but they would not listen.
13 So then, the word of the LORD *to them will become: Do this, do that, a rule for this, a rule for that; a little here, a little there— so that as they go they will fall backward; they will be injured and snared and captured.*

Read! - I cannot read (Isaiah 29)

Isaiah 29 is another prophetic passage in the Bible, which consists of both enigmatic and noticeable statements about early history of Islam, including the very first revelation to Prophet Muhammad$_{pbuh}$. It starts with a warning to *Ariel*, a disputed word.

Isaiah 29:1 (NIV)
Woe to you, Ariel, Ariel, the city where David settled! Add year to year, and let your cycle of festivals go on.

Cambridge Bible for Schools and Colleges gives two doubtful interpretations for the verse:

Cambridge Bible for Schools and Colleges[50]

1. Jerusalem's time of joyous security shall speedily come to an end. **Ho Ariel, Ariel, city where David encamped! (R.V.).** *Of the word "Ariel" two explanations (both ancient) are given. (a) That which renders it* "Lion of God" *is undoubtedly the one most naturally suggested by the form of the word. It is also thought to be confirmed by the proper name 'ar'çlî in* Genesis 46:16; Numbers 26:17; *and the "lion-like men" ('ărîçl) of* 2 Samuel 23:20; 1 Chronicles 11:22; *although* all these analogies are very doubtful *(cf. ch.* Isaiah 33:7*).* But is it suitable in the present context? Hardly, *unless we take* Isaiah 29:2 *to mean that Jerusalem when driven to bay, will exhibit a prowess worthy of her mystic appellation; which is not at all the idea of the passage. The name is in any case a strange one for a city, and it would be difficult to account for its selection by Isaiah. (b) The other (and preferable) explanation is given by the Targum[1], and is supported by a word which occurs in two forms (har'çl and 'ărî'êl) in* Ezekiel 43:15 *f. It appears to mean "altar-hearth"[2]; and occurs, probably in the same sense, in the inscription of the Moabite Stone[3]. The translation here will be either* **"hearth of God"** *or (better) simply* "*altar-hearth*." *How Isaiah was led to such a designation we shall see from* Isaiah 29:2.

In the above quotation, Ariel thought to be either "Lion of God" (another metaphor!) or "altar hearth". The first interpretation is very doubtful, as even the source itself has pointed it out. Simply, interpreting a metaphor with another metaphoric statement does not clarify anything. It even makes the statement more complicated. The second interpretation, "altar hearth", is also refutable because the subsequent verse rejects such interpretation. It says that Ariel will be *like* an altar hearth; the simulation proves that they are not same.

Isaiah 29:2
NIV
Yet I will besiege Ariel; she will mourn and lament, she will be to me like an altar hearth.

Then it says that you people do not understand this vision because God has made you sleep.

9 Be stunned and amazed, blind yourselves and be sightless; be drunk, but not from wine, stagger, but not from beer.
10 The Lord has brought over you a deep sleep: He has sealed your eyes (the prophets); he has covered your heads (the seers).

Verse 10 is referring to false prophets. Some interpreters place "the prophets" and "the seers" in brackets. It may indicate that these verses have gone through changes.

Then, verses 11 and 12 have a statement, which at first look, they sound unnecessary to be there, because they have already been mentioned in the previous verses. In my opinion, these two verses are hidden prophecies in the context, rather than repetition of a statement.

11 For you this whole vision is nothing but words sealed in a scroll. And if you give the scroll to someone who can read, and say, "Read this, please", they will answer, "I can't; it is sealed." 12 Or if you give the scroll to someone who cannot read, and say, "Read this, please", they will answer, "I don't know how to read."

Verse 11 means that your learned men and women do not want to read the scroll (revelation) saying that it is sealed, yet *they can open and read it*. Today many learned people refuse reading the Quran. Verse 11 may indicate this reality. It can also mean that they cannot decode the revelation.

The verse 12 says that an unlearned man will also say that he cannot read it. In this case, for a different reason: he is not learned. It is interesting that how verse 12 portrays the story of the first revelation to Prophet Muhammad$_{pbuh}$, when he was asked by Angel Gabriel to read. "I cannot read", he replied. Because, he was not learned.

Some Bible interpreters may say that they easily understand the meaning of these verses! However, Isaiah himself states contrary. (*11 For you this whole vision is nothing but words sealed in a scroll.*)

Verse 14 challenges the wisdom of wise and the intelligence of the intelligent.

14 Therefore once more I will astound these people with wonder upon wonder; the wisdom of the wise will perish, the intelligence of the intelligent will vanish."

It is exactly what the Quran says in three places: [26]

Quran 17:88
Say: "If the whole of mankind and Jinns[a] were to gather together to produce the like of this Qur'an, they could not produce the like thereof, even if they backed up each other with help and support.

Quran 11:13
Or they may say, "He forged it", Say, "Bring ye then ten suras forged, like unto it, and call (to your aid) whomsoever ye can, other than Allah!- If ye speak the truth!

Quran 2:23
And if ye are in doubt as to what We have revealed from time to time to Our servant, then produce a Sura like thereunto; and call your witnesses or helpers (If there are any) besides Allah, if your (doubts) are true.

Verse 17 of Isaiah 29 is plainly predicting the *turning a nation of no fertility* (no divine leadership) to *a nation of fertility.*

17 In a very short time, will not Lebanon be turned into a fertile field and the fertile field seem like a forest?

Next verses are even more interesting:

18 In that day the deaf will hear the words of the scroll, and out of gloom and darkness the eyes of the blind will see.

This means the one who could not understand the truth and the nation who were in darkness will receive the truth and light. They are not Jews for sure. Jews had received revelations many times,

---

[a] Jinns are metaphysical, creatures created from fire and living in world just like us but not visible to human eyes. They, unlike angels, possess the power of choice to choose between good and evil. There is a chapter in the Quran named Al-Jinn.

contrary to Arabs who never had a written revelation from God, prior to Islam.

Verse 19 mentions another future event:

19 Once more the humble will rejoice in the Lord; *the needy will rejoice in the Holy One of Israel.*

No doubt, if the verse is intact, it is about the humble people who accept the God of Jacob. The Holy One is mentioned in several places in the Bible such as Isaiah 40:25, 1 Samuel 6:20, Habakkuk 1:12, and so on, all referring to God.

Verse 24 completes the prophecy:

24 Those who are wayward in spirit will gain understanding; those who complain will accept instruction."

Again, it is about people who were wayward (disobedient, fractious, and intractable); this may refer to any nation, including Arabs.

In summary, Isaiah 29 is a prophetic passage concerning a nation in darkness, without revelation. The chapter has focused on two matters: a person who is able to read but do not want to read and a person who is given revelation but cannot read. The factual interpretation for the first part is Israelites who rejected the Christ and for the second part is Prophet Muhammad$_{pbuh}$, who were not learned when the Quran was revealed to him.

An Everlasting Scroll and Five People (Isaiah 30)

Chapter 30 of Isaiah talks about the Israelite who consulted Egypt and Pharaoh instead of God, they chose the enemy of God instead of Him. The entire chapter is metaphoric. I do not know why the interpreters have taken it literal.

Jews are called *obstinate children* in verse one, who chose Egypt and Pharaoh instead of God. Verse 5 predicts a shameful end to this.

Isaiah Chapter 30
NIV
1 "Woe to the obstinate children", declares the LORD, "to those who carry out plans that are not mine, forming an alliance, but not by my Spirit, heaping sin upon sin;
2 who go down to Egypt without consulting me; who look for help to Pharaoh's protection, to Egypt's shade for refuge.
3 But Pharaoh's protection will be to your shame, Egypt's shade will bring you disgrace.
4 Though they have officials in Zoan and their envoys have arrived in Hanes,
5 everyone will be put to shame because of a people useless to them, who bring neither help nor advantage, but only shame and disgrace."

Verse 6 goes to Negev[a], a place in southern Palestine and Iraq near the River Euphrates (called Najaf in the local language). However, verse 7 goes back again to Egypt. It clearly shows that the Egypt in this passage is not the *land* or *people of Egypt* but a symbol of devilish power. It is not the only time names are being used

---

[a] The word Negev is discussed in Chapter 4 – Imam Hussain in the Bible, under "Sufyani and Mahdi (Isaiah 21)".

symbolically in the Bible. The Bible is an abundant source of figurative statements, such as *Song of the Vineyard* (Isa. 5:1-7), *I am the true Vine* (John 15:1-6), *I, wisdom, dwell with prudence* (Prov. 8:12), *Drink water from your own cistern, and fresh water from your own well* (Prov. 5:15), *A man reaps what he sows* (Gal. 6:7b) and so forth.

6 A prophecy concerning the animals of the Negev: Through a land of hardship and distress, of lions and lionesses, of adders and darting snakes, the envoys carry their riches on donkeys' backs, their treasures on the humps of camels, to that unprofitable nation, 7 to Egypt, whose help is utterly useless. Therefore I call her Rahab the Do-Nothing.

Verse 8 talks about a scroll, an everlasting witness:

8 Go now, write it on a tablet for them, inscribe it on a scroll, that for the days to come it may be an everlasting witness.

Verse 17 is also interesting:

17 A thousand will flee at the threat of one; at the threat of five you will all flee away, till you are left like a flagstaff on a mountaintop, like a banner on a hill."

I could not find any interpretation for verse 17 from any exegeses, except what is commonly said, "It represents victory of the underestimated power of God over exaggerated force of devil". The question, or better to say *the objection*, for such interpretation is "why at the threat of *five* you will all flee away"; why not six or seven or ... other numbers? The answer is clear: there is a meaning in the *five*, but the Bible scholars have ignored it. Not even one commentary mentions any importance for the number five in the verse.

We have to use historical facts to pull out the real meaning of verse 17. "A thousand will flee at the threat of one and at the threat of five you will all flee away" has a message, may be eschatological, chronological or both.

The first one, eschatological message, could only be true by coming of the final man of God, the Mahdi$_{pbuh}$ in Islamic belief, the second coming of Jesus$_{pbuh}$ in Christianity, or Meshiach in Jewish faith. Nevertheless, it has not happened yet.

The second one, chronological message, of the *five* in particular, has only one application; and that is the Five members of the household of the Prophet of Islam, known as the Ahl –al Bait. They are undoubtedly famous among all Muslims. This is the same "5" that God gave to Abraham when He said: "No longer will you be called Abram, your name will be Abraham, for I have made you a father of many nations." (Genesis 17:5) Letter ה "h", given to Abram in the verse, equals number 5 in Hebrew numeric system. Please note the number of the verse (5). Interestingly the verse in Isaiah 30, which states the importance of the number 5 is verse 17, correlating to chapter 17 of Genesis.

This is after Abraham's first son, Ishmael, was born. It is coherent and concurrent with Genesis 17:20, where God promises to bless Ishmael, to make him fruitful and to bring forth twelve princes from Meodmeod (See Chapter 2 – The Prophet and Twelve Princes). When we read Isaiah 30, we will find more proof for this interpretation.

Isaiah 30:21 brings up another fact:

21 Whether you turn to the right or to the left, your ears will hear a voice behind you, saying, "This is the way; walk in it."

What can be around children of Jacob except the children of Ismael, the Muslims? We read in the Holy Quran:

Quran (Al-Nahl) 16:125[26]
Invite (all) to the Way of thy Lord with wisdom and beautiful preaching; and argue with them in ways that are best and most gracious: for thy Lord knoweth best, who have strayed from His Path, and who receive guidance.

Interestingly the passage is about Abraham$_{pbuh}$, as it says:

Quran (Al-Nahl) 16:120-124[26]
120 Abraham was indeed a model, devoutly obedient to Allah, (and) true in Faith, and he joined not gods with Allah: 121 He showed his gratitude for the favours of Allah, who chose him, and guided him to a Straight Way. 122 And We gave him Good in this world, and he will be, in the Hereafter, in the ranks of the Righteous. 123 So We have taught thee the inspired (Message), "Follow the ways of Abraham the True in Faith, and he joined not gods with Allah." 124 The Sabbath was only made (strict) for those who disagreed (as to its observance); But Allah will judge between them on the Day of Judgment, as to their differences.

Isaiah 30:25 is most likely talking about the event of Karbala. Its eschatological possibility is also high. In verse 26, we find a good evidence for attributing these metaphors to the coming of Islam.

25 In the day of great slaughter, when the towers fall, streams of water will flow on every high mountain and every lofty hill. 26 The moon will shine like the sun, and the sunlight will be seven times brighter, like the light of seven full days, when the LORD binds up the bruises of his people and heals the wounds he inflicted.

It talks about *Mekka* (but translated to: "their wounds"), it is the second word from last in Hebrew (see Figure 65 and Figure 66). The common Bible translations have interpreted *Makkah* as if it is from Hebrew word "nakah"!

[There are other forms of the word *Mekka* in the Bible such as Meka, Maka and so on.]

Below is the rendered translation:

Isaiah 30:26
The moon will shine like the sun, and the sunlight will be seven times brighter, like the light of seven full days, when the LORD binds up the fracture of his people and heals the bruise of Makkah (Makkeh).

Verse 27 states: "the name of the Lord comes from far". The common biblical interpreters are referring it to Seir or Sinai!

27 See, the Name of the LORD comes from afar, with burning anger and dense clouds of smoke; his lips are full of wrath, and his tongue is a consuming fire.

Verse 31 completes the prophecy:

31 The voice of the LORD will shatter Assyria; with his rod he will strike them down

Assyria is an area covering northern Iraq, Syria, Turkey and Iran; its capital, Neinawa (Nineveh), is the area where event of Karbala took place. Figure 67 is the definition of Assyria according to ATS Bible Dictionary.

Figure 65

4347. makkah or makkeh[1]

Strong's Concordance

makkah or makkeh: a blow, wound, slaughter

Original Word: מַכָּה
Part of Speech: Noun Feminine
Transliteration: makkah or makkeh
Phonetic Spelling: (mak-kaw')
Short Definition: slaughter

NAS Exhaustive Concordance

Word Origin
from nakah
Definition
a blow, wound, slaughter
NASB Translation
blow (1), casualties (1), crushed (1), disasters (1), inflicted (1), injury (1), plague (3), plagues (4), slaughter (14), stripes (1), strokes (2), wound (8), wounded (1), wounds (9).

THE SPIRIT OF TRUTH   Chapter 6 – Isaiah and Islam

Figure 66
Isaiah 30:26[1]

▲ **Isaiah 30:26** ▼

Isaiah 30 Interlinear

Strong's	Hebrew	Transliteration	English	Part
1961 [e]	וְהָיָה	wə-hā-yāh	and shall be	Verb
216 [e]	אוֹר	'ō-wr-	26	Noun
3842 [e]	הַלְּבָנָה	hal-lə-ḇā-nāh	Moreover the light of the moon	Noun
216 [e]	כְּאוֹר	kə-'ō-wr	as the light	Noun
2535 [e]	הַחַמָּה	ha-ḥam-māh,	of the sun	Noun
216 [e]	וְאוֹר	wə-'ō-wr	and the light	Noun
2535 [e]	הַחַמָּה	ha-ḥam-māh	of the sun	Noun
1961 [e]	יִהְיֶה	yih-yeh	shall be	Verb
7659 [e]	שִׁבְעָתַיִם	šiḇ-'ā-ṯa-yim,	sevenfold	Noun
216 [e]	כְּאוֹר	kə-'ō-wr	as the light	Noun
7651 [e]	שִׁבְעַת	šiḇ-'aṯ	of seven	Noun
3117 [e]	הַיָּמִים	hay-yā-mîm;	days	Noun
3117 [e]	בְּיוֹם	bə-yō-wm,	on the day	Noun
2280 [e]	חֲבֹשׁ	ḥă-ḇōš	binds up	Verb
3068 [e]	יְהוָה	Yah-weh	that the LORD	Noun
853 [e]	אֶת־	'eṯ-	-	Acc
7667 [e]	שֶׁבֶר	še-ḇer	the breach	Noun
5971 [e]	עַמּוֹ	'am-mōw,	of his people	Noun
4347 [e]	מַכָּתוֹ	mak-kā-ṯōw	of their wound	Noun
4273 [e]	וּמַחַץ	ū-ma-ḥaṣ	and the stroke	Noun
7495 [e]	יִרְפָּא	yir-pā	heals	Verb
			s	-

319

Figure 67

ATS Bible Dictionary[51]

Assyria

A celebrated country and empire, had its name from Ahur, or Assur, the second son of Shem, who settled in that region, Genesis 10:22. In the Bible the name Assyria is employed in three different significations: namely, 1. Assyria ancient and proper lay east of the Tigris, between Armenia, Susiana, and Media, and appears to have comprehended the six provinces attributed to it by Ptolemy, namely, Arrapachis, Adiabene, Arbelis, (now Erbil,) Calachene, (Heb. Halah- 2 Kings 17:6,) Apollonias, and Sittacne. It is the region which mostly comprises the modern Kurdistan and the pashalik of Mosul. Of these provinces, Adiabene was the most fertile and important; in it was situated Nineveh the capital; and the term Assyria, in its most narrow sense, seems sometimes to have meant only this province. 2. Most generally, Assyria means the Kingdom of Assyria, including Babylonia and Mesopotamia, and extending to the Euphrates, which is therefore used by Isaiah as an image of this empire, Isaiah 7:20; 8:7. In one instance, the idea of the empire predominates so as to exclude that of Assyria proper, namely, Genesis 2:14, where the Hiddekel or Tigris is said to flow eastward of Assyria. 3. After the overthrow of the Assyrian state, the name continued to be applied to those countries which had been formerly under its dominion, namely, (a) To Babylonia, 2 Kings 23:29; Jeremiah 2:18. (b) To Persia, Ezra 6:22, where Darius is also called king of Assyria.

The coded letters in verses 32 and 33 add up even more mystery to the cryptic prophecies of Isaiah 30. (Read from right to left)

30:32   at the end of verse   (ק :במ [בה כ])   (q: m b [k h f])
30:33   in the middle   (ק היא) [הוא כ]   (q a y h) [k a v h]
And at the end: ס (s)

No comment is given to these letters so far. Perhaps, what I could relate them to, is that they stand for important phrases discussed throughout the chapter. If we take them as Islamic names and terminologies, we are not contradicting the context and in fact, they are very relevant to it.

(Read from right to left)
Isaiah 30:32 *(ק :במ [בה כ])*   *(q: m b [k h f])*

- Possibility 1:

Furqan, Hitgalut, Kitab/Kalemah, Bi Muhammad$_{pbuh}$, Quran.
It means: *Furqan, Revelation, Book /Word, to Muhammad$_{pbuh}$, Quran*

- Possibility 2:

Fahadza Kitabun Bi Muhammad: Quran
Meaning: *This is the book through/to Muhammad: Quran*

Isaiah 30:33 ס *(ק היא) [הוא כ] s (q a y h) [k a v h]*

h: Hitgalut (Revelation) or number 5 (the household of the Prophet)
v: Va (and)   a: Allah   k: Kitab (book) or Kalimah (word)
h: Hitgalut (Revelation) or number 5 (the household of the Prophet)   y: yah (Oh)   a: Allah
q: Quran   s: Salute (Arabic: Salawat) or Salaat (Prayer)

My Messenger, My Muslim (Isaiah 42:19)

Isaiah 42, another seriously disputed passage, gives details of the one whom God is pleased. God calls him "<u>my servant</u>", "my messenger", "my Muslim" who *will bring justice to the nations; a meek, mild, gentle, quiet, and humble teacher of the Islands.* He is called "Zediq" in Hebrew, "a guidance for Gentiles", "chosen" (in Hebrew: baw-kheer'); *new song he will sing and Kedar will rejoice,* says the Isaiah.

There are many opinions about who "the servant" is in Isaiah 42, the following three are the main ones:

1. Some believe that the "servant" in Isaiah 42 is the Israelite, Jacob and his people.
2. Some say, it is Cyrus the Great, the king of Persia.
3. According to mainstream Christianity, it is Jesus Christ$_{pbuh}$.

The following lines are examining chapter 42 to clarify the truth.

Isaiah 42 (NIV)
*1 "Here is my servant, whom I uphold, my **chosen one** in whom **I delight**; I will put my Spirit on him, and he will bring justice to the **nations**.*

The word translated to "nations" in Hebrew Bible is גוים (gō-w-yim). No doubt, it means Non-Jews (Gentiles), as the KJB also translates so:

Isaiah 42:1(KJB)
Behold my servant, whom I uphold; mine elect, in whom my soul delighteth; I have put my spirit upon him: he shall bring forth judgment to the <u>Gentiles</u>.

Verses 2 and 3 are emphasizing his humble, quiet and just manner.

2 He will not shout or cry out, or raise his voice in the streets. 3 A bruised reed he will not break, and a smoldering wick he will not snuff out. In faithfulness he will bring forth justice;

Verse 4 is about his Just government in the lands far from Judea, "the islands". It may have an end time prophecy too.

*4 he will not falter or be discouraged till he establishes justice on earth. In his teaching the islands will put their hope."
5 This is what God the* LORD *says— the Creator of the heavens, who stretches them out, who spreads out the earth with all that springs from it, who gives breath to its people, and life to those who walk on it.*

In verse 6, he is called צדק "ṣe-deq", translated to "righteousness". He is also guidance (light) to Gentiles. (Table 47)

6 "I, the LORD, *have called you **in righteousness**; I will take hold of your hand. I will keep you and will make you to be a covenant for the people and a **light for the Gentiles**,
7 to open eyes that are blind, to free captives from prison and to release from the dungeon those who sit in darkness.
8 "I am the* LORD; *that is my name! I will not yield my glory to another or my praise to idols.*

Some have taken the first part of verse 7 (*to open eyes that are blind*) literally, relating it to Jesus[pbuh]. But, at the same time, they have considered the rest of verse (*to free captives from prison and to release from the dungeon those who sit in darkness*) as symbolic statements.

Table 47

Text Analysis[1]   **Isaiah 42:6**

Str	Translit	Hebrew	English	Morph
589 [e]	'ă-nî	אֲנִי	I [am]	Pro
3068 [e]	Yah-weh	יְהוָה	the LORD	Noun
7121 [e]	qə-rā-tî-kā	קְרָאתִיךָ	have called you	Verb
6664 [e]	bə-ṣe-deq	בְצֶדֶק	in righteousness	Noun

In verses 9 and 10, we are told that the revelation will be different from the old one; and it is going to be a new song (not Hebrew), from a far place.

*9 See, the former things have taken place, and **new things I declare**; before they spring into being I announce them to you." 10 Sing to the* LORD ***a new song***, *his praise from the ends of the earth, you who go down to the sea, and all that is in it, you islands, and all who live in them.*

In verse 11, it is perfectly pointed out that the passage is about Arabia, where Kedar[a] lives:

11 Let the wilderness and its towns raise their voices; **let the settlements where Kedar lives rejoice.** *Let the* **people of Sela**[b] *sing for joy; let them shout from the mountaintops.*
12 Let them give glory to the LORD *and proclaim his praise in the islands.*

Verses 11 and 12 illustrate the pilgrimage to Mekka and Azan, *call for prayer*. The verses after, take a furious and warlike mood:

13 The LORD *will march out like a champion, like a warrior he will stir up his zeal; with a shout he will raise the battle cry and will triumph over his enemies. 14 "For a long time I have kept silent, I have been quiet and held myself back. But now, like a woman in childbirth, I cry out, I gasp and pant. 15 I will lay waste the mountains and hills and dry up all their vegetation; I will turn rivers into islands and dry up the pools.*

Verse 16 is again emphasizing a revelation to people who never had guidance, people living in darkness:

16 I will lead the blind by ways they have not known, along unfamiliar paths I will guide them; I will turn the darkness into light before them and make the rough places smooth. These are the things I will do; I will not forsake them.

Verses 17 and 18 remind that the idol worshipers are the subject of the prophecy:

---

[a] Kedar (or Qidar) is the second son of Ishmael$_{pbuh}$. (Genesis 25:13)
[b] Sela is said to be the city of Edomites. Edom is another name of Esau, brother of Jacob. Another opinion on that is the desert of Arabia. (See Barnes' Notes on the Bible)

17 But those who trust in idols, who say to images, 'You are our gods,' will be turned back in utter shame. 18 "Hear, you deaf; look, you blind, and see!

Isaiah 42 in verse 19 clarifies that the messenger is called "Muslim". The word משלם "m-šul-lām" is translated to "covenant". In some Bibles, it is written exactly as "Muslim" (See Figure 68 – Persian Bible).

Figure 68[a]

۱۸ ای کران بشنوید و ای کوران نظر کنید تا ببینید. ۱۹ کیست که مثل بنده من کور باشد و کیست که کر باشد، مثل مُسلم من و کور مانند بنده خداوند؟ ۲۰ چیزهای بسیار می‌بینی امّا نگاه نمی‌داری. گوش‌ها باز است امّا نمی‌شنود. ۲۱ خداوند را به خاطر عدل خود پسند آمد که شریعت خویش را تعظیم و تکریم نماید. ۲۲ لیکن

He is also called the servant of the LORD, in Arabic عبدالله "Abdullah". Abdullah is another epithet of the Prophet and his father's name as well. Furthermore, the Quran calls the Prophet "His servant" (Quran 17:1, 18:1, 25:1 …):

Quran 18:1[26]
Praise be to Allah, Who hath sent to His Servant the Book, and hath allowed therein no Crookedness.

The Arabic translation of the Smith & Van Dyke avoided use of m-šul-lām by translating it to كامل "kaamel", meaning "perfect". I

---

[a] https://www.razgah.com/ (accessed February 9, 2017)

understand the reason, because it is a conclusive proof for every reader that Isaiah is prophesying the *Muslim* Prophet; so they translated it to "perfect". (See below)

Arabic: Smith & Van Dyke[1] أشعياء ٤٢:١٩

من هو اعمى الا عبدي واصم كرسولي الذي أرسله. من هو اعمى كالكامل واعمى كعبد الرب.

Some English translations, such as NIV, write *"covenant with me"*.

Isaiah 42:19
NIV
19 Who is blind but my servant, and deaf like **the messenger I send**? *Who is blind like the one in* <u>**covenant with me,**</u> *blind like* **the servant of the LORD**?

Here is the rendered translation:

Isaiah 42:19
Who is blind but my servant, and deaf like **the messenger I send**?
Who is blind like **the Muslim***, blind like* **the servant of he LORD**?

If I had to translate it into Arabic, no Arab would think that it is foretelling anyone other than prophet Muhammad_{pbuh}. This is how it would look like in Arabic:

من هو اعمى الا عبدي واصم كرسولي الذي أرسله. من هو اعمى كالمسلم واعمى كالعبد الله.

Re-rendering the English translation makes it even more transparent:

Isaiah 42:19
Who is blind but my servant, and deaf like **the messenger I send**?
Who is blind like the **Muslim***, blind like* **the Abdu-Allah**?

327

What "blind" likely could mean here is that he himself cannot see the truth, cannot read the scroll, and has no vision of his own. He will be sent by God, as a Muslim, and whatever he sees is from God not himself, opposing the idea of "a visionary or dreamlike revelation" proposed by some so called "scholars".

Believing that the blindness of the messenger of God is literal has no evidence; or taking it as a spiritual defection and decisiveness makes no sense at all. How a messenger of God can guide people if he himself is misguided. Therefore, a reasonable interpretation of the *blind* is that he must be an *illiterate* and *unlearned* man. That comes to reality with Prophet Muhammad_pbuh.

Some commentaries attribute *blind* and *deaf* messenger to the Jews who is "perfect"; here is one of them:

Figure 69

Barnes' Notes on the Bible[1]

Who is blind, but my servant? ... As he that is perfect - (כמשלם kîmeshullâm). A great variety of interpretations has been offered on this word - arising from the difficulty of giving the appellation 'perfect' to a people so corrupt as were the Jews in the time of Isaiah. Jerome renders it, Qui venundatus est - 'He that is sold.' The Syriac renders it, 'Who is blind as the prince?' Symmachus renders it, Ὡς ὁ τέλειος hōs ho teleios; and Kimchi in a similar manner by תמים tâmîym - 'perfect.'

However, Ellicott's Commentary could not miss the point. It mentions the connection between "m-šul-lām" and Muslim. (Figure 70)

Figure 70

Ellicott's Commentary for English Readers[1]

(19) **Deaf, as my messenger . . .**—The work of the messenger of God had been the ideal of Isaiah, as it was of *the* servant in whom the ideal was realised (Romans 10:15; Isaiah 42:1). But how could a blind and deaf messenger, like the actual Israel, do his work effectually? (Psalm 123:2).

As he that is perfect.—Strictly speaking, *the devoted,* or *surrendered one.* The Hebrew *meshullam* is interesting, as connected with the modern *Moslem* and *Islam,* the man *resigned* to the will of God. The frequent use of this, or a cognate form, as a proper name after the exile (1Chronicles 9:21; Ezra 8:6; Ezra 10:15; Nehemiah 3:4) may (on either assumption as to the date of 2 Isaiah) be connected with it by some link of causation. Other meanings given to it have been "perfect" as in the Authorised Version, "confident," "recompensed," "meritorious."

It is very hard to understand that why such a simple word should be complicated to the "scholars". I have met people of different nationalities; Asian, Russian, Greek, German, British, Scandinavian, South American, African and so forth. Some happened to ask if I am a Muslim. I replied them: "yes". I never thought *how they knew the word "Muslim"*. No one in my lifetime has come across asking me what "Muslim" is.

Now I wished I could meet Isaiah and have the honour of a short conversation with him. I would clarify with him if he really called the Jews "the idol worshipers" not the Yahweh worshipers, "the

Muslim" not Jewish, "Kedar" not Judea or Israelite, and "Gentiles" not Jews.

Well, let us be honest; no need to meet Isaiah, just read his words the way they are. No one can do a better job than what Isaiah has done. There is a reason for calling him "The Prince of Hebrew Prophets"; he is not vague, fearful or incomprehensible. He is formidable and straightforward in his numerous prophecies. He has never left a prophetic passage without clear evidence on the subject of his prophecy. Nevertheless, why so many confusions and disputes exist amongst exegetes? The answer lies under the manipulation of the words and context. They interpret it, as they like, rather than reading it the way it is. This has been an ongoing story.

After Ahmed (Isaiah 59)

Isaiah chapter 59 is another outstanding text filled with prophetic statements. It is very enlightening to spend days studying this chapter. Christians see it through the teachings of Church Fathers. Jews see it through their own way. I like to see it the way it is written in the Hebrew text.

It is commonly believed that Isaiah, in this chapter, is addressing the Israelite and prophesying coming of the Messiah. The following examination, using only the Hebrew text refutes such claim. The chapter points out that Isaiah is talking about Gentiles, not Jews. He mentions exalted Islamic figures such as, Ahmed (Prophet Muhammad$_{pbuh}$), Lady Sediqa$_{pbuh}$ (the Prophet's daughter), and Imam Naqi$_{pbuh}$ (Imam Al-Hadi, the tenth Imam).

Isaiah 59 is about the early Islamic era: Right after the Prophet's death, people did not follow the guidance and turned away from the right path and therefore justice departed from their society and God left them alone. Isaiah affirms that Jesus$_{pbuh}$ will be absent in the timeline of the prophecy, but his name has been interpreted as "salvation" or "deliverance".

Verses 1 to 7 explain the reason for separation of God from people:

Isaiah 59 (NIV)
1 Surely the arm of the LORD *is not too short to save, nor his ear too dull to hear. 2 But your iniquities have separated you from your God; your sins have hidden his face from you, so that he will not hear. 3 For your hands are stained with blood, your fingers with guilt. Your lips have spoken falsely, and your tongue mutters wicked things. 4 No one calls for justice; no one pleads a case with integrity. They rely on empty arguments, they utter lies; they conceive trouble and give birth to evil. 5 They hatch the eggs of vipers and spin a spider's web. Whoever eats their eggs will die,*

and when one is broken, an adder is hatched. 6 Their cobwebs are useless for clothing; they cannot cover themselves with what they make. Their deeds are evil deeds, and acts of violence are in their hands.

To whom are these verses addressed, Israelites, Gentiles, or both? The answer comes in the following verses:

7 Their feet rush into sin; they are swift to shed innocent blood. They pursue evil schemes; acts of violence mark their ways. 8 The way of peace they do not know; there is no justice in their paths. They have turned them into crooked roads; no one who walks along them will know peace.

Verse 7 contains a well-known word to Muslims: נקי *nā-qî*, translated to "innocent". (See Table 48) He is the tenth Imam of Shi'ite Muslims who became Imam at the age of 7. Is it a coincident to have his name in verse 7?

Imam Naqi$_{pbuh}$, also known as "Al-Hadi" (meaning "the Guide"), lived in Medina until age of 30. He trained many people during his life. His miracles made some people to call him "God". The Imam strictly denounced those people and ordered his followers to exonerate from such thoughts.

At the age of 30, he was summoned to Samarra (in Iraq) by the Abbasid Caliph, Al-Mutawakkil. [Jesus$_{pbuh}$ started his ministry at age of 30.] It was an era of mistreatment and custody toward the Imam. There, the Caliph and his authorities treated him rough. He was poisoned at the age of 40 by the Caliph and was buried in Samarra. He was Imam for 33 years. [Jesus$_{pbuh}$ lived for the same number of years before his ascension.]

Verse 8 gives evidence: Islam (from Hebrew שלום *šā-lō-wm*). It occurs twice in the verse; but translated to "peace". (Table 49)

Below are the Hebrew texts and the analysis of verses 7 and 8:

Isaiah 59:7 WLC (Consonants Only) [1]

רגליהם לרע ירצו וימהרו לשפך דם נקי מחשבותיהם מחשבות און שד ושבר במסלותם:

Isaiah 59:8 WLC (Consonants Only) [1]

דרך שלום לא ידעו ואין משפט במעגלותם נתיבותיהם עקשו להם כל דרך בה לא ידע שלום:

Table 48

Text Analysis[1] Isaiah 59:7

Str	Translit	Hebrew	English	Morph
7272 [e]	raḡ-lê-hem	רַגְלֵיהֶם	Their feet	Noun
7451 [e]	lā-raʿ	לָרַע	to evil	Adj
7323 [e]	yā-ru-ṣū,	יָרֻצוּ	run	Verb
4116 [e]	wî-ma-hă-rū,	וִימַהֲרוּ	they make haste	Verb
8210 [e]	liš-pōk	לִשְׁפֹּךְ	to shed	Verb
1818 [e]	dām	דָּם	blood	Noun
5355 [e]	nā-qî;	נָקִי	innocent	Adj
4284 [e]	maḥ-šə-ḇō-w-tê-hem	מַחְשְׁבוֹתֵיהֶם	their thoughts [are]	Noun
4284 [e]	maḥ-šə-ḇō-wt	מַחְשְׁבוֹת	thoughts	Noun
205 [e]	'ā-wen,	אָוֶן	of iniquity	Noun
7701 [e]	šōḏ	שֹׁד	wasting	Noun
7667 [e]	wā-še-ḇer	וָשֶׁבֶר	and destruction [are]	Noun
4546 [e]	bim-sil-lō-w-tām.	בִּמְסִלּוֹתָם׃	in their paths	Noun

Table 49
Text Analysis[1]   Isaiah 59:8

Str	Translit	Hebrew	English	Morph
1870 [e]	de-rek	דֶּרֶךְ	The way	Noun
7965 [e]	šā-lō-wm	שָׁלוֹם	of peace	Noun
3808 [e]	lō	לֹא	not	Adv
3045 [e]	yā-dā-'ū,	יָדָעוּ	do they know	Verb
369 [e]	wə-'ên	וְאֵין	and no	Prt
4941 [e]	miš-pāṭ	מִשְׁפָּט	[there is] judgment	Noun
4570 [e]	bə-ma'-gə-lō-w-tām;	בְּמַעְגְּלוֹתָם	in their tracks	Noun
5410 [e]	nə-tî-ḇō-w-tê-hem	נְתִיבוֹתֵיהֶם	paths	Noun
6140 [e]	'iq-qə-šū	עִקְּשׁוּ	they have made them	Verb
1992 [e]	lā-hem,	לָהֶם	like	Pro
3605 [e]	kōl	כֹּל	whoever	Noun
1869 [e]	dō-rêk	דֹּרֵךְ	goes	Verb
	bāh,	בָּהּ	in	Prep
3808 [e]	lō	לֹא	not	Adv
3045 [e]	yā-da'	יָדַע	do know	Verb
7965 [e]	šā-lō-wm.	שָׁלוֹם׃	peace	Noun

335

Rendered translation:

Isaiah 59:7, 8
7 Their feet rush into sin; they are swift to shed blood of Naqi. They pursue evil schemes; acts of violence mark their ways.
8 The way of Islam they do not know; there is no justice in their paths. They have turned them into crooked roads; no one who walks along them will know Islam.

Continuing to the next verses:

NIV
9 So justice is far from us, and righteousness does not reach us. We look for light, but all is darkness; for brightness, but we walk in deep shadows. 10 Like the blind we grope along the wall, feeling our way like people without eyes. At midday we stumble as if it were twilight; among the strong, we are like the dead. 11 We all growl like bears; we moan mournfully like doves. We look for justice, but find none; for deliverance, but it is far away.

Verse 11 in Hebrew says that לִישׁוּעָה *lî-šū-'āh* (meaning "for Jesus") is away. It emphasizes that Jesus$_{pbuh}$ is absent, physically and theologically. However, îšū'āh (Jesus) is translated to "deliverance" or "salvation". (Table 50[1])

Table 50
Text Analysis[1]   Isaiah 59:11

3444 [e]	lî-šū-'āh[a]	לִישׁוּעָה	For salvation	Noun
7368 [e]	rā-hă-qāh	רָחֲקָה	[but] it is far off	Verb
4480 [e]	mim-men-nū.	מִמֶּנּוּ׃	from	Prep

Rendered translation:
Isaiah 59:11
We all growl like bears; we moan mournfully like doves. We look for justice, but find none; for Jesus is far away.

The verse is talking about the absence of Jesus[pbuh] and lack of Justice in the era when these prophecies are to take place.

As shown in Table 51 and Table 52, verses 14 and 15 have an equivocal phrase: אמת 'ĕ-met, pronounced as "ehmet". It is translated to "truth". As it was explained in Chapter 2 – The Prophet and Twelve Princes, under "Ehmet and Ahmed", Ehmet is indeed Ahmed, which is another name of Prophet Muhammad[pbuh].

---

[a] lî-šū-'āh consists of "le" and "ishua" means: "for (because) Jesus".

Table 51

Text Analysis[1]   Isaiah 59:14

Str	Translit	Hebrew	English	Morph
5253 [e]	wə-hus-saḡ	וְהֻסַּג	and is turned away	Verb
268 [e]	'ā-ḥō-wr	אָחוֹר	backward	Subst
4941 [e]	miš-pāṭ,	מִשְׁפָּט	judgment	Noun
6666 [e]	ū-ṣə-ḏā-qāh	וּצְדָקָה	and justice	Noun
7350 [e]	mê-rā-ḥō-wq	מֵרָחוֹק	afar off	Adj
5975 [e]	ta-'ă-mōḏ;	תַּעֲמֹד	stands	Verb
3588 [e]	kî-	כִּי־	for	Conj
3782 [e]	kā-šə-lāh	כָשְׁלָה	is fallen	Verb
7339 [e]	bā-rə-ḥō-wb	בָרְחוֹב	in the street	Noun
571 [e]	'ĕ-meṯ,	אֱמֶת	for truth	Noun
5229 [e]	ū-nə-ḵō-ḥāh	וּנְכֹחָה	and equity	Adj
3808 [e]	lō-	לֹא־	not	Adv
3201 [e]	ṯū-ḵal	תוּכַל	do	Verb
935 [e]	lā-ḇō-w.	לָבוֹא׃	enter	Verb

Table 52

Text Analysis[1] Isaiah 59:15

Str	Translit	Hebrew	English	Morph
1961 [e]	wat-tə-hî	וַתְּהִי	and fails	Verb
571 [e]	hā-'ĕ-met	הָאֱמֶת	truth	Noun
5737 [e]	ne'-de-ret,	נֶעְדֶּרֶת	fails	Verb
5493 [e]	wə-sār	וְסָר	[that] and he departs	Verb
7451 [e]	mê-rā'	מֵרָע	from evil	Adj
7997 [e]	miš-tō-w-lêl;	מִשְׁתּוֹלֵל	makes himself a prey	Verb
7200 [e]	way-yar	וַיַּרְא	and saw	Verb
3068 [e]	Yah-weh	יְהוָה	the LORD	Noun
7489 [e]	way-yê-ra'	וַיֵּרַע	and it displeased	Verb
5869 [e]	bə-'ê-nāw	בְּעֵינָיו	in His sight	Noun
3588 [e]	kî-	כִּי־	that	Conj
369 [e]	'ên	אֵין	not	Prt
4941 [e]	miš-pāṭ.	מִשְׁפָּט׃	[there was] judgment	Noun

339

Isaiah 59:14 WLC (Consonants Only) [1]
והסג אחור משפט וצדקה מרחוק תעמד כי־כשלה ברחוב אמת ונכחה לא־תוכל לבוא:

Isaiah 59:15 WLC (Consonants Only) [1]
ותהי האמת נעדרת וסר מרע משתולל וירא יהוה וירע בעיניו כי־אין משפט:

Isaiah 59:14, 15
NIV
14 So justice is driven back, and righteousness stands at a distance; truth has stumbled in the streets, honesty cannot enter. 15 Truth is nowhere to be found, and whoever shuns evil becomes a prey. The LORD looked and was displeased that there was no justice.

If we keep אמת ('ĕ-met) as it is, the result is remarkable. It illustrates the history of early Islam right after the death of the Prophet.

Rendered translation:
14 So justice is driven back, and righteousness stands at a distance; Ahmed has stumbled in the streets, honesty cannot enter. 15 Ahmed is gone, and whoever shuns evil becomes a prey. The LORD looked and was displeased that there was no justice.

As a complementary to what is said, verse 16 appears to be foretelling the story of Imam Ali$_{pbuh}$, whom the Muslims gave their allegiance at the time of the Prophet but they turned their back to him after the Prophet's death. In this verse, he is pictured as a man who has no helper but his own righteousness and helmet. He will punish the enemies accordingly; will help the poor, and finally the

West will be afraid of the name of Lord. Below is the NIV translation.

Isaiah 59:16
NIV
He saw that there was no one, he was appalled that there was no one to intervene; so his own arm achieved salvation for him, and his own righteousness sustained him.

The "righteousness" is a translation of Hebrew צדקת *ṣid-qā-ṯ*; identical to Arabic صديقة "*seddiqat*" (or "seddigah"), which is the epithet of Prophet Muhammad's daughter_pbuh, the wife of Imam Ali_pbuh. She was the supporter of the Imam. Shortly after her father, she passed away due to an inroad into her house. This is explained in verses 14, 15 and 16.

Rendered translation of verse 16:

He saw that there was no one, he was appalled that there was no one to intervene; so his own arm achieved salvation for him, and his Seddiqah sustained him.

Verse 17 explains figuratively his righteousness and his defensive wars: (NIV)

17 He put on righteousness as his breastplate, and the helmet of salvation on his head; he put on the garments of vengeance and wrapped himself in zeal as in a cloak.

There are two words in verses 16 and 17, צִדְקָתוֹ *ṣid-qā-ṯōw* and צְדָקָה *ṣə-ḏā-qāh*; despite the different spellings, both are translated to "righteousness". However, for every Arab speaker the first word (צִדְקָתוֹ *ṣid-qā-ṯōw*) is nothing but a name, as It is pointed out in the rendered translation of verse 16.

Verse 18 emphasizes his fearlessness to his enemies and his kindness to poor and strangers (islands).

18 According to what they have done, so will he repay wrath to his enemies and retribution to his foes; he will repay the islands their due.

Verse 19 starts with an interesting phrase, "from the West":

19 From the west, people will fear the name of the LORD, and from the rising of the sun, they will revere his glory. For he will come like a pent-up flood that the breath of the LORD drives along.

The question is "west of what?" Is this about Israelite? There is no west to the habitats of Israelite. It must be talking about an eastern land that has an opposing western land.

The last verse of this chapter, verse 20, makes it clear that the prophesied one is not from Zion but *to Zion*, not from Israelite, not even to Israelite but *to the Israelite who repent their sins*.

20 "The Redeemer will come to Zion, to those in Jacob who repent of their sins",

The early history of Islam confirms that many Jews accepted truthfulness of the Prophet of Islam, not to mention, even today, many are embracing it. As stated earlier, Jesus$_{pbuh}$ also said that People of Jerusalem would not see him again unless they welcome the one who comes in the name of God:

Matthew 23:37-39
NIV
37 "Jerusalem, Jerusalem, you who kill the prophets and stone those sent to you, how often I have longed to gather your children together, as a hen gathers her chicks under her wings, and you

were not willing. 38 Look, your house is left to you desolate. 39 For I tell you, you will not see me again until you say, 'Blessed is he who comes in the name of the Lord.

This is a confirmation of the truthfulness of Prophet Muhammad$_{pbuh}$ who came in the name of God. The Quran is the only Holy Book that begins with this statement: "In the name of God, The most beneficent, The most merciful."

Matthew 23:37-39 explicitly explains that there will be no guidance from Jerusalem after Jesus$_{pbuh}$ because they have killed the prophets and stoned them to death. They will not even see Jesus$_{pbuh}$ if they do not accept the one who comes in the name of God. It reminds me another statement of Jesus$_{pbuh}$ that reassures no more revelation to come from Jerusalem:

Matthew 21:43
NIV
"Therefore I tell you that the kingdom of God will be taken away from you and given to a people who will produce its fruit."

Chapter 7 – Hajj, the Pilgrimage

The Symbol of Submission and Unity

The story of Hajj is beyond mankind's imagination. What is it about? What does it do to us? When did it come to us? And, why in Mekka? The action of circling the Cube, Ka'ba, is not limited to mankind, it is for entire universe; all shall submit to the will of the Almighty in harmony, willingly or unwillingly. However, we are given the privilege of choice.

There is nothing on pause, silence, or quiescence; all the seen and unseen are moving: circling around The One, as a symbol of submission. Electrons revolve around nuclei, planets around stars, stars around the core of galaxies, galaxies around the core of universes, multiverses around their core, and all are moving in harmony around The One. We are not an exception in the move, but in the choice.

Hajj is not a production of 1400-year-old Muslim tradition. In my opinion, it goes back to the creation of mankind. The Bible is not in shortage of words on Hajj. It mentions the Hajj in Exodus 5:1, 10:9, 12:14 and 13:6.

Genesis 22:2 reads that God ordered Abraham$_{pbuh}$ to take his *only* son for sacrifice to the land of Morriah (Marwah) ("The only son" here is assumed to be Isaac$_{pbuh}$, but historically speaking only Ishmael$_{pbuh}$ was his *only* son because he was the first son who was born 13 years before Isaac).

In Genesis, we are told that Abraham$_{pbuh}$ was 86 years old when Hagar$_{pbuh}$ gave birth to Ishmael$_{pbuh}$, and Isaac$_{pbuh}$ from Sarah$_{pbuh}$ was born when Abraham$_{pbuh}$ was a hundred. Who was Hagar? She was Sarah's maid. After a proposal given by Sarah$_{pbuh}$, she became second wife of Abraham$_{pbuh}$.

Genesis 16:16 (NIV)
Abram was eighty-six years old when Hagar bore him Ishmael.

Genesis 21:5 (NIV)
Abraham was a hundred years old when his son Isaac was born to him.

Word Hajj in Hebrew is חָגַג "chagag" (Figure 71). It is mentioned in the Bible, in several verses. In the following lines, we will examine only a few of these verses.

Figure 71

2287. chagag[1]

Strong's Concordance

chagag: to make a pilgrimage, keep a pilgrim feast

Original Word: חָגַג
Part of Speech: Verb
Transliteration: chagag
Phonetic Spelling: (khaw-gag')
Short Definition: celebrate

Brown-Driver-Briggs

[חָגַג] verb **make pilgrimage, keep a pilgrim-feast** (Arabic ‎حَجَّ‎ betake oneself to or towards an object of reverence; make a pilgrimage to Mecaa;

Moses and Hajj

Moses_pbuh mentions the pilgrimage / "festival" in the following verses. "Festival" is a translation of Hebrew חג "ḥāḡ". In Arabic, it is حج "hajj". (See Figure 71)

Exodus 5:1[a]
NIV
Afterward Moses and Aaron went to Pharaoh and said, "This is what the LORD, the God of Israel, says: 'Let my people go, so that they may hold a <u>festival</u> to me in the wilderness.'"

Exodus 12:14[b]
NIV
"This is a day you are to commemorate; for the generations to come you shall celebrate it as a <u>festival</u> to the LORD--a lasting ordinance.

Exodus 13:6
NIV
For seven days eat bread made without yeast and on the seventh day hold a <u>festival</u> to the LORD.

---

[a] Note numbers (5 and 1), demonstrates the role of 5 (corresponding to letter *h* in Hebrew, given to Abraham, and 5 households of Islam) and 1 (the oneness of God). It is interesting how the Hajj is beautifully mentioned in relation with these numbers. The word "my people" (in Hebrew עמי "'am-mî" , Arabic امّتى "Ummati") also reflects the concept of *one nation* under One God.

[b] Again numbers 12 and 14, a meaningful and supernaturally arranged to be where it supposed to be, consonant with the 14 Infallibles and the 12 Imams of Islam.

Moses_pbuh was directed to perform Hajj upon going out from Egypt, from the land of slavery to the land of freedom, from Pyramids to Ka'ba. That is why even today Jewish rabbis tie a black wooden cube, called "the phylactery"[a], around their left arm and forehead as a symbol of performing Hajj. The strap of the phylactery must be turned around the arm 7 times, just as Muslims circle the Ka'ba 7 times during the pilgrimage; and the 7 days of the special food regulations (Exodus 13:6) also commemorate the ceremony of Hajj.

As we read in the following verses, Moses_pbuh was indeed ordered to go to Mekka not Palestine.

Exodus 13:17-18
NIV
17 When Pharaoh let the people go, God did not lead them on the road through the Philistine country, though that was shorter. For God said, "If they face war, they might change their minds and return to Egypt."
18 So God led the people around by the desert road toward the Red Sea. The Israelites went up out of Egypt ready for battle.

---

[a] The phylactery contains four passages of the Torah: Ex. 13:1-10, 13: 11-16; Deu. 6:4-9 and 11:13-21.

Moses, the Tradition of Sacrifice and Ashura

Exodus 12:3 is ordering Israelite to separate a lamb per family as a sacrifice on the 10th day of Tishrei, which is exactly the 10th of Muharram, called "Ashura". That is the day Imam Hussain$_{pbuh}$ was martyred. It is discussed in Chapter 4 – Imam Hussain in the Bible, under "Ashura in the Bible".

Exodus 12:3
NIV
Tell the whole community of Israel that on the tenth day of this month each man is to take a lamb for his family, one for each household.

Every Muslim Pilgrim sacrifices a lamb/Sheep during Hajj, just as every Jewish family is required to offer a lamb, as mentioned in Exodus 12:3. [Number 12 reflects the 12 Imams and number 3 represents the third Imam, Hussain$_{pbuh}$, who was martyred on the 10th of Muharram.]

The story of Moses$_{pbuh}$ performing Hajj in Mekka is widely known to scholars. For instance, Dennis Avi Lipkin, in his book *Return to Mecca*, has articulated it in detail.

We Muslims believe in the unity of the Abrahamic faiths with no boundaries and borders. Islam is the only monotheistic faith keeps the message of unity alive, even today. Because, in Islam, every being was created as a Muslim, a submitter to the will of God. All Prophets are Muslims, all living and non-livings are Muslims.

David and Hajj

David (or perhaps someone from his offspring) prays to God and calls for his help. He dreams of the pilgrimage and wishes luck to perform it. As we read in Psalm 42:

Psalm 42
NIV
1 As the deer pants for streams of water, so my soul pants for you, my God. 2 My soul thirsts for God, for the living God. When can I go and meet with God? 3 My tears have been my food day and night, while people say to me all day long, "Where is your God?"

Then, in verse 4, he clarifies where he wishes to go:

4 These things I remember as I pour out my soul: how I used to go to the <u>house of God</u> under the protection of the Mighty One with shouts of joy and praise among the <u>festive</u> throng.

The Hebrew word translated to "house of God" is בית אלהים bêṯ 'ĕ-lō-hîm. It is بيت الله "beitu Allah" in Arabic, a famous name for Kaaba. In addition, "Festive" is from חוגג ḥō-w-ḡêḡ, or Hajj in Arabic. (See Figure 71 and Table 53)

Table 53

Text Analysis[1]   Psalm 42:4

Str	Translit	Hebrew	English	Morph
428 [e]	'êl-leh	אֵלֶּה	These	Pro
2142 [e]	'ez-kə-rāh	אֶזְכְּרָה ׀	When I remember	Verb
8210 [e]	wə-'eš-pə-kāh	וְאֶשְׁפְּכָה	[things] I pour out	Verb
5921 [e]	'ā-lay	עָלַי ׀	in	Prep
5315 [e]	nap̄-šî,	נַפְשִׁי	my soul	Noun
3588 [e]	kî	כִּי	for	Conj
5674 [e]	'e-'ĕ-ḇōr	אֶעֱבֹר ׀	I had gone	Verb
5519 [e]	bas-sāḵ	בַּסָּךְ	with the throng	Noun
1718 [e]	'ed-dad-dêm,	אֶדַּדֵּם	I went	Verb
5704 [e]	'ad-	עַד-	with them to	Prep
1004 [e]	bêṯ	בֵּית	to the house	Noun
430 [e]	'ĕ-lō-hîm	אֱלֹהִים	of God	Noun
6963 [e]	bə-qō-wl-	בְּקוֹל-	With the voice	Noun
7440 [e]	rin-nāh	רִנָּה	of joy	Noun
8426 [e]	wə-tō-w-dāh,	וְתוֹדָה	and praise	Noun
1995 [e]	hā-mō-wn	הָמוֹן	with a multitude	Noun
2287 [e]	ḥō-w-ḡêḡ	חוֹגֵג׃	that kept holy day	Verb

Chapter 8 – Imam Mahdi in the Bible

Who is Imam Mahdi?

Imam Muhammad Al-Mahdi[a]$_{pbuh}$ is the only son of Imam Hassan Al-Askari$_{pbuh}$, the eleventh Imam, and Lady Narjes Khatoon$_{pbuh}$, the granddaughter of the Roman Emperor. Lady Narjes' journey from the Roman palace to the house of Imam Askari was revealed to her in a dream. In short, she traveled with slaves, pretending to be one of them, and was sold as a slave. Eventually, she married to Imam Hassan Al-Askeri$_{pbuh}$.

On the 15th of Sha'ban 255 AH/ 869 AD, she gave birth to her only son, Imam Mahdi$_{pbuh}$, in total secrecy, because danger was at her doorstep; the ruler knew that Imam Hassan Al-Askari$_{pbuh}$ will be the father of the savior who will overthrow kings and rulers. Divine measures were taken to protect the newborn son from Al-Mu'tamid, the ruler.

Imam Hassan Al-Askari$_{pbuh}$ was poisoned and martyred at the age of 28 when Imam Mahdi$_{pbuh}$ was five years old. The five-year-old Imam led the funeral prayer while the Ruler himself was amongst the prayers.

Imam Mahdi$_{pbuh}$ was not seen again by people for nearly 70 years after the funeral, with an exception to his four deputies, known as *Safeer*. This period is called "The Minor Occultation".

In 329 AH / 941 AD, the fourth Safeer announced an order by Imam Mahdi$_{pbuh}$ that the deputy would soon die, the deputyship would end, and the Major Occultation would begin. The fourth deputy died six days later.

---

[a] Other spellings: Mehdi, Mehdy, Mahdy

Mahdi in Different Faiths

The word *Mahdi*, in Sanskrit, is the contraction of "Ma Adi" (Primordial Mother) in the same way that *Maitreya*, the returning Savior according to Buddha, is the contraction of "Ma Treya" (compare with Mother Threefold, Trimorphic Protennoi [a] or Trigunatmika).

In Sikhism, he is called *Aykaa Mayee*. Madai is the name of the deified ancestor of the Kachin people of Myanmar, according to the indigenous Kachin religion. Maidyo Mah is the first man who believed in Zoroaster.

Searching the final savior in different civilizations and faiths takes us on an endless journey; therefore, I picked one of the oldest known religions, namely Zoroastrianism, as a sample of non-Hebrew faiths. It is believed that ancient Iranians, centuries before Christ, were given a Book through Prophet Zoroaster[pbuh], the holy book of Avesta.

The Holy Quran has mentioned the followers of Zoroaster as *Majoos* (Al-Hajj, 22:17). Unfortunately, some translators of the Quran, such as Pickthall and Yusufali, have interpreted it as "Maggians". Avesta, as it will be discussed shortly, opposes this interpretation.

---

[a] Trimorphic Protennoi is a Gnostic text from the New Testament apocrypha.

Mahdi in Avesta

Even a quick search in my ancestral holy book of Avesta reveals the evidence for the truthfulness of Islam. By just scratching the surface, we find words equivalent to "Ameen", "Ahmed", "people who submit to the will of God", "Mekka", "the true religion", "Maidyo Mah, Born in the Middle of Month" and "the three promised ones". Avesta foretells a divine reward of "Garonemana to the Pure Man of Magkha".

Soshians, Airyaman, Adzan and Islam

In Zoroastrianism, savior is called Soshiant[a], or Soshians, meaning "the one who brings benefit", or in a wider scale, "the savior". In Avesta, it is used for Zoroaster and for *three promised persons*.[52] The prophecy of *three promised persons* is very well known in Judaism and Christianity, as it is explained in Chapter 2 – The Prophet and Twelve Princes, under "The Three Awaited Figures (John 1:19 - 21)".

Airyaman is an epithet of the Savior, Soshiant. It means *helper, friend, and healer of sicknesses brought by devil.* (Yasna 54.1)[b] He is the best, the greatest, and the most influential in overthrowing the devil.[53, 59] (See Yasht 3.5 in Figure 73) It is

---

[a] Other spellings: Saoshyant and Saoshiant
[b] Yasna texts are part of the Avesta (Zoroastrian scriptures). It constitutes 72 chapters altogether, also includes 17 chapters comprising the five Gathas (in Persian هات). These five Gathas are Prophet Zoroaster's direct words.

equivalent to the Parakleet or the Spirit of Truth of the Gospel of John.

Airyaman has an apparent similarity with the Arabic "Al-Ameen", the epithet of both Prophet Muhammad and Imam Mahdi $_{pbut}$. The standing epithet of the savior is astvat-ərəta, "embodying righteousness", which has "Truth" (arta/asha), as an element of the name (See Yasna 48.12). *Righteousness* and *Truth*, "Ameen" and "Ehmet" in Arabic and Hebrew respectively, are related to Prophet Muhammad and Imam Mahdi $_{pbut}$.

Airyaman of Avesta is a synonym to Mahimen and Parakleet. The book of Revelation (19:11) mentions Mahimen. (We will discuss Mahimen shortly.) The Gospel of John (chapters 14 and 16) makes a great deal of Parakleet. (See Chapter 2 – The Prophet and Twelve Princes, under "Parakleet")

In Zoroastrian Book of Worship, Yasna, we read:

Yasna 48.12[54]
The Saoshyants and Saviors of the world are indeed wise and follow duty's call guided by Vohuman[a]. There deeds are inspired by Asha[b] and on in tune with Thy teachings, O Mazda. They are, in truth, vanquishers of hate and anger and producers of love and peace.

[Yasna 48:12 may also represent the 12 Imams numericaly; 4 + 8 = 12, that is also the verse number.]

---

[a] "Vohuman" is Rightness of deeds grounded in good mind.
[b] Asha means "God's will", "desirable" and "the angel of Truth and Justice."

The call for prayer, Adzan in Muslim tradition, is the *Duty's Call* in the Yasna. *Duty's call guided by Vohuman* can be interpreted as "the Adzan call guided by Righteous." The concept of Yasna 48.12 will be apparent by replacing *righteous* with *Ameen.*

The statement *There deeds are inspired by Asha* (Go's will) *and on in tune with Thy teachings* is the exact explanation of being a Muslim, *a total submission to God's will.* The last statement, *producers of love and peace,* is what the Islam is about. (Peace is one of the meanings of Islam.)

Garonemana to the Pure Man of Magkha

(Yasna 51.15 and Yasht 3.4)

Yasna 51.15 is talking about the Mekkans and the followers of their religion. In the following translation, the word مگه (Magkha)[a] is interpreted as "Magians". "Magians" are people who follow true religion, because the word مگه (Magkha) means "the true religion". Some believe that it means "the place of worship and praise", while others suggest using it without translating, as a definite noun.[55] Dr. Jalil Doustkhah explains the concept of Magka and the variety of translations given to it, but he suggests using it without interpretation because none of the translations gives an adequate meaning to the word. (See Figure 72)

Yasna 51.15[54]
The reward which Zoroaster has promised the Magians (مگه Magkha) and all the followers of this religion is Garo-Nemana or the House of Songs and Praise, the Paradise. This abode has been the House on High from Eternity, where Ahura Mazda dwells. This reward which is a divine blessing and can only be attained by pure thought and truth, I promise to you.

Studying the above verse in depth reveals a few important points:

1. "Magians", *from* مگه *Magkha*, are the followers of a true religiom.
2. "Garo-Nemana" is the promised reward.
3. The place, "this abode", is the house of God.
4. This reward, "Garo-Nemana", is a Divine Blessing.

---

[a] In Azeri, the language of Azerbaijan where Zoroastrianism perhaps started, the word Mekka is pronounced identical to Avestal مگه (Magkha).

As mentioned earlier, the Holy Quran calls Zoroastrians مجوس *Majoos* (The Quran 22:17). Some have interpreted the word "Majoos" wrongly as "Magains", from Latin "Mage", meaning "magic". Magian is "a believer of the religion of Magic".

Since magic is condemned in both Zoroastrianism[56] and Islam (The Holy Quran 2:102), neither the Quranic *Majoos* nor the Avestan *Magkha* are the *Magians*. I believe the Quranic *Majoos* are مغ *Mogh, the followers of Zoroastrian*, not "Magians".

In my opinion, the مگ *Magkha* in Yasna 51.15 must be a prophetic term, referring to Mekka. The verse itself provides the evidence that they are neither the followers of Zoroaster nor the followers of Magicians.

Once again, Dr. Jalil Doustkhah writes that none of the interpretations or meanings given by Scholars to مگ (Magkha) contains clarity or adequacy. He explains that changes have occurred in the usage and meaning of the word مگ (Magkha) throughout time. (See Figure 72) His decision to use the term مگ (Magkha) without interpretation was probably the wisest measure to take.

Moreover, we must keep in mind that Avestan scholars are facing numerous difficulties in understanding the true meanings of many words in the Avesta. Dr. Kenneth Sylvan Launfal Guthir, in his book titled *The Hymns of Zoroaster*, writes:

The difficulties of Avestan writing are great in themselves, for the letters are both numerous and difficult to form and to distinguish both in enunciation and representation....
There are places and words generally given up as hopelessly insoluble or corrupt.[57]

THE SPIRIT OF TRUTH   Chapter 8 – Imam Mahdi in the Bible

Figure 72
مگه (Magkha) In Avesta[58]

پیوست / ۱۰۵۵

شکوه» که برخی از پژوهندگان، آن را با واژهٔ «مَگْهَه» در سنسکریت که به معنی «دارایی»، «پاداش» و «دهش» است، خویشاوند می‌دانند. در گزارش پهلوی اوستا، این واژه به "makih" به معنی «مهی و بزرگی» برگردانده شده و برای روشنگری بیشتر، افزوده شده است: «آپیچَکیه» = ویژگی).

در دوره‌های متأخر، «مغ» به معنی «موبد» یا «آتُربان» و نیز «پیرو دین زرتشتی» بکار رفته است. در گاهان از این واژه نشانی نمی‌بینیم و احتمالاً کاربرد آن مربوط به دوران تدوین اوستای نو و شاخهٔ غربی دین زرتشتی است. اما چندین بار از «مَگَه» و «مَگَوَن» سخن به میان آمده است.

. . . .

باشد. (← موبد، دربارهٔ «مغ» همچنین← زرتشت، ص۴۹)

مَگَوَن: واژه‌ای است گاهانی که ما آن را به همین صورت در این گزارش آورده‌ایم و برآنیم که به مفهوم هموند یا عضو «مگه» بکار رفته است. (← مگه)

مَگَه: واژه‌ای است گاهانی که ما آن را به همین صورت در این گزارش آورده‌ایم و برآنیم که به مفهوم جرگه یا انجمن پذیرندگان و پیروان پیام و آموزش زرتشت بکار رفته است.

برخی از پژوهندگان، این واژه را با «مغ» همریشه پنداشته و به معنی «آیین مغ» یا «انجمن برادری مغان» و نظایر آن گرفته‌اند. «مسینا» می‌گوید «مگه» به معنی «هدیهٔ الهی» و «دین راستین» است. «نیبرگ» از اجتماع زرتشت و یارانش، تصویری‌ک گروه شَمَنی دارد و می‌گوید واژهٔ «مگه» در اصل به معنی گروه خوانندگانی بوده که در انجمن گاهانی سرود می‌خوانده‌اند و بعدها به معنای جای سرودخوانی گاهانی و برگذاری آیین نیایش بکار رفته و هنگامی که این سرودخوانی کهن فراموش شده، به معنی جای راندن دیوان درآمده که همان

۱۰۵۶/اوستا

«برشنوم گاه» در «وندیداد» است. (← برشنوم گاه)

این معانی و تعبیرهای دیگری که اوستاشناسان تاکنون برای این واژه پیشنهاد کرده‌اند، هیچ کدام روشنگر و رسا نیست و ما ترجیح دادیم که در حال حاضر، صورت اصلی آن را بکار بریم. (← مگون)

The context of Yasna 51.15 strongly suggests that it has to be a prophetic statement, *a promised reward*. Zoroaster repeats the promise twice in this verse. Obviously, the promise was a divine blessing to the followers of مَغْ *Magkha*, and only can be attained by pure thought and truth.

Avesta, in Yasht 3.4, makes it clearer by expressing that it belongs to the pure man. (Figure 73) That is "The Infallible Man" in Islamic believe.

Yasht 3.4[59]
To the pure man belongs Garo-nemas, none of the wicked can approach to Garo-nemas, to the dwelling pure in joy, manifest Ahura-Mazda.

A combination of Yasna 51.15 and Yasht 3.4 reveals a secret: "Garonemana to the pure man of Magkha". It means *the Quran to the infallible man of Mekka*. [The first letter of the word *Quran* in Arabic is ق that is the "g" in Latin. Since "g" may sound ج (j) as well, hence to avoid any wrong pronunciation, it is written with "q".]

[Note the numerical message of Yasna 51.15 and Yasht 3.4 (5 + 1 + 5 +1 = 12 and 3 x 4 = 12); similar to Yasna 48:12, (4 +8 = 12)]

Figure 73

Garo-Nemana In Yasht Ardibihist XIX (3)[59]

28   KHORDAH-AVESTA.

XIX. (3). YASHT ARDIBIHIST.*

In the name, etc. May the Amshaspand Ardibihist increase in great majesty, may he come. Of all my sins, etc.

To Asha-vahista, the fairest, to Airyama-ishya, to strength created by Mazda, to Çaŏka the good, endowed with far-seeing eyes, created by Mazda, pure, be satisfaction, etc. Asha-vahista, the fairest Amĕsha-çpĕnta, praise we. Airyama-ishya praise we. Strength created by Mazda praise we. Çaŏka, the good, endued with far-seeing eyes, created by Mazda, pure, praise we.

1. Ahura-Mazda spake to the holy Zarathustra: As to what then belongs to the assistance of Asha-vahista, O holy Zarathustra, (so is he) Psalmist, Zaŏta, Praiser, Reader, Offerer, Lauder, Celebrator of good, effecting that the bright lights shine for the praise and adoration of us, Amĕsha-çpĕntas.†

2. Then spake Zarathustra: Speak the words, the true words, O Ahura-Mazda, how are the succours ‡ of Asha-vahista become as Singer, Zaŏta, Praiser, Reader, Offerer, Lauder, Celebrator of good, effecting that the good lights may shine to the praise and adoration of you, Amĕsha-çpĕntas?

3. I will praise Asha-vahista: if I praise Asha-vahista, then praise I him as the helper of the other Amĕsha-çpĕntas, whom Mazda protects through good thoughts, whom Mazda protects through good works, whom Mazda protects through good words.

4. To the pure man belongs Garo-nemâna, none of the wicked can approach to Garo-nemâna, to the dwelling pure in joy, manifest, Ahura-Mazda.

5. He (Asha-vahista) smites all the sorcerers and Pairikas belonging to Aṅra-mainyus through Airyama,§(which is) the greatest of the Mańthras, the best of the Mańthras, the fairest of the Mańthras, the most fairest of the Mańthras, the strong of the

Maidyo Mah, Airyaman and Aishyo

(Yasna 53.2 and 54.1)

Yasna 53.2 has the name of *Maidyo Mah*, the cousin of Zoroaster. Maidyo was the first man who believed in Zoroaster. The word "Maidyo Mah" literally means "the one who is born in middle of the month"[60]. (Figure 74) Imam Mahdi$_{pbuh}$ was born in 15th of the month of Shaaban.

Yasna 53.2[54]
So, let all strive with thought, word and deed to satisfy Mazda. Let each one choose to perform good deeds as his worship. Kavi Vishtaspa, the faithful devotee of Zoroaster together with <u>Maidyo-Mah</u> and Frashaoshtra are treading the path of Truth and have chosen the Faith inspired and revealed by the Saoshyant, or the Savior of Mankind, taught by Ahura.

In Yasna 54.1, we read that Airyaman or airyémaa is to come to help the men and women of Zarathustra, and the poet asks for his rewards.

Yasna 54.1
Aa airyémaa aishyo^a rafedhraai jantû,
Nerebyaschaa naairibyaschaa Zarathushtrahé,
Vanghéush rafedhraai manangho,
Yaa daénaa vairîm hanaat mîzhdem,
Ashahyaa yaasaa ashim,
Yaam ishyaam ahuro masataa mazdaao!

Translation (by Ali A. Jafarey)[61]
May the desired Fellowship come

---

[a] It is from اشه (Asha), meaning "God's will", "desirable" and "the angel of Truth and Justice."

for the support of the men and women of Zarathushtra,
for the support of good mind,
so that the conscience of every person earns
the choice reward, the reward of righteousness,
a wish regarded by the Wise God.

The above verse is called Â Airyemâ Ishyâ,[a] Closing stanza or the end Gatha of Avesta. The verse apparently is a wish/prayer for coming of Airyaman, translated to *Fellowship, the highest unit of human society.*[62]

Ali A. Jafarey writes in the book, THE GATHAS, OUR GUIDE: *A Airyema Ishya is a prayer which wishes us a worthy world of unity, unity through the Good Conscience, unity through the Fellowship it establishes. It is a beautiful benediction with which Asho Zarathushtra concludes his inspired and inspiring songs—TheGathas—of divine love and sublime guidance.*[63]

The word *aishyo* is translated to "the desired". This is the exact meaning of Hebrew "Mahammad", "Hamda" and "Hemdat", as we read in the Song of Solomon 5:16 (NLV, ESV, NASB, and more) and many other books of the Bible. (See Chapter 2 – The Prophet and Twelve Princes, under "Hamda and Hem-daṯ") In addition, the similar pronunciation of *aishyo* and *Yeshwa* (Jesus) is very remarkable.

The airyaman ishya is "the greatest, best, fairest, most fearful, most firm, most victorious, and the most healing" of all formulas (Yasht 3.5). The Yasna verse, immediately following the prayer, considers the airyaman ishya "the greatest uttering of asha" (Yasna 54.2).

---

[a] Other spellings: *A Airyeman Ishya* and *Aa airyémaa aishyo*

The similar pronunciation of *Aishyo* and *Yeshwa* in contrast to the equivalent meaning of *Aishyo* and *Muhammad* defines the Islamic end-time prophecy of simultaneous re-appearances of Jesus (Yeshwa) and Muhammad (Al-Mahdi) pbut.

Figure 74

"Maidyo Mah" in Avesta[60]

پیوست / ۱۰۵۳

در میانهٔ ماه، هنگام پُر ماه (بَدرِ تمام) و بار سوم در پایان ماه، هنگامی که ماه دیگر باره باریک می‌نماید. (ــــ ماه)

ماه یشت: نام هفتمین یشت از یشتهای بیست و یک گانهٔ اوستاست در ستایش و نیایش ماه که از یشتهای کوتاه به شمار می‌آید و تنها ۷ بند دارد.

ماهیّه: نام ایزد نگاهبان ماه است.

مَئِتَخ: نام کوهی است. (زام. بند ٤)

مَدیو ماهِ سِپیتمان: (در اوستا «مَیذیویی یا مَیذیویی ماونگهَه» و در پهلوی «مَتیوک ماه» به معنی «در میانهٔ ماه زاییده») بنا بر سنتهای دینی مزداپرستان و اشاره‌هایی در اوستای نو و متنهای پارسی میانه، نام پسر عموی زرتشت و نخستین پذیرفتار و پیرو دین زرتشت است. مدیوماه پسر «آراستی» و از خاندان «سپیتمان» است. (ــــ سپیتمان)

Mahdi in the Bible

The Bible prophecy on the matter of the final savior is a significant topic in the world of Judaism and Christianity. Indeed, it is the mother of separation between these two.

The Islamic tradition in the matter may appear to some bible believers as irrelevant or even an opposing position. However, as we will be defining in the next pages, both Old and New Testaments are pointing out that the Mahdi is the final and true savior of the nations. He is related to Ario-Semitic-Roman genealogy. He is from Arians, Arabs, Jews and Roman Christians. He is from Persia, Arabia, Rome and Jerusalem. He is the promised one of Avesta, Tanakh, Gospels and Quran.

He is a descendant of Prophet Muhammad$_{pbuh}$, Simon [a] and Shahrbanoo,[b] the daughter of Yazdgerd, the Sassanian King of Persia.

---

[a] Simon or Peter was the first Disciple of Jesus. He is the forefather of Lady Narjes, Mother of Mahdi.
[b] Lady Shahrbanoo was wife of Imam Hussain, and the mother of Imam Sejjad$_{pbuh}$, the fourth Imam.

Madai

The Book of Genesis (10:2) writes that Madai was the third son of Japheth, and the 16th grandson of Noah (Book of Jubilee 10:50-51). He was married to a daughter of Shem.

Some Biblical scholars assumed that Iranians are Madai, Media or Medes. A close study rejects this assumption. For example, in Esther 1:3 and 1:14, 18, 19, these phrases appear side by side, *Persia and Media* or *Persia and Medes*, assuring that they might be related to each other but not the same.

According to Hitchcock's Bible Names Dictionary, the phrase "Madai" literally means "a measure" and "judging", also "a garment." (See below)

Figure 75

Hitchcock's Bible Names Dictionary[1]

Madai

a measure; judging; a garment

Ali Elam and Mahdi

The Biblical prophecies about Imam Mahdi$_{pbuh}$ are scattered throughout the Bible. Isaiah 21, as explained in Chapter 4 – Imam Hussain in the Bible, under "Sufyani and Mahdi (Isaiah 21)", is one of the prophetic statements about Imam Mahdi$_{pbuh}$.

Isaiah 21:1, 2
A prophecy against the Desert by yam: 1 Like Sufians sweeping through Nejef, an invader comes from the desert, from Noraa (Neinawa). 2 A dire vision has been shown to me: The traitor betrays, the looter takes loot. Ali ê-lām portray Mahdi! I will bring to an end all the groaning.

Repairer of the Broken Ghadeer

Another passage that explains Imam Mahdi's advent from Mekka is Isaiah 58. (It is discussed in Chapter 6 – Isaiah and Islam) Below is the rendered translation of Isiah 58:1, 12. Interestingly, the chapter has 14 verses, representing the 14 infallibles in Shi'ite Islam.

Isaiah 58: 1, 12
*1 "Recite by Quran (qə-rā ḇə-ḡā-rō-wn[a]), do not hold back. Raise your voice like a trumpet. Declare to my people their rebellion and to the descendants of Jacob their sins.
12 You will rebuild from Mekka (mim-mə-ḵā[b]) the ancient ruins and will raise up the foundations of generation and generation; you will be called Repairer of Broken Ghadeer (גדר gō-ḏêr), Restorer of Streets with Dwellings.*

As mentioned before, these two verses are brilliant explanations of the Quran (as the first announcement of Isaiah 58) and someone who will repair the broken Ghadeer. "Repairer", in Arabic, is جابر (Jabir). It is one of Imam Mahdi's nicknames. The verse number (12) may also represent Imam Mahdi[pbuh] numerically; he is the 12th Imam.

---

[a] "קְרָא בְגָרוֹן" (qə-rā ḇə-ḡā-rō-wn) is translated "Shout it aloud" (NIV)
[b] "מִמְּךָ" (mim-mə-ḵā) is translated to "some of you", "of", "your people", and so on.

The Occultation and Mahimen

Moreover, the book of Revelation has excellent passages about Imam Mahdi's Occultation and re-appearance, as explained in Chapter 2 – The Prophet and Twelve Princes, under" The 12 Stars of a Lady (Revelation 12)"

The Bible talks about a lady who has 12 stars on her crown, she gives birth to a son. He goes on occultation and will return with an iron sword to rule nations. It is in chapter 12 of the Book of Revelation. [a numerical indication of the 12th Imam]

Chapter 19 of Revelation has another prophecy about Imam Mahdi$_{pbuh}$, although it could also indicate Prophet Muhammad$_{pbuh}$. Right at the beginning, it talks about Furqan, the Holy Quran[a], but the word *Furqan* is translated to "salvation".

Revelation 19
NIV
1 After this I heard what sounded like the roar of a great multitude in heaven shouting: Salvation (Furqana) *and glory and power belong to our God, "Hallelujah!*

Rendered translation:

Revelation 19:1
And after these things I heard a great voice of a crowd in heaven, saying, Glory to Furqan, the Praise and might belongs to Allah.

"Hallelujah" is equivalent to Arabic "Alhamdulel-Allah", meaning "Praise be to Allah". Revelation 19:1 not only mentions the Holy Quran but also gives another sign; the heavenly voice says, "The

---

[a] See Chapter 5 – Quran In The Bible.

Praise and might belongs to Allah." This is exactly how the Quran starts:

The Quran, Chapter 1:1-2[26]
1 In the name of Allah, Most Gracious, Most Merciful.
2 Praise be to Allah, the Cherisher and Sustainer of the worlds;

Having the name and the opening chapter of the Holy Quran in Revelation 19:1 ensures that the context is about Islam.

Continuing to Revelation 19:

2 for true and just are his judgments. He has condemned the great prostitute who corrupted the earth by her adulteries. He has avenged on her the blood of his servants." 3 And again they shouted: "Hallelujah! The smoke from her goes up for ever and ever." 4 The twenty-four elders and the four living creatures fell down and worshiped God, who was seated on the throne. And they cried: "Amen, Hallelujah!" 5 Then a voice came from the throne, saying: "Praise our God, all you his servants, you who fear him, both great and small!" 6 Then I heard what sounded like a great multitude, like the roar of rushing waters and like loud peals of thunder, shouting: "Hallelujah! For our Lord God Almighty reigns. 7 Let us rejoice and be glad and give him glory! For the wedding of the Lamb has come, and his bride has made herself ready. 8 Fine linen, bright and clean, was given her to wear." (Fine linen stands for the righteous acts of God's holy people.)

"The Holy People" in Hebrew is "hasid"; that is "Al-Seyid" in Arabic, the title of the Prophet and his descendants.

Verse 9 clarifies that it is talking about "the true words of God." It is not talking about any book but the Quran because the name is there, right at the beginning.

9 Then the angel said to me, "Write this: Blessed are those who are invited to the wedding supper of the Lamb!" And he added, "These are the true words of God."

10 At this I fell at his feet to worship him. But he said to me, "Don't do that! I am a fellow servant with you and with your brothers and sisters who hold to the testimony of Jesus. Worship God! For it is the Spirit of prophecy who bears testimony to Jesus."

Therefore, verse 10 must be opposing the common Christian belief of worshiping Jesus$_{pbuh}$ or the Holy Spirit. It says, *"Worship God! For it is the Spirit of prophecy who bears testimony to Jesus;"* meaning if you want to bear testimony to Jesus, worship God alone. Islam has made a same statement regarding Trinity. We read in the Quran:

The Quran, Chapter 1[26]

1 In the name of Allah, Most Gracious, Most Merciful.
2 Praise be to Allah, the Cherisher and Sustainer of the worlds;
3 Most Gracious, Most Merciful;
4 Master of the Day of Judgment.
5 Thee do we worship, and Thine aid we seek.
6 Show us the straight way,
7 The way of those on whom Thou hast bestowed Thy Grace, those whose (portion) is not wrath, and who go not astray.

Revelation 19:11 gives even his name, Mahimen but translated to "Faithful and True." (See Figure 76)

11 I saw heaven standing open and there before me was a white horse, whose rider is called Faithful and True. With justice he judges and wages war.

We have discussed about the "true" and "Faithful" which are Ahmed and Ameen; the well-known name and nickname of the Prophet of Islam and may apply to Al-Mahdi$_{pbuh}$ whose name is also same. The white horse is also well known in the Islamic tradition as the horse of the Prophet and Al-Mahdi $_{pbut}$. *"With justice he judges and wages war*" is very fitting statement, describing the defensive wars of both.

In Peshitta (Figure 76), we see the word "Faithful" as ܡܗܝܡܢܐ mhymnᵓ (from ēman). It means "trustworthy", the exact meaning of Arabic "Ameen." (Figure 77)

Figure 76

Peshitta[31]

- Revelation 19:11

ܘܚܙܝܬ ܫܡܝܐ ܕܦܬܝܚ ܘܗܐ ܣܘܣܝܐ ܚܘܪܐ ܘܕܝܬܒ ܥܠܘܗܝ ܡܬܩܪܐ ܡܗܝܡܢܐ ܘܫܪܝܪܐ ܘܒܟܐܢܘܬܐ ܕܐܢ ܘܡܩܪܒ ܀ (analyze)

Revelation 19:11 - وخزيت شميا دڤتيخ وها سوسيا خورا وديتب علوهي متقرا مهيمنا وشريرا وبكانوتا دان ومقرب .

Revelation 19:11 - wḥzyt šmyᵓ dptyḥ wh ᵓ swsyᵓ ḥwrᵓ wdytb ᶜlwhy mtqrᵓ mhymnᵓ wšryrᵓ wbkᵓnwtᵓ dᵓn wmqrb . .

Figure 77

mhymn A02[31]

mhymn (mhay/ēman) adj. **trustworthy, faithful**	Q p.p (or active? see note)

1 trustworthy, faithful, reliable Com. --(b) + ܐܝܢ : I am permitted Syr. --(b) trustee Syr. (b.1) a title: translating Hebrew סריס, as in Hebrew and Akkadian not always literally a eunuch Hat, Syr. 1 literal eunuch Syr.
 2 believer CPA, Syr, JBA.
 3 as an interjection: by faith! (for Hebrew נאם**)** Sam.
 4 deposit Sam.

Verse 12 states that he has *a name* written on him that only he himself knows it. Verse 13 has a clear statement on the matter of his other name. It says that his name is the Word of God

12 His eyes are like blazing fire, and on his head are many crowns. He has a name written on him that no one knows but him himself. 13 He is dressed in a robe dipped in blood, and his name is the Word of God.

At first look, verses 12 and 13 may appear inconsistent. However, if we take a careful look at the verses, we will not find any inconsistency at all. Verse 12 reads: "He has *a name* written on him that no one knows but him himself". Here it is not about his known name, but *a name* that no one knows except him. Verse 13 gives a clue on *his name*: "the Word of God". Both Jesus and Imam Mahdi ₚbut are called كلمة الله (kalimatullah); meaning *word of God*, and only Mahdi_pbuh is called Mohaymin or Ameen.

As it is explained earlier, Revelation in general and chapter 19 in particular is not a historic record but a prophetic text. If we assume that it is a prediction of Jesus' second coming, then we must accept that the Revelation is prophesying both Jesus and Mahdi ₚbut, because Jesus_pbuh was never called Ameen. The context of Revelation 19 is also far from being a Christo messianic prophecy. The remaining verses illustrate a great battle between Ameen and the entire world.

14 The armies of heaven were following him, riding on white horses and dressed in fine linen, white and clean. 15 Coming out of his mouth is a sharp sword with which to strike down the nations. "He will rule them with an iron scepter." He treads the winepress of the fury of the wrath of God Almighty. 16 On his robe and on his thigh he has this name written: KING OF KINGS AND LORD OF LORDS

"King of Kings" is also a nickname of Imam Mahdi$_{pbuh}$, امیرالامرا *Ameer al-Omaraa* in Arabic. I do not know any meaningful interpretation for these verses except the revelation of the Quran and the coming of Imam Mahdi$_{pbuh}$. In verse 16, the robe can be an indication of his lineage, and the thigh may reflect his offspring.

Rest of the chapter is about the victorious ending of the war:

17 And I saw an angel standing in the sun, who cried in a loud voice to all the birds flying in midair, "Come, gather together for the great supper of God, 18 so that you may eat the flesh of kings, generals, and the mighty, of horses and their riders, and the flesh of all people, free and slave, great and small." 19 Then I saw the beast and the kings of the earth and their armies gathered together to wage war against the rider on the horse and his army. 20 But the beast was captured, and with it the false prophet who had performed the signs on its behalf. With these signs he had deluded those who had received the mark of the beast and worshiped its image. The two of them were thrown alive into the fiery lake of burning sulfur. 21 The rest were killed with the sword coming out of the mouth of the rider on the horse, and all the birds gorged themselves on their flesh.

Verse 20 condemns worshiping images. Many Christian places of worship filled with images of Mary, Jesus, Angels and Saints. The believers have become conditioned to pray in the presence of these images because they are part of the divinity in today's Christian theology. It is also noticeable that the beast will have a prophet, the false prophet, and he will be destroyed by Ameen.

I have no doubt that these prophecies are related to Imam Mahdi$_{pbuh}$.

A Closing Statement

The Biblical prophecies on the advent of Islam are evidence for the truthfulness of Islam. There is no matter in the Bible as highly outstanding as Islam. The original languages of the Bible, as well as some translations, still have a plethora of evidence about the divine source of the Holy Quran.

The very first verse of the Bible mentions that *Elohim* created the Heavens and the Earth; it is the same God in the Quran: Allah. The very first commandment of the Torah and the foremost teaching of Jesus$_{pbuh}$ is also the first and most important principle of the Islamic theology, the Monotheism. The very first blessing that God promised to Abraham$_{pbuh}$ was his fruitfulness through Ishmael$_{pbuh}$ and then Isaac$_{pbuh}$. The last and ultimate prophecy of the Bible is the advent of Islam; the revelation of the Quran, the 12 Imams from Mekka, and the Mahdi the Judge, the King of Kings, the Ruler of Rulers, and the prince of Shalowm (Islam) who is to stablish the Kingdom of Heaven on Earth,

I have not read nor heard of a single book comparable to the Bible in the prophetic plenitude about Islam. That is why I have called the Bible "the Herald of Quran". I believe and have evidently exhibited through this book that the most magnificent mission of the Bible is leading its believers to Islam; howbeit every one of us must obtain the tolerance and acceptance of the differences in the opinions. Then we will be rewarded by achieving the state of intelligence and spirituality, which is the main purpose of the divine religions.

This humble book of mine is dedicated to you, the reader who knows no boundary in embracing the Truth. With hope of peace and unity, I close my words. May Allah open our hearts to his mercy.

A'meen.

REFERENCES

[1] http://biblehub.com/ (accessed 2017 March 10)
[2] Dr. Hugh Ross in *Fulfilled Prophecy: Evidence for the Reliability of the Bible*, article dated: August 22, 2003, http://www.reasons.org. (accessed 2017 March 20)
[3] Michael H. Hart – *The 100, A Ranking of The Most Influencial Persons In History*, Second Edition, A Citadel Press Book, 1992, pages 3 and 4
[4] Dr. Maurice Bucaille, *"THE BIBLE, The QUR'AN and Science", The Holy Scriptures Examined in the Light of Modern Knowledge*, Translated from the French By Alastair D. Pannell and The Author, Publised by *Thrike Tarsile Qur'an, Inc.*, ISBN 1-879402-98-X, First U.S. Edition 2003
[5] Heinrich Graetz, *History of the Jews* – Volume VI, COSIMO CLASSIC, New York 2009, P. 148
[6] Kelly Bulkeley, Kate Adams, Patricia M. Davis, *Dreaming in Christianity and Islam: Culture, Conflict, and Creativity* – Rugers University Press, New Brunswick, New Jersey, and London 2009, P. 179
[7] Muhammad Asad, *The Road to Macca*, Academic Trust, 1998
[8] Josef W. Meri, Editor, Medieval Islamic Civilization: An Encyclopedia – Rutledge Tailor & Francis Group – New York 2006, P. 666
[9] Thomas Hauser, *Muhammad Ali: His Life and Times* - Simon & Schuster Publishing company 1991
[10] http://radaris.com/p/Sachini/Stretchen/ (accessed: 2017 January 10)
[11] *The Fathers of the Church, Eusebius Pamphili, Ecclesiastical History*, Books 1-5, translated by Roy J. Deferrari, The Catholic University Of America Press, Washington, DC, pages 174, 175
[12] *Explanation of the Sayings of the Lord* [cited by Eusebius in History of the Church 3:39]
[13] Aron D. Rudin, *A Brief Introduction to the Semitic Languages*, Gorgias Press 2010
[14] Daniel Norén (811201-5618), *An Arabic Hebrew comparative Study of Genesis 1-3*, GOTHENBURG UNIVERSITY, 2011, P. 16
[15] Dr. Bart D. Ehrman, *Misquoting Jesus* - Harper Collins Publishers – New York 2005, P. 89, 90
[16] Dr. Bart D. Ehrman, *Misquoting Jesus* - Harper Collins Publishers – New York 2005, P. 98
[17] https://www.biblegateway.com (accessed 2017 March 15)

[18] http://biblehub.com/niv/1_john/5.htm (accessed 2017 March 10)
[19] http://biblehub.com/niv/1_john/5.htm (see the footnotes) (accessed: 2017 March 10)
[20] Stephen J. Patterson – *The God of Jesus: The Historical Jesus and the Search for Meaning*, Trinity Press International, Harrisburg Pennsylvania the USA, P. 76
[21] Dr. Bart D. Ehrman, *Studies in the Textual Criticism of the New Testament*, ... Leiden, Netherlands 2006, P. 196
[22] D. M. Murdock, Acharya S, Robert M. Price, *Who Was Jesus? Fingerprints of the Christ*, Stellar House Publishing, the USA 2011, P. 42
[23] Dr. Bart D. Ehrman, *Misquoting Jesus* - Harper Collins Publishers – New York 2005, P. 66
[24] https://www.biblegateway.com/passage/?search=Mark+16:9-20 (accessed 2017 March 15)
[25] Professor Thomas McElwain, *Islam in the Bible*, Adams & McElwain Publishers, Puijonrinne 7, 70200 Kuopio, Finland, P. 174
[26] http://www.parsquran.com/; Yusufali translation (accessed 2017 March 10)
[27] http://www.doitinhebrew.com/ (accessed 2017 March 10)
[28] Daniel Norén (811201-5618), *An Arabic Hebrew comparative Study of Genesis 1-3*, GOTHENBURG UNIVERSITY, 2011, P.8, 9
[29] Edward Lipinski, *Semitic Languages*, Outline of A Comparative Grammar, 1997, Peeters, P. 150
[30] http://www.almaany.com/ (accessed 2017 March 10)
[31] Lars J. Lindgren, Dukhrana Biblical Research Society, Department of Linguistics and Philosophy at Uppsala University, http://dukhrana.com/peshitta/ (accessed 2017 March 10)
[32] Steve Urick, *Signs of the Second Coming of Jesus Christ and the End of the World*, Author House, Bloomington, IN, The USA 2009, ISBN 978-1-4389-7501-6 (sc)
[33] George Jordac, *The Voice of Human Justice*, Translator: M. Fazal Haq, Ansariyan Publications, P. 505
[34] Professor Thomas McElwain, *Shi'ite Beliefs in the Bible*, The London Lectures (2001-2002) –Adams & McElwain Publishers – Puijonrinne 770200 Kuopio, Finland – Lecture 9, P. 99, 100
[35] http://www.aoal.org/Hebrew/AudioBible/ (accessed 2017 March 15)

[36] لجامعة ١٠:٢٠ Arabic: Smith & Van Dyke, from Biblehub.com (accessed March 2017 10)
[37] Dr. S. Manzoor Rizvi, *Unique Sacrifice of Imam Hussain for Humanity*, Message of Peace Inc., Bloomfield, USA
[38] S. V. Ahmed Ali, *Saving Monotheism in the Sands of Karbala*, Tahrike Tarsile Quran, Incorporated, 2009
[39] *The Encyclopaedia Britannica*: A Dictionary of Arts, Sciences, and ..., Volume 6, edited by Thomas Spencer Baynes, Page 729
[40] David J. Gibson, *The Land of Eden Located*, 1964, Chapter Four, ttp://nabataea.net/eden4.html (accessed 2017 March 15)
[41] Thomas Hieke, Tobias Nicklas, *The day of Aronement: Its Interpretations in Early Jewish and Christian Traditions*, Leiden – Boston, USA, p. 58
[42] Al-Biruni, *"Al-Athar al-Baḳiyyah"*, ed. Sachau, p. 326
[43] https://en.oxforddictionaries.com/definition/najaf (accessed 2017 March 15)
[44] http://www.codexsinaiticus.org/ (accessed 2017 March 15)
[45] Dr. Bart D. Ehrman, *Misquoting Jesus* - Harper Collins Publishers – New York 2005, P. 66
[46] https://www.biblegateway.com/passage/?search=Mark+16:9-20 (accessed 2017 March 15)
[47] Stephen J. Patterson – *The God of Jesus: The Historical Jesus and the Search for Meaning*, Trinity Press International, Harrisburg Pennsylvania the USA, P. 76
[48] Dr. Bart D. Ehrman, *Studies in the Textual Criticism of the New Testament*, ... Leiden, Netherlands 2006, P. 196
[49] D. M. Murdock, Acharya S, Robert M. Price, *Who Was Jesus? Fingerprints of the Christ*, Stellar House Publishing, the USA 2011, P. 42
[50] http://biblehub.com/commentaries/cambridge/isaiah/29.htm (accessed 2017 March 10)
[51] http://biblehub.com/topical/a/assyria.htm (accessed 2017 March 10)
[52] Jalil Doustkhah, Phd., *Avesta:Tthe Ancient Iranian Hymns and Texts*, Volume 2, Morvarid Publication, 1385 Hijri Shamsi, ISBN 964-6026-17-6, P. 1011
[53] Jalil Doustkhah, Phd., *Avesta:Tthe Ancient Iranian Hymns and Texts*, Volume 2, Morvarid Publication, 1385 Hijri Shamsi, ISBN 964-6026-17-6, P. 939, 940

[54] Mobed Firouz Azargoshasb, *Translation of Gathas, The Holy Songs Of Zarathushtra*, the Council of Iranian Mobeds of North America, March 1988, From www.Zarathushtra.com (accessed 2017 March 26)

[55] Jalil Doustkhah, Phd., *Avesta:Tthe Ancient Iranian Hymns and Texts*, Volume 2, Morvarid Publication, 1385 Hijri Shamsi, ISBN 964-6026-17-6, P. 1055, 1056

[56] Jalil Doustkhah, Phd., *Avesta:Tthe Ancient Iranian Hymns and Texts*, Volume 2, Morvarid Publication, 1385 Hijri Shamsi, ISBN 964-6026-17-6, P. 1055

[57] Dr. Kenneth Sylvan Launfal Guthir, *The Hymns of Zoroaster*, THE PLATONIST PRESS, Teocalli, No. Yonkers, N. Y., U. S. A, 1914, P.131

[58] Jalil Doustkhah, Phd., *Avesta:The Ancient Iranian Hymns and Texts*, Volume 2, Morvarid Publication, 1385 Hijri Shamsi, ISBN 964-6026-17-6, P. 1055, 1056

[59] Arthur Henry Bleeck, *AVESTA, THE RELIGIOUS BOOKS OF THE PARSEES*, HERTFORD, 1864

[60] Jalil Doustkhah, Phd., *Avesta:Tthe Ancient Iranian Hymns and Texts*, Volume 2, Morvarid Publication, 1385 Hijri Shamsi, ISBN 964-6026-17-6, P. 1053

[61] *THE GATHAS, OUR GUIDE, the thought-provoking divine songs of Zarathushtra*, translated by Ali A. Jafarey USHTA PUBLICATION, Cypress, CA., U.S.A., 1989 P. 54

[62] *THE GATHAS, OUR GUIDE, the thought-provoking divine songs of Zarathushtra*, translated by Ali A. Jafarey USHTA PUBLICATION, Cypress, CA., U.S.A., 1989 P. 68

[63] *THE GATHAS, OUR GUIDE, the thought-provoking divine songs of Zarathushtra*, translated by Ali A. Jafarey USHTA PUBLICATION, Cypress, CA., U.S.A., 1989 P. 67

www.ingramcontent.com/pod-product-compliance
Lightning Source LLC
Chambersburg PA
CBHW031131160426
43193CB00008B/102